Studies in Perception and Action VIII

Thirteenth International Conference on Perception and Action

July 5–10, 2005
Monterey, California, USA

Edited by

Harry Heft
Denison University

Kerry L. Marsh
University of Connecticut

T0347149

Routledge
Taylor & Francis Group

LONDON AND NEW YORK

First published 2005 by Lawrence Erlbaum Associates, Inc.,
10 Industrial Avenue
Mahwah, New Jersey 07430-2262

This edition published 2013 by Routledge

711 Third Avenue   2 Park Square,
New York   Milton Park, Abingdon,
NY 10017   Oxfordshire OX14 4RN

First issued in paperback 2016

Routledge is an imprint of the Taylor & Francis Group, an informa business

Cover design by Claudia Carello

Includes bibliographical references and index.

ISBN 13:978-0-415-65210-0 (pbk)
ISBN 13:978-0-8058-5553-1 (hbk)

Table of Contents

Preface ix

Meeting History xi

Contributors xii

Affordances

Enacting the Perception of the Affordances of Potential Tools I: The Case of
Children Hammering
B. Bril & J. Foucart 3

Perceiving the Obstacle Step-Acrossability After the Maximal Exercise Test
S. Cornus, G. Walther, T. Rupp, & L. Rasseneur 7

Enacting the Perception of the Affordances of Potential Tools II: The Case of
Chimpanzees Nut-Cracking
J. Foucart, S. Hirata, K. Fuwa, & B. Bril 10

Perceiving Whether or Not Another Person Can Use a Step to Reach an Object
V.C. Ramenzoni, M. Riley, T. Davis, & J. Snyder 15

Posting Balls Through Holes: Effect of Hole-Size and Background Texture on
Action Initiation Time and the Perception of Affordances
Gert-Jan Pepping & Joanne Smith 19

Comfort as a Determinant of the Location of Critical Boundaries in the Act of
Reaching
Sara Stasik & Leonard S. Mark 23

Feeling and Seeing to Avoid Tripping
Kona R. Taylor & Jeffrey B. Wagman 27

Postural Sway Supports Affordance Perception
Chih-Mei Yang, Thomas A. Stoffregen, & Benoît G. Bardy 31

Interpersonal Perception and Dynamics

The Salience of Actions over Faces for Young Infants
*Lorraine E. Bahrick, Mariana Vaillant-Molina, Melissa A. Shuman, Laura
C. Batista, Lisa C. Newell, Irina Castellanos, & Traci S. Williams* 37

Verbal Constraints on Interpersonal Coordination
Aimee A. Baker, Kevin Shockley, Michael J. Richardson, & Carol A Fowler 41

Interpersonal Coordination among Articulations, Gesticulations, and Breathing
Movements: A Case of Articulation of /a/ and Flexion of the Wrist
Nobuhiro Furuyama, Koji Hayashi, & Hiroyuki Mishima 45

The Interpersonal Phase Entrainment of Rocking Chair Movements
   *Justin R. L. Goodman, Robert W. Isenhower, Kerry L. Marsh, R. C.
   Schmidt, & Michael J. Richardson* 49

The Specificity of Intrapersonal and Interpersonal Affordance Boundaries:
   Intrinsic versus Extrinsic Metrics
   *Robert W. Isenhower, Kerry L. Marsh, Claudia Carello, Reuben M. Baron,
   & Michael J. Richardson* 54

Coordination of Self-Disclosure and Gossip in Adolescent Conversations
   S. Stavros Valenti, Morgan Anderson, Karen Chin, & Jocelyn Schwartz 59

Control of Locomotion

Integrating Target Interception & Obstacle Avoidance
   Hugo Bruggeman & William H. Warren 65

Estimating TTC (time-to-collision) of Non-Rigid Approaching Objects
   Hirokazau Doi & Kazuhiro Ueda 69

The Role of Calibration in Visually-Guided Braking
   Brett R. Fajen 73

Velocity Control of a Harbor Porpoise (*Phocoena phocoena*): A Case Study
   *Kiyohide Ito, Takashi Matsuishi, Ayumi Ito, Yuji Kojima, Atsuko
   Miyashita, & Mamoru Aoyama* 77

Basic Strategies of Target Search by Smell
   E. E. Kadar, P. Fisher, & G. S. Virk 82

Dynamic Touch

CyARM: Direct Perception Device by Dynamic Touch
   *Junichi Akita, Kiyohide Ito, Takanori Komatsu, Tetsuo Ono,
   & Makoto Okamoto* 87

Peripheral Neuropathy and Length Perception by Dynamic Touch
   Claudia Carello, Jeffrey Kinsella-Shaw, & Eric Amazeen 91

Haptic Perception of Rod Length in Force Pattern
   Tin-cheung Chan 95

Do Children and Adults Use Haptic Information When Selecting Tools for
   Simple Power and Precision Tasks?
   S. E. Cummins-Sebree, A. M. Tollner, & K. Shockley 99

Perceived Heaviness with Variation in Rotational Inertia or Static Moment
   *Steven J. Harrison, Stacy Lopresti-Goodman, Robert W. Isenhower,
   Alen Hajnal, & Jeffrey Kinsella-Shaw* 103

The Orientation of T-Shaped Objects Cannot Be Perceived by Dynamic Touch
Christopher C. Pagano 107

Spatial Distortions in Active Tactile Exploration
W. L. Ben Sachtler, Philip M. Grove, Thomas E. von Wiegand,
& S. James Biggs 111

Perceiving Affordances of Hockey Sticks
Alison M. Tollner, Philip Hove, & Michael A. Riley 115

"How Heavy?" Does Not Depend on Which Hand
Jeffrey B. Wagman & Students in Psychology 331.04 119

Perception and Interception of Moving Objects

Hand Trajectories for Catching Balls on Horizontal, Linear Trajectories
Ryan Arzamarski, Steven J. Harrison, & Claire F. Michaels 125

Effects of Attention on Performance in Baseball Batting
Brooke Castaneda & Rob Gray 129

The Influence of Symmetry on Perception of Thrown, Oblong, Symmetrical
Projectiles in 3D
Igor Dolgov, Michael K. McBeath, & Thomas G. Sugar 132

An Information-Based Account of Lateral Interception: Coupling of Hand
Movements to Optics in Novel Trajectories
Alen Hajnal, Robert W. Isenhower, Steven J. Harrison, &
Claire F. Michaels 136

The Effects of Task Constraints on the Perceptual Guidance of Interceptive
Reaching Toward a Moving Target
Joanne Smith & Gert-Jan Pepping 139

Audition

The Influence of Presentation Method on Auditory Length Perception
Brent C. Kirkwood 145

Hearing Silent Shapes: Identifying the Shape of a Sound-Obstructing Surface
Ryan L. Robart & Lawrence D. Rosenblum 149

Hearing Space: Identifying Rooms by Reflected Sound
Ryan L. Robart & Lawrence D. Rosenblum 153

The Role of Instrument Properties in Music Performance: Variations in Sound
and Movements Induced by Baroque-Violin Playing
R. Goasdoué & B. Bril 157

Does Length Sound Like What Length Feels Like?
  Jeffrey B. Wagman, Kimberly M. Hopkins, & Jennifer L. Minarik 162

Intermodal and Bimodal Perception-Action

Coupling Movement to Acoustic Flow in Sighted Adults
  ChungGon Kim, Thomas Stoffregen, Kiyohide Ito & Benoît Bardy....... 169

Intermodal Specification of Egocentric Distance in a Target Reaching Task
  Bruno Mantel, Benoît G. Bardy, & Thomas A. Stoffregen 173

Exploiting New Perception-Action Solutions in Ball Bouncing
  A. Morice, I. A. Siegler, & B. G. Bardy 177

The Effects of Bimodal and Unimodal Familiarization on Infants' Memory for
  Unimodal Events
  Joe Schmutz, Dan Hyde, Seth Gunderson, Katie Gordon, & Ross Flom . 181

Optical Gain and the Perception of Heaviness.
  Matt Streit & Kevin Shockley 185

Action and Coordination Dynamics

Stability and Variability of Rhythmic Coordination with Compromised Haptic
  Perceptual Systems
  *Claudia Carello, Geraldine L. Pellecchia, Polemnia G. Amazeen
  & M .T. Turvey*... 191

(De)Stabilization of Required vs. Spontaneous Postural Dynamics with
  Learning
  Elise Faugloire, Benoît G. Bardy, & Thomas A. Stoffregen 195

Effects of Task and Individual Characteristics on Microslips of Action
  Naoya Hirose 199

Complexity and Stability in Isometric Force Production
  S. Lee Hong, Jacob J. Sosnoff, & Karl M. Newell 203

A New Method for Studying Non-Stationary Signals in Human Movement: The
  Cross-Wavelet Transform
  *Johann Issartel, Ludovic Marin, Thomas Bardainne, Phillipe Gaillot,
  & Marielle Cadopi* 207

Stability of Coordination Between Upper and Lower Body Rhythms During
  Treadmill Walking: Response to Changes in Walking Speed
  B. A. Kay, T. G. Rhodes, A. Hajnal, & R. W. Isenhower 211

Effects of Coordination Stability on Simple Reaction Time in Dual Task Performance
Annie J. Olmstead, Ryan Arzamarski, Miguel Moreno, & Geraldine L. Pellecchia... 214

Postural Stabilization

Postural Stabilization of Looking: Eye Movement Data
Cedrick T. Bonnet, Thomas A. Stoffregen & Benoît G. Bardy 221

Intention to Sway Stabilizes Postural Coordination
Olivier Oullier, Benoît G. Bardy, Reinoud J. Bootsma, & Thomas A. Stoffregen 225

Effects of Concurrent Memory Task on the Maintenance of Upright Stance
V. C. Ramenzoni & Michael A. Riley 229

Explicitly Minimizing Postural Sway While Performing a Visuo-Spatial Cognitive Task
Nichole E. Saunders & Michael A. Riley 234

Picture Perception and Distance Perception

Falling Towards a Theory of the Vertical-Horizontal Illusion
Russell E. Jackson 241

Perspective Picture Perception: A Test of the ART Theory
Igor Juricevic & John Kennedy 245

Object Constancy: Object Orientation Affects Relative Depth in Perspective Pictures?
Igor Juricevic & John Kennedy.. 249

Pedagogy

Using EPAID to Design Doctoral Minors
Judith Effken, Gerri Lamb, Marylyn McEwen, Joyce Verran, Deborah Vincent, & Michael Young 257

Author index 261

Keyword index 265

Preface

Since 1991, the edited book series Studies in Perception and Action has appeared in conjunction with the biennial International Conference on Perception and Action (ICPA). This conference provides an opportunity for individuals who share interests in ecological psychology to come together to present current research, to exchange ideas, and to resume continuing conversations on theoretical and methodological concerns. A particularly important feature of these meetings is the poster sessions because they allow for intensive, face-to-face dialogues between conference attendees and researchers displaying their latest work. This book series has become a way of preserving these peer-reviewed works beyond the stimulating days of the meetings, and in the process making them available for scrutiny by a wider audience. These collections of brief research reports are representative of research in ecological psychology and allied areas, and collectively, they convey much of the intellectual excitement of this international meeting.

This volume is the 8th in the series, and it presents the posters offered at the ICPA XIII conference held in the Asilomar Conference Center, Monterey, California, July 5-10, 2005. The overall conference organizer was Lawrence Rosenblum, University of California, Riverside. The editors of the preceding volumes in this series have shown considerable acumen and care in bringing each collection to fruition, and we hope our effort approaches the standards that they have set.

A significant challenge we faced in assembling this collection was organizing these diverse papers into a coherent set of categories. Most problematic for us, as for previous editors, was that many papers would not easily fit under a single heading, but instead cut across several. While recognizing the limitations of our imposed order, we feel that it offers an initial structure for the reader. As a further aid for more detailed study, we have provided an index of keywords. It should be noted that we have engaged in a minimum of editing to ensure that the submissions convey the authors' intent and to preserve the flavor of the poster sessions.

Twelve years ago the editors of the second volume Stavros Valenti and John Pittenger expressed the hope that "the poster book will become a tradition of the International Conferences on Event Perception and Action, promoting the poster format as a valuable medium for communicating scientific research." We can now say with confidence that this hope has been realized, and we are very pleased to continue this noteworthy tradition.

We thank William Mace of the International Society for Ecological Psychology (ISEP) for his advice and guidance. Also, we express our gratitude to Claudia Carello for her fine work on the cover design, and for her forbearance in our deliberations. Early in the planning process the advice of prior editors Greg Burton and Sheena Rogers was invaluable, and we are most grateful to them. Denison University Computing Services kindly facilitated our work, and for this assistance we give thanks to Teri Beamer and Charlie Reitsma. Finally, and on behalf of ISEP, we are pleased to acknowledge the contributions of Art

Lizza and Lori Stone of Lawrence Erlbaum Associates (LEA) and to express our gratitude to LEA for its continuing commitment to this series.

Harry Heft
Kerry L. Marsh

Meeting History

1. 1981 – Storrs, CT, USA
2. 1983 – Nashville, TN, USA
3. 1985 – Uppsala, SWEDEN
4. 1987 – Trieste, ITALY
5. 1989 – Miami, OH, USA
6. 1991 – Amsterdam, NETHERLANDS
7. 1993 – Vancouver, CANADA
8. 1995 – Marseilles, FRANCE
9. 1997 – Toronto, CANADA
10. 1999 – Edinburgh, SCOTLAND
11. 2001 – Storrs, CT, USA
12. 2003 – Gold Coast, QLD, AUSTRALIA
13. 2005 – Monterey, CA, USA

Contributors

Junichi Akita, Kanazawa University, Kakuma, Kanazawa, 920-1192, Japan. E-mail: akita@is.t.kanazawa-u.ac.jp

Eric Amazeen, Dept. of Psychology, Arizona State University, Tempe, AZ 85287, USA.

Polemnia G. Amazeen, Dept. of Psychology, Arizona State University, Tempe, AZ 85287, USA.

Morgan Anderson, Department of Psychology, 135 Hofstra University, Hempstead, NY 11549, USA.

Mamoru Aoyama, Otaru Aquarium, Japan.

Ryan Arzamarski, Center for the Ecological Study of Perception and Action, 406 Babbidge Road, Unit 1020, University of Connecticut, Storrs, CT 06269-1020, USA. E-mail: ryan.arzarmarski@uconn.edu

Lorraine E. Bahrick, Florida International University, 11200 SW 8th St., Department of Psychology, DM 115, Miami, FL 33199, USA. E-mail: bahrick@fiu.edu

Aimee A. Baker, Department of Psychology, ML 0376, 429 Dyer Hall, University of Cincinnati, Cincinnati, OH, 45221-0376, USA. E-mail: bakerax@email.uc.edu

Thomas Bardainne, Geophysic Imagery Laboratory, University of "Pau et des pays de l'Adour", Pau, France. E-mail: thomas.bardainne@univ-pau.fr

Benoît G. Bardy, Research Center in Sport Sciences, UFR STAPS, Université Paris XI, Bat.335, 91405 ORSAY Cedex, France. E-mail: benoit.bardy@staps.u-psud.fr

Reuben M. Baron, Department of Psychology, 406 Babbidge Road, Unit 1020, University of Connecticut, Storrs, CT 06269-1020, USA. E-mail: rmbaron@uconn.edu

Laura C. Batista, Florida International University, 11200 SW 8th St., Department of Psychology, DM 115, Miami, FL 33199, USA, batistal@fiu.edu

S. James Biggs, Research Laboratory of Electronics (36-789), Massachusetts Institute of Technology, 77 Massachusetts Avenue, Cambridge, MA, 02139, USA. E-mail: jbiggs@mit.edu

Cedrick Bonnet, School of Kinesiology, University of Minnesota, Minneapolis, MN, 55414, USA.

Reinhoud J. Bootsma, Laboratoire Mouvement et Perception (UMR 6152), CNRS-Université de la Méditerranée, 163, avenue de Luminy CP910, 13288 Marseille cedex 09, France. E-mail: bootsma@laps.univ-mrs.fr

Blandine Bril, Groupe de Recherche Apprentissage et Contexte, École des Hautes Études en Sciences Sociales, 54 Bd Raspail, 75006 Paris, France. E-mail: blandine.bril@ehess.fr

Hugo Bruggeman, Post Doctoral Fellow, Dept. of Cognitive and Linguistic Sciences, Brown University, Box 1978, Providence, RI 02912-1978, USA. E-mail: hugo@brown.edu

Marielle Cadopi, Motor Efficiency and Motor Deficiency Laboratory, University of Montpellier 1, France. E-mail: marielle.cadopi@univ-montp1.fr

Claudia Carello, Center for the Ecological Study of Perception and Action, 406 Babbidge Road, Unit 1020, University of Connecticut, Storrs, CT 06269-1020, USA. E-mail: claudia.carello@uconn.edu

Brooke Castaneda, Department of Applied Psychology, Arizona State University East, 7001 E. Williams Field Road, Building 140, Mesa, AZ 85212, USA. E-mail: radford@asu.edu

Irina Castellanos, Florida International University, 11200 SW 8th St., Department of Psychology, DM 115, Miami, FL 33199, USA. E-mail: irina.castellanos@fiu.edu

Tin-Cheung Chan, Department of Psychology, Chinese University of Hong Kong Shatin, NT, Hong Kong SAR, China. Email: tcchan@cuhk.edu.hk

Karen Chin, Department of Psychology, 135 Hofstra University, Hempstead, NY 11549, USA.

Sabine Cornus, Equipe d'Accueil en Sciences du Sport, Strasbourg, URF STAPS, Universite Marc Bloch, 14 Rue Rene Descartes 67084 Strasbourg, France. E-Mail: cornus@umb.u-strasbg.fr

S. Cummins-Sebree, Raymond Walters College, Cincinnati, OH, USA.

T. Davis, Perceptual-Motor Dynamics Laboratory, Department of Psychology, University of Cincinnati, OH, 45219, USA, E-mail: sabateh@sbcglobal.net

Hirokazu Doi, Department of General System Studies, University of Tokyo, 8-1, Komaba 3-chome, Meguro-ku, Tokyo 153-8902, Japan. E-mail: doi@pri.kyoto-u.ac.jp

Igor Dolgov, Department of Psychology, Arizona State University, P.O. Box 871104, Tempe, AZ 85287-1104, USA. E-mail: Igor.Dolgov@asu.edu

Judith Effken, University of Arizona College of Nursing, PO Box 210203, Tucson, AZ 85721-0203, USA. E-mail: jeffken@nursing.arizona.edu

Brett R. Fajen, Department of Cognitive Science, Carnegie Building 308, Rensselaer Polytechnic Institute, 110 8th Street, Troy, NY 12180-3590, USA. E-mail: fajenb@rpi.edu

Elise Faugloire, Human Factors Research Laboratory, Cooke Hall, 1900 University Ave SE, Minneapolis, MN 55455, USA. E-mail: elise_faugloire@umn.edu

Paul C. Fisher, ParsecUK, Arundel, BN18 0QP, UK.
E-mail: Support@ParsecUK.com

Ross Flom, Department of Psychology, 1001 Kimball Tower, Brigham Young University, Provo, UT 84602, USA. Email: flom@byu.edu

Julie Foucart, Groupe de Recherche Apprentissage et Contexte, École des Hautes Études en Sciences Sociales, 54 Bd Raspail, 75006 Paris, France. E-mail: julie.foucart@ehess.fr

Carol A. Fowler, Haskins Laboratories, 300 George St., New Haven, CT, 06511, USA. E-mail: Carol.Fowler@haskins.yale.edu

Nobuhiro Furuyama, National Institute of Informatics, Japan, 2-1-2 Hitotsubashi, Chiyoda-ku, Tokyo 101-8430, Japan.
E-mail: furuyama@nii.ac.jp

K. Fuwa, Hayashibara Great Apes Research Institute - GARI, Okayama, Japan

Phillipe Gaillot, Center for Deep Earth Exploration, Japan Agency for Marine-Earth Science and Technology, Yokohama Kanagawa, Japan. E-mail: gaillotp@jamstec.go.jp

Remi Goasdoué, Groupe de Recherche Apprentissage et Contexte, École des Hautes Études en Sciences Sociales, 54 Bd Raspail, 75006 Paris, France. E-mail: remi.goasdoue@libertysurf.fr

Justin R. L. Goodman, Center for the Ecological Study of Perception and Action, 406 Babbidge Road, Unit 1020, University of Connecticut, Storrs, CT 06269-1020, USA. E-mail: justin.goodman@uconn.edu

Katie Gordon, Department of Psychology, 1001 Kimball Tower, Brigham Young University, Provo, UT 84602, USA.

Rob Gray, Department of Applied Psychology, Arizona State University East, 7001 E. Williams Field Road, Building 140, Mesa, AZ 85212, USA. E-mail: robgray@asu.edu

Philip M. Grove, School of Psychology, The University of New South Wales, Sydney NSW 2052, Australia. E-mail: p.grove@unsw.edu.au

Seth Gunderson, Department of Psychology, 1001 Kimball Tower, Brigham Young University, Provo, UT 84602, USA.

Alen Hajnal, Center for the Ecological Study of Perception and Action, 406 Babbidge Road, Unit 1020, University of Connecticut, Storrs, CT 06269-1020, USA. E-mail: alen.hajnal@uconn.edu

Steven J. Harrison, Center for the Ecological Study of Perception and Action, 406 Babbidge Road, Unit 1020, University of Connecticut, Storrs, CT 06269-1020, USA. E-mail: steven.harrison@uconn.edu

Koji Hayashi, The University of Tokyo, 7-3-1 Hongo, Bunkyo-ku, Tokyo 113-0033, Japan. E-mail: hayashi@educhan.p.u-tokyo.ac.jp

S. Hirata, Hayashibara Great Apes Research Institute - GARI, Okayama, Japan.

Naoya Hirose, School of Human Sciences, Sugiyama Jogakuen University, 37-234 Takenoyama, Iwasaki-cho, Nisshin, Aichi, 470-0131, Japan. Email: nhirose@hs.sugiyama-u.ac.jp

Lee S. Hong, Department of Kinesiology, The Pennsylvania State University, 266 Recreation Building, University Park, PA 16802, USA. E-mail: slh343@psu.edu

Kimberly M. Hopkins, Kimberly M., Department of Psychology, Campus Box 4620, Illinois State University, Normal, IL, 61790, USA.

Philip Hove, Department of Psychology, University of Cincinnati, USA and Whirlpool Corporation, Benton Harbor, MI, 49022, USA. E-mail: philip_hove@whirlpool.com

Dan Hyde, Department of Psychology, 1001 Kimball Tower, Brigham Young University, Provo, UT 84602, USA.

Robert W. Isenhower, Center for the Ecological Study of Perception and Action, 406 Babbidge Road, Unit 1020, University of Connecticut, Storrs, CT 06269-1020, USA. E-mail: robert.isenhower@uconn.edu

Johann Issartel, Motor Efficiency and Motor Deficiency Laboratory, University of Montpellier 1, France. E-mail: johann.issartel@univ-montp1.fr

Ayumi Ito, School of Systems Information Science, Future University-Hakodate, Japan.

Kiyohide Ito, Future University-Hakodate, 116-2 Kamedanakano, Hakodate, 041-8655, Japan.

Russell Jackson, Psychology Department, University of Texas at Austin, 1 University Station: A8000, Austin, Texas 78712-1189, USA. E-mail: russelljackson@mail.utexas.edu

Igor Juricevic, Department of Psychology, University of Toronto -- Psychology, 1265 Military Trail, Toronto, Ontario, M1C 1A4, Canada. E-mail: igorphd@hotmail.com

E. E. Kadar, Department of Psychology, University of Portsmouth, Portsmouth, PO1 2DY, UK. E-mail: endre.kadar@port.ac.uk

Bruce A. Kay, Center for the Ecological Study of Perception and Action, 406 Babbidge Road, Unit 1020, University of Connecticut, Storrs, CT 06269-1020, USA. E-mail: bruce.kay@uconn.edu

John M. Kennedy, Department of Psychology, University of Toronto -- Psychology, 1265 Military Trail, Toronto, Ontario, M1C 1A4, Canada. E-mail: kennedy@banks.scar.utoronoto.ca.

ChungGon Kim, School of Kinesiology, University of Minnesota, Minneapolis, MN, 55414, USA.

Jeffrey Kinsella-Shaw, Department of Physical Therapy, School of Allied Health, 358 Mansfield Road, Unit 2101, Storrs, CT 06269-2101, USA. E-mail: jeffrey.kinsella-shaw@uconn.edu

Brent C. Kirkwood, Technical University of Denmark, Acoustic Technology, Ørsteds Plads, Building 352, DK-2800 Kgs. Lyngby Denmark. E-mail: bki@oersted.dtu.dk

Yuji Kojima, School of Systems Information Science, Future University-Hakodate, Japan.

Takanori Komatsu, Future University-Hakodate, 116-2 Kamedanakano, Hakodate, 041-8655, Japan.

Gerri Lamb, University of Arizona College of Nursing, PO Box 210203, Tucson, AZ 85721-0203, USA. E-mail: glamb@nursing.arizona.edu

Stacy Lopresti-Goodman, Center for the Ecological Study of Perception and Action, 406 Babbidge Road, Unit 1020, University of Connecticut, Storrs, CT 06269-1020, USA. E-mail: Stacy.Lopresti-goodman@uconn.edu

Bruno Mantel, Center for Research in Sport Sciences, University of Paris Sud XI, Bat.335, 91405 Orsay Cedex, France.
E-mail: bruno.mantel@staps.u-psud.fr

Ludovic Marin, Motor Efficiency and Motor Deficiency Laboratory, University of Montpellier 1, France. E-mail: ludovic.marin@univ-montp1.fr

Leonard S. Mark, Department of Psychology, Miami University Oxford, OH 45056, USA. E-mail: markls@muohio.edu

Kerry L. Marsh, Department of Psychology, 406 Babbidge Road, Unit 1020, University of Connecticut, Storrs, CT 06269-1020, USA. E-mail: Kerry.L.Marsh@uconn.edu

Takashi Matsuishi, Graduate School of Fisheries Sciences, Hokkaido University, Japan.

Michael K. McBeath, Department of Psychology, Arizona State University, P.O. Box, 871104, Tempe, AZ 85287-1104, USA.
E-mail: Michael.McBeath@asu.edu

Marylyn McEwen, University of Arizona College of Nursing, PO Box 210203, Tucson, AZ 85721-0203, USA. E-mail: mmcewen@nursing.arizona.edu

Claire F. Michaels, Center for the Ecological Study of Perception and Action, 406 Babbidge Road, Unit 1020, University of Connecticut, Storrs, CT 06269-1020, USA. E-mail: claire.michaels@uconn.edu

Jennifer L. Minarik, Department of Psychology, Campus Box 4620, Illinois State University, Normal, IL, USA 61790

Hiroyuki Mishima, University of Fukui, 3-9-1 Bunkyo, Fukui-shi, Fukui 910-8507, Japan. E-mail: a980014@icpc00.icpc.fukui-u.ac.jp

Atsuko Miyashita, Graduate School of Fisheries Sciences, Hokkaido University, Japan.

Miguel Moreno, Center for the Ecological Study of Perception and Action, 406 Babbidge Road, Unit 1020, University of Connecticut, Storrs, CT 06269-1020, USA. Email: miguel.moreno@uconn.edu

M. Antoine Morice, UFR STAPS, Université Paris Sud XI, Centre de recherche en sciences du sport, Bât. 335, 91405 ORSAY Cedex, France. E-mail: antoine.morice@staps.u-psud.fr

Karl M. Newell, College of Health and Human Development, The Pennsylvania State University, 201 Henderson, University Park, PA 16802, USA. E-mail: kmn1@psu.edu

Lisa C. Newell, Florida International University, 11200 SW 8th St., Department of Psychology, DM 115, Miami, FL 33199, USA.

Makoto Okamoto, Future University-Hakodate, 116-2 Kamedanakano, Hakodate, 041-8655, Japan.

Annie J. Olmstead, Center for the Ecological Study of Perception and Action, 406 Babbidge Road, Unit 1020, University of Connecticut, Storrs, CT 06269-1020, USA. E-mail: anne.olmstead@uconn.edu

Tetsuo Ono, Future University-Hakodate, 116-2 Kamedanakano, Hakodate, 041-8655, Japan

Olivier Oullier, Research Associate, Laboratoire Mouvement et Perception (UMR 6152) CNRS-Université de la Méditerranée, 163, avenue de Luminy CP910, 13288 Marseille cedex 09, France. E-mail: oullier@laps.univ-mrs.fr

Christopher C. Pagano, Department of Psychology, 418 Brackett Hall, Clemson University, Clemson, SC 29634-1355, USA. E-mail: cpagano@clemson.edu

Geraldine L. Pellecchia, Department of Physical Therapy, School of Allied Health, 358 Mansfield Road, Unit 2101, Storrs, CT 06269-2101, USA. E-mail: geraldine.pellecchia@uconn.edu

Gert-Jan Pepping, Perception-in-Action Laboratories, Moray House School of Education, The University of Edinburgh, St. Leonard's Land, Holyrood Road, Edinburgh, EH8 8AQ, UK. E-mail: g.j.pepping@ed.ac.uk

V. C. Ramenzoni, Perceptual-Motor Dynamics Laboratory, Department of Psychology, University of Cincinnati, OH, 45219, USA. E-mail: ramenzvc@email.uc.edu

L. Rasseneur, Equipe d'Accueil en Sciences du Sport, Strasbourg, URF STAPS, Universite Marc Bloch, 14 Rue Rene Descartes 67084 Strasbourg, France. E-mail: laurence.rasseneur@umb.u-strasbg.fr

Theo G. Rhodes, Center for the Ecological Study of Perception and Action, 406 Babbidge Road, Unit 1020, University of Connecticut, Storrs, CT 06269-1020, USA. Email: theo.rhodes@uconn.edu

Michael J. Richardson, Center for the Ecological Study of Perception and Action, 406 Babbidge Road, Unit 1020, University of Connecticut, Storrs, CT, 06269-1020, USA. E-mail: Michael.Richardson@uconn.edu

M. A. Riley, Perceptual-Motor Dynamics Laboratory, Department of Psychology, University of Cincinnati, Cincinnati,OH, 45219, USA. E-mail: rileym@email.uc.edu

Ryan L. Robart, Department of Psychology, University of California, Riverside, CA 92521, USA. E-mail: rroba001@student.ucr.edu

Lawrence D. Rosenblum, Department of Psychology, University of California, Riverside, CA 92521, USA. E-mail: rosenblu@citrus.ucr.edu

T. Rupp, Equipe d'Accueil Efficience et Déficience Motrices, Montpellier, UFR STAPS, 700 Ave du Pic St Loup 34090 Montpellier, France. E-Mail: thomas.rupp@univ-montp1.fr

W. L. Ben Sachtler,, School of Psychology, The University of New South Wales, Sydney NSW 2052, Australia. E-mail: bensan@unsw.edu.au

Nichole E. Saunders, Perceptual-Motor Dynamics Laboratory, Department of Psychology, University of Cincinnati, Cincinnati, OH 45219, USA.

R. C. Schmidt, Department of Psychology, College of the Holy Cross, College Street, Box 38A, Worcester, MA, 01610, USA. E-mail: rschmidt@holycross.edu

Joe Schmutz, Department of Psychology, 1001 Kimball Tower, Brigham Young University, Provo, UT 84602, USA.

Jocelyn Schwartz, Department of Psychology, 135 Hofstra University, Hempstead, NY 11549 USA.

Kevin D. Shockley, Department of Psychology, ML 0376, 429 Dyer Hall, University of Cincinnati, Cincinnati, OH, 45221-0376, USA. E-mail: Kevin.Shockley@uc.edu

Melissa A. Shuman, Florida International University, 11200 SW 8th St., Department of Psychology, DM 115, Miami, FL 33199, USA. E-mail: melissa.shuman@fiu.edu

I. A. Siegler, Institut Universitaire de France, 103 bd St Michel, 75005 Paris, France.

Joanne Smith, Perception-in-Action Laboratories, Moray House School of Education, The University of Edinburgh, St. Leonard's Land, Holyrood Road, Edinburgh, EH8 8AQ, UK.
E-mail: joanne_smith@education.ed.ac.uk

J. Snyder, Perceptual-Motor Dynamics Laboratory, Department of Psychology, University of Cincinnati, Cincinnati, OH, 45219, USA.
E-mail: snyderjl@email.uc.edu

Jacob J. Sosnoff, Department of Kinesiology, The Pennsylvania State University, 266 Recreation Building, University Park, PA 16802, USA.
E-mail: jjs388@psu.edu

Sara Stasik, Department of Psychology, Miami University, Oxford, Ohio, 45056, USA.

Thomas A. Stoffregen, Human Factors Research Laboratory, School of Kinesiology, 1900 University Avenue S.E., University of Minnesota, Minneapolis, MN 55414, USA. E-mail: tas@umn.edu

Matt Streit, Department of Psychology, ML 0376, 214 Dyer Hall, University of Cincinnati, Cincinnati, OH 45221-0376 USA.
E-mail: streitms@email.uc.edu

Thomas G. Sugar, Department of Mechanical & Aerospace Engineering, Arizona State University, P.O. Box 876106, Tempe, AZ 85287-6106, USA. E-mail: Thomas.Sugar@asu.edu

Kona R. Taylor, Department of Psychology, Campus Box 4620, Illinois State University, Normal, IL 61790, USA. E-mail: kona211@hotmail.com

Alison M. Tollner, Department of Psychology, University of Cincinnati, Cincinnati, OH, 45219, USA. E-mail: tollneam@email.uc.edu

Affordances

Studies in Perception and Action VIII
H. Heft & K. L. Marsh (Eds.)
© *2005 Lawrence Erlbaum Associates, Inc.*

Enacting the Perception of the Affordances of Potential Tools I: The Case of Children Hammering

B. Bril & J. Foucart

Groupe de Recherche Apprentissage et Contexte,
École des Hautes Etudes en Sciences Sociales, Paris, France

Tool use offers a privileged situation for an analysis of how children enact the perception of affordances of objects as tools. When confronted with a given task, the child has to solve a multidimensional problem: What should be the main features of the action to be performed? And correlatively what kind of tool is adapted to solve the motor problem at hand?

In this study we analyzed the development of tool selection when children aged 3 to 12 years are given the task of cracking nuts. If we consider that performing an action necessitates exploiting the constraints of the task and particularly the physics of the system involved (Roux et al., 2000; Goldfield et al. 1993), then the choice of an adequate tool to perform a specific action requires perceiving the relation between the tool properties and the task properties–what van Leeuwen et al. (1994) call second order affordances. Functional tool use depends on (a) the choice of the adequate tool and (b) the functional manipulation of the tool (Gibson, 1977). *Identifying information* that specifies affordances appears as a critical challenge for the understanding of tool use expertise.

Nut-cracking is defined as a task which consists of producing the right amount of kinetic energy and transferring it to the nut in order to produce an adequate deformation of the shell so that it breaks. Consequently the child must discover a way to produce this transfer of energy; that is (1) to produce some kinetic energy, (2) to find the right tools so that it is possible, on the one hand, to produce kinetic energy and, on the other hand, not to lose the energy during the impact. If, for example, the nut is lying on a soft support, the energy will be absorbed by the support, and it will be impossible to crack the nut. Consequently the way the action must be carried out depends on several factors, i.e. the weight of the hammer, the support surface, the object to be hit, the velocity of the hammer, the orientation of the trajectory, etc.

Method

Sixty children aged 3 to 13 divided into six age groups had to crack open 15 nuts (5 different species, some well known to the child, others totally unknown). For the experiment the child who was sitting on a soft gymnastic carpet was offered 21 objects as potential tools of various degrees of functionality (Figure 1). In addition, a group of 6 young adults considered as the expert group participated in a similar experiment. All of the sessions were videotaped.

Figure 1. Display of the 21 objects offered as potential hammers to crack open nuts.

Results

Except for the younger group of children (3 years of age), almost every participant operated upon the nut by means of percussive movements. But the 3 years old were very different from the other children in their actions, and most of them failed to crack open the nuts. Furthermore, they tried many different ways of breaking the nut; the use of a hammer represented less than 50% of the total actions performed on the nuts. For the older children up to 10 years of age, the metal hammer (manufactured tool) represented 40 to 50% of the choices. In the oldest group and in the adult group, the metal hammer represented 65% of the total choices. When the metal hammer was not chosen, a stone was used in most cases. The use of a second tool, i.e. an anvil, was exceptional for the youngest children. In groups 3 and 4 (that is, around 8 to 10 years) it became more common, but it was still used in less than 50% of the percussive movements. It becomes almost systematic in the oldest age group (12-13 years) and in the adult group.

The exploratory behavior of the children changed a great deal with age. Here again the youngest group activity stood clearly apart. Figure 2 indicates the number of different hammers chosen, and the number of times a child changed hammer during the whole session. The number of different hammers picked up during a session was as high as 9.4 for the 4-5 years old children, and dropped to 4.4 and 2.5 tools for the oldest children and the adults respectively. The number of times a child changed hammers was even greater and reached 22 times in the 4-5 years old children, but dropped to 10.5 times in the 12-13 years old group.

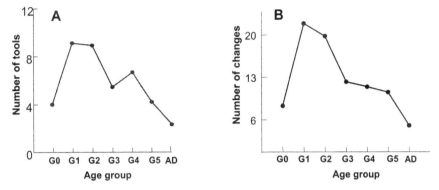

Figure 2. Exploratory behavior depending on the age group (G0: 3 years; G5: 12/13 years, AD: adults): (A) Average number of different tools picked up by a child during a session; (B) Average number of changes of tool for a child during one session.

Discussion

This experiment shows that nut cracking is not such an easy task, at least for urban children with little experience. The youngest children, aged 3 years did not succeed, which means that they did not master the constraints of the task: they performed inappropriate actions that did not fit the demands of the task, the correlate being an inadequate tool choice. However from 4 years of age the action choice was appropriate, but the choice of the tool was still far from optimal. Most of the time the nut was positioned on the soft ground; in this condition energy is mainly dissipated in the soft ground which makes it difficult to fracture the shell of the nut. However, the children tended to overcome this situation by using a heavier stone as hammer. This suggests that they were aware of the necessity to produce a certain amount of kinetic energy, but they were not sensitive to the necessity of avoiding its dissipation in the ground. (This capacity of action does not, of course, imply a conceptualization of these properties of the action). The necessity to use an anvil, which offsets the effects of the slight elastic ground surface, was apprehended around 12 years of age. Note that the use of heavy stone hammer decreased significantly, while the use of an anvil increased (Figure 3).

The developmental trend of learning the affordances of a task that require the production of a controlled amount of kinetic energy for, e.g., nut cracking, suggests that choosing the right tool, that is, learning the affordances of the tools, depends on the discovery of numerous task properties.

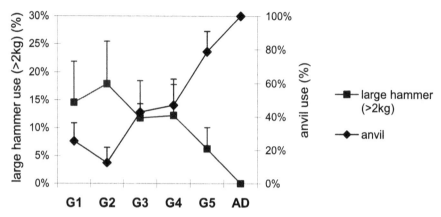

Figure 3. Frequency of use of a large hammer (weight greater than 2 kg) and use of an anvil in each age group.

References

Goldfield, E. C., Kay, B. A., & Warren, W. H., Jr. (1993). Infant bouncing: The assembly and tuning of action systems. *Child Development, 64*, 1128-1142.

Roux, V.,Bril, B., Dietrich, G. (1995) Skills and learning difficulties involved in stone knapping. *World Archeology, 27*, 63-87.

van Leeuwen, L., Smitsman, A., & van Leeuwen, C. (1994). Affordance, perceptual complexity, and the development of tool use. *Journal of Experimental Psychology, 20*, 174-191.

Gibson, J. J. (1977). The theory of affordances. In R. Shaw & J. Bransford (Eds.), *Perceiving, acting, and knowing* (pp. 67-82). Hillsdale: Lawrence Erlbaum Associates.

Acknowledgements. Thanks to all the children who have participated to this experiment. This work was supported by a Grant from the French Ministry of Research, ACI 3T 02 20440 awarded to Blandine Bril.

Studies in Perception and Action VIII
H. Heft & K. L. Marsh (Eds.)
© *2005 Lawrence Erlbaum Associates, Inc.*

Perceiving the Obstacle Step-Acrossability after the Maximal Exercise Test

S. Cornus[1], G. Walther[2], T. Rupp[3], & L. Rasseneur[1]

[1]Equipe d'Accueil en Sciences du Sport, Strasbourg, France
[2]Jeune Equipe en Physiologie des Adaptations Cardiovasculaires à
l'Exercice, Avignon, France
[3]Equipe d'Accueil Efficience et Déficiences Motrices, Montpellier,
France

Affordance perception must be considered as an interaction between the capabilities of the actor and the situation. For example, this perception depends on the psychological and developmental characteristics of the actor. Different states of actor, such as anxiety (e.g., Bootsma, Bakker, Van Snippenberg, & Tdlohreg, 1992) or expertise level (e.g., Pijpers & Bakker, 1993) can alter the precision of affordance perception. But also, this perception can be altered by the situation. Jiang and Mark (1994) showed that the gap depth altered the perception of affordances. The relevance of the interaction between the capabilities of the actor and the situation had been developed in many studies. However, few studies have examined the importance of the physiological factors in the perception of affordances. The aim of this study was to analyze the effect of the maximal exercise test on the precision of affordances perception. In order to address this effect, we compared two obstacle stepping judging tasks to an obstacle stepping across task.

Method

Nine subjects (*M* age = 19 years, *SD* = 3.56) performed three tasks: an obstacle stepping across task and two obstacle step-acrossability judging tasks before and after a maximal exercise test. In the stepping across task, subjects had to walk naturally and step across a flat 1 m wide obstacle located on average 10 m from the starting point. During this displacement, subjects had to judge the obstacle step-acrossability: (1) when they arrived in the space placed at 3 m from the obstacle (J1: judging task 1); (2) when they put their foot in order to step across the obstacle (J2: judging task 2). The obstacles ranged in length from 0.60 m to 1.20 m (length increments = 0.05 m). Four series, two increasing and two decreasing, were presented in a counterbalanced order (n = 13). During the maximal exercise test, subjects were instructed to keep the pedalling rate constant (between 70 and 80 rpm) throughout the test. The work-load was increased stepwise by 20 W every minute until volitional exhaustion (Lonsdorfer, Londofer-Wolf, Rasseneur, Oswald-Mammosser, Richard, & Doutreleau, 2001). The actual (or judged) critical stepping across size (before or after the exercise) was defined as the obstacle size beyond which the subject changed (or judged s/he had to change) from stepping across to jumping over the obstacle. The accuracy of judged obstacle step-acrossability can be expressed as a percentage of absolute error (Cornus, Montagne, & Laurent, 1999). Using the actual critical stepping across size before the exercise as a baseline, the formula for the percentage of absolute error was: (Scaled critical values - 1)*100.

Results

A student's t-test showed that the mean percentage of absolute error obtained on the judging task 2 before the exercise (J2b: $M = 2.27\%$, $SD = 0.82$) was significantly different from the mean percentage obtained on the judging task 1 after, $t(8) = - 2.84$, $p = .022$ (J1a: $M = 4.95\%$, $SD = 3.02$), on the judging task 2 after, $t(8) = - 2.82$, $p = .023$ (J2a: $M = 5.89\%$, $SD = 3.87$), and on the stepping across task after, $t(8) = - 2.49$, $p = .037$, (Sa: $M = 5.34\%$, $SD = 3.35$) (Figure 1). The mean percentage of absolute error obtained on the judging task 2 before the exercise (J2b) was not significantly different from the mean percentage obtained on the judging task 1 before, $t(8) = - 2.84$, $p = .022$ (J1b: $M = 4.07\%$, $SD = 3.83$) (Figure 1).

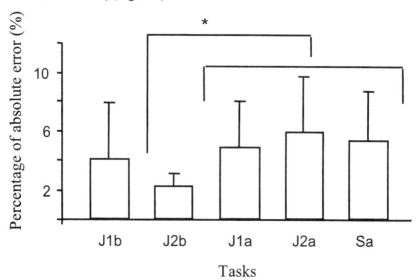

Figure 1. Mean percentage of absolute error obtained on the judging task 1 (J1) and on the judging task 2 (J2) before (b) and after (a) the exercise, and mean percentage of absolute error obtained on the stepping across task after the exercise (Sa).

Discussion

The percentages of absolute error obtained after the exercise were greater than the percentages obtained before the exercise. This maximal exercise seems to alter the precision of the processes of affordance perception. But contrary to Cornus et al. (1999), this perturbation was observed in the stepping across task and in the judging task. The analytic processes to judge the obstacle step-across-ability and the perceptive processes to step across the obstacle were less accurate after the maximal exercise test. Depending on the situation, the accuracy of perceived or judged obstacle step-acrossability must be considered as the interaction between visuo-motor capabilities and physiological capabilities of the actor.

References

Bootsma, R. J., Bakker, F. C., Van Snippenberg, F. E. J., & Tdlohreg, C. W. (1992). The effects of anxiety on perceiving the reachability of passing objects. *Ecological Psychology, 4*, 1-16.

Cornus, S., Montagne, G., & Laurent, M. (1999). Perception of a stepping-across affordance. *Ecological Psychology, 11*, 249-267.

Lonsdorfer, J., Londofer-Wolf, E., Rasseneur, L., Oswald-Mammosser, M., Richard, R., & Doutreleau, S. (2001). Rééducation de l'asthmatique et sport: pour une préparation physique personnalisée. *Revue Française d'Allergologie et d'Immunologie Clinique, 41*, 316-24.

Pijpers, R. J., & Bakker, F. C. (1993). Perceiving affordances in climbing. In S. S. Valenti & J. B. Pittenger (Eds.), *Studies in perception in action II* (pp. 85-88). Hillsdale, NJ: Lawrence Erlbaum Associates, Inc.

Studies in Perception and Action VIII
H. Heft & K. L. Marsh (Eds.)
© *2005 Lawrence Erlbaum Associates, Inc.*

Enacting the Perception of the Affordances of Potential Tools II: The Case of Chimpanzees Nut-Cracking

J. Foucart[1], S. Hirata[2], K. Fuwa[2], & B. Bril[1]

[1]EHESS, Groupe de Recherche "Apprentissage et Contexte", Paris, France
[2]Hayashibara Great Apes Research Institute, GARI, Okayama, Japan

For centuries the capacity to use tools has been considered as the landmark of humankind. Now it is well known that non-human primates and even birds are tool users (Beck, 1980). However, apart from humans, chimpanzees are the only animal showing diversified and regular tool use activities in the wild as well as in captivity. In the wild they have been observed to select appropriate tools or to modify an object to obtain an optimal tool. In a nut cracking task, chimpanzees are capable of selecting appropriate hammers and anvils –i.e. size, shape, material (Boesch & Boesch, 1981). This capacity to perceive the functionality of tools has been confirmed in captivity using experimental settings (Visalberghi, 2000).

The aim of the present study was to analyze the capacity of captive chimpanzees to perceive the affordances (Gibson, 1977) of unfamiliar tools while engaged in a familiar task. We evaluated the aptitude of five juvenile chimpanzees for successfully cracking nuts, when unfamiliar tools varying in their degree of functionality are offered. They were trained a few months earlier to crack open nuts with stone hammers.

Method

Participants in the study were 5 juvenile chimpanzees from GARI, two males and three females aged 6 to 9.5 years. Due to technical constraints and the rapid decrease of motivation of the younger chimpanzees, we attempted to make the investigation experiment as similar as possible to one conducted with children by partitioning it into two experiments, one considering hammer choices (Experiment 1), and the second considering anvil choices (Experiment 2). Prior to the experiments, two habituation sessions were conducted. The chimpanzees were encouraged to manipulate the objects that will be offered as potential tools in the subsequent experiments. Each chimpanzee was tested individually by the second and third authors. All sessions were videotaped.

Experiment 1: Hammer choice

The chimpanzee had to crack open a total of 14 nuts from three different species (5 artificial, 5 macadamia and 4 Brazilian nuts) on a familiar anvil (a flat stone with cavities). Each chimpanzee was offered eight objects characterized by different degrees of functionality as hammers (Figure 1a), due to their weight, shape and substance (four pieces of wood, a primate toy, two pieces of foam and one plastic bottle). The nuts were given one by one, in an unvarying order (artificial, macadamia and Brazil). The eight objects were placed in an open box. The chimpanzee could take whatever object he/she wanted and could change as many times as he/she wanted. Once the nut was cracked, the hammer was put back into the box. After each success he/she was given a piece of fruit as reward. Two sessions were completed.

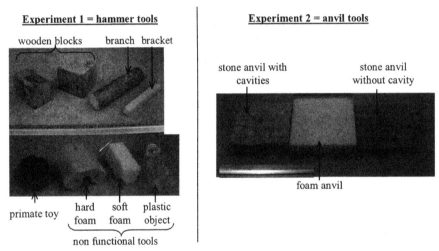

Figure 1. Potential tools provided for the hammer experiment (on the left) and the anvil experiment (on the right)

Experiment 2: Anvil choice

This experiment was similar to Experiment 1, but the choice concerned the anvils and not the hammer. Each chimpanzee was offered simultaneously 3 unfamiliar square anvils varying in their degree of functionality (one piece of foam, two stone anvils, one smooth, and the surface of the other one was carved with cavities). The anvils were arranged in a row (Figure 1b). Three sessions were conducted in order to change the layout of the anvils and minimize a choice of anvil due to the characteristics of the layout. The anvils were permuted for each session, in order to have a different anvil at the central position. In addition to avoid directing the chimpanzee's choice, the nut was given from the side of the non functional anvil. The hammer was a familiar one (a stone weighing approximately 600 g).

Analysis

A time series analysis was performed on the videotapes. Action strategies were analyzed with respect to the following variables: total number of tools selected during one session (the minimum number is equal to the number of nuts, one tool may be chosen several times); number of different tools chosen; number of times the chimpanzee switched one tool for another; number of strikes; number of changes of the position of the nut on the anvil; number of changes of the orientation of the hammer and of the nut.

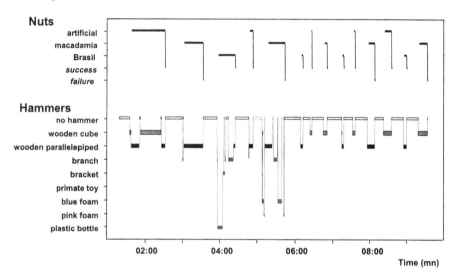

Figure 2. Example of the results of the time series analysis from Experiment 1. The upper part of the graph gives the time needed to crack each nut ended with a success or failure. The lower part of the graph gives the successive choice of hammers: in this example the hammers most often chosen are the wooden cube and the wooden parallelepiped.

Results and Discussion

We give here the results from one male, Zamba, 9 years old.

Experiment 1: Hammer choice

Due to the type of hammer (recall that familiar hammers were stones weighing 600g, while the heaviest piece of wood was about 270 g): the number of failures was quite high: 4 during the first session, and 7 during the second session. Zamba's motivation was lower during the second session. This is clearly suggested when looking at the number of strikes before giving up (especially for macadamia). Surrender happens after 24 strikes during the first session, but after only 10.4 during the second session.

In both sessions, non functional objects were hardly selected: only three times during each session, while pieces of wood were selected 18 and 13 times during the first and second sessions, respectively. However, the two biggest pieces of wood were selected preferentially (16 and 11 times, respectively). The primate toy and the bracket were never chosen. However the choice of a non functional object does not seem to be clearly associated with one particular type of nut.

The striking behavior indicates some kind of understanding of the functionality of the tools as well. On average the number of strikes performed in a row with a non functional tool was less than half compared with the number of strikes performed when a more functional tool is used (wooden object) (5.2 ± 2.2 and 13.3 ± 2.4 strikes, respectively). Except in the cases of low motivation, unsuccessful strikes were followed by discard of the tool and the choice of another one. This happened 7 times during the first session, but twice only during the second session. Another interesting behavior, the reorientation of the piece of wood in the hand, was observed as well (three times during the second session). These exploratory behaviors reveal an understanding of the proper action to be performed.

Experiment 2: Anvil choice

Whatever the position of the non functional anvils, Zamba never chose the foam anvil. The smooth anvil was chosen only once when the anvil was positioned in front of him. This choice corresponds to the first nut of the session. However, after 7 strikes Zamba shifted to the stone anvil with cavities which was subsequently used during the whole session. Two other traits of Zamba behavior showed a clear understanding of the best fit between tool and nut cracking action: (1) if the nut happened to slip on the foam anvil or on the smooth stone one, the chimpanzee stopped his action and placed the nut back on the anvil with cavities; (2) Zamba changed the position or the orientation of the nut 11 times.

Conclusions

While these results are preliminary and concern one chimpanzee only, they show that (1) when offered different unknown objects as tools he preferentially chose the most functional ones; (2) when he failed to crack the nut, he tried another tool or repositioned the tool in his hand or the nut on the anvil; (3) when an inadequate tool was chosen he did not persevere in the ineffective action.

This experiment suggests that acquiring a motor skill (here nut cracking) involves learning the affordances of the task. That is, the chimpanzee was able to detect the relevant properties of the objects offered as potential tools in relation to the demand of the task at hand, even when these objects are unfamiliar to him.

References

Beck, B. B. (1980). *Animal tool behavior*. New York: Garland STPM Press.

Boesch, C., & Boesch, H. (1981). Sex differences in the use of natural hammers by wild chimpanzees: a preliminary report. *Journal of Human Evolution, 10*(7), 585-593.

Gibson, J. J. (1977). The theory of affordances. In R. Shaw & J. Bransford (Eds.), *Perceiving, acting, and knowing* (pp. 67-82). Hillsdale: Lawrence Erlbaum Associates.

Visalberghi, E. (2000). Tool use behavior and the understanding of causality in primates. In E. Thommen & H. Kilcher (Eds.), *Comparer ou prédire. Exemple de recherche en psychologie comparative aujourd'hui* (pp. 17-35). Fribourg Suisse: Editions Universitaires.

Acknowledgements

We are very grateful to the GARI staff for their help during the experiments. This work was supported by the French Ministry of Education and Research (ACI 3T, 02 2 0440) awarded to B. Bril.

Studies in Perception and Action VIII
H. Heft & K. L. Marsh (Eds.)
© *2005 Lawrence Erlbaum Associates, Inc.*

Perceiving Whether or Not Another Person Can Use a Step to Reach an Object

V. C. Ramenzoni, M. A. Riley, T. Davis, & J. Snyder

Perceptual-Motor Dynamics Laboratory, Department of Psychology
University of Cincinnati, OH, USA

Perhaps one of the most complex issues surrounding the theory of affordances concerns their ontology. In Gibson's (1979/1986) account an affordance does not refer to either subjective properties of an agent or objective properties of the world, but to the relation between the world and agent. An affordance describes a potential for action—the capacity of an object or environmental surface to enable an agent to perform an action. In that respect, affordances are animal-specific. They exist relative to the action capabilities of particular actors. Nevertheless, according to Gibson an affordance possesses ontological reality independently of the particular actor and the actor's intentions. This suggests that an agent should be as capable of perceiving affordances for himself/herself as perceiving affordances for other agents. However, little evidence supports this hypothesis. Until recently (Stoffregen, Gorday, Sheng, & Flynn, 1999), the ability to perceive affordances for other agents has received little attention in the literature compared to the abundance of research on the ability to perceive affordances for oneself. This project extends a recent line of research that has shown people can perceive whether they could use steps of different heights to reach an object suspended at various heights. We explored the perceiver's capacity to perceive whether another actor could reach an object if the actor were to stand on steps of varying heights, and whether those perceptions would be influenced by the actor's reaching height. Furthermore, we explored whether the perception of the affordance was affected by the distance between the actor and the participant.

Method

Ten undergraduate participants (5 females, 5 males) from the University of Cincinnati received course credit for participation in this study. All participants had normal or corrected-to-normal vision. Experimental procedures were approved by the University of Cincinnati Institutional Review Board, and participants signed an informed consent form prior to participation in the experiment. The apparatus consisted of an adjustable step and a small cylindrical object suspended from the ceiling by a rope (see Figure 1). Three step heights (49.5 cm, 64.5 cm, & 79.5 cm) were used. Each participant completed

24 randomized trials (2 trials per condition). Participants stood barefoot in a fixed location throughout the experiment and were instructed to close their eyes between trials. On each trial, participants were asked to provide a reachability judgment for either a short (reaching height = 1.85 m) or tall (reaching height = 2.17 m) actor. During each trial either the tall or short actor stood barefoot, with the arms suspended at the sides, at one of three distances from the perceiver (next to the perceiver, 1.5 m away from the perceiver and directly beside the apparatus, or 3 m from the perceiver). Reachability judgments were obtained using the method of limits. An experimenter raised or lowered (counterbalanced across trials) the to-be-reached object until the perceiver indicated that it was just reachable by the actor if the actor were to stand on the step. The actors never actually stood on the step or reached for the object. After each trial, raw reachability judgments were obtained by measuring the distance between the object and the step.

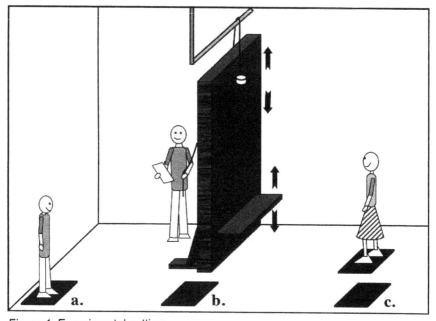

Figure 1. Experimental setting.

Results

ANOVAs were conducted on the raw reachability values (extrinsic metric) and on the ratio of those values to the actors' actual reaching heights (intrinsic metric). Judgments for the two actors differed for the raw reachability values, $F(1,7) = 54.51$, $p < .05$, but not for the intrinsically scaled reachability values ($p > .05$) (see Figure 2). Ratios near unity for both actors (short: 0.991; tall: 0.953) indicated that the perceived reachability boundaries were fairly accurate, but overall there was a tendency to underestimate reaching ability. Main effects for distance between the actor and perceiver, $F(4,28) = 4.11$, $p < .05$, and for step height, $F(4,28) = 14.93$, $p < .05$, were also found for the intrinsic metrics. In general, accuracy diminished for the closest distance and as a function of increases in step height. A step height × distance interaction, $F(4,28) = 49.97$, $p < .05$, indicated that the intrinsically scaled reachability boundaries differed between the actor-middle and actor-far conditions only for the middle step height, whereas ratios for the actor-close condition were lower than the other distance conditions for all step heights. An actor × step height interaction, $F(2,14) = 4.32$, $p < .05$, indicated that reachability judgments for the two actors were most similar for the highest step and diverged for lower step heights.

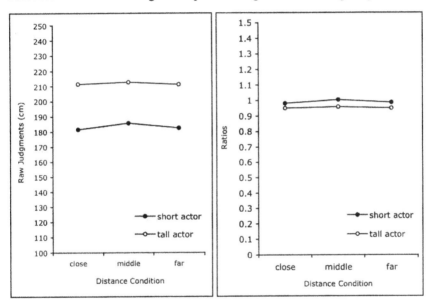

Figure 2. The graph on the left shows the raw reachability values obtained for each actor for the three distances, averaged across step height. The graph on the right shows the ratio of the raw reachability values to the reaching height of each actor for the three distances, averaged across step height.

Discussion

The results showed that participants were generally capable of perceiving the affordance of reachability via a step for another actor. An overall tendency to underestimate reaching ability was observed for both actors (on average there were underestimations of about 3 cm and 5 cm for the short and tall actor, respectively), which is similar to underestimations we have observed in experiments on step-reachability judgments for oneself (on average 7 cm). However, the observed dependency of reachability judgments on combinations of actor, step height, and actor distance raise some questions about the information specifying the affordance of reachability via a step. Interactions between step height and actor and between step height and actor distance indicate that the perception of the affordance is constrained by several factors, including the height of the step, the actor's height and reaching ability, and the distance between the actor and the perceiver. Nevertheless, the fact that participants could perceive the affordance of reachability via a step for agents with distinct action capabilities suggests that affordances can be perceived independently of the action capabilities of the perceiver. In principle, these results provide empirical support for the independent ontological status of affordances. In other words, affordances seem to be constitutive features of the environment-agent system, and are therefore available for other agents to perceive.

References

Gibson, J.J. (1986). *The ecological approach to visual perception.* Hillsdale, NJ: Erlbaum. [Original work published in 1979]
Stoffregen, T. A., Gorday, K. M., Sheng, Y-Y., & Flynn, S. B. (1999). Perceiving affordances for another person's actions. *Journal of Experimental Psychology: Human Perception & Performance, 25,* 120-136.

Studies in Perception and Action VIII
H. Heft & K. L. Marsh (Eds.)
© *2005 Lawrence Erlbaum Associates, Inc.*

Posting Balls through Holes: Effect of Hole-Size and Background Texture on Action Initiation Time and the Perception of Affordances

Gert-Jan Pepping & Joanne Smith

Perception-in-Action Laboratories, Moray House School of Education,
The University of Edinburgh, Scotland

Hick's law describes the relation between response uncertainty and reaction time. The law predicts that in a forced choice situation reaction time increases with increased stimulus-response uncertainty presented by a task. Traditional interpretations of the law focus on task *complexity* and take reaction time differences to result from differences in information processing demands by the brain. A more satisfactory interpretation from an ecological viewpoint, argues that reaction time differences should be understood as the result of differences in the speed of affordance detection (Michaels, 1988). From this viewpoint reaction time is seen as the time it takes to explore the environment to find the relevant information specifying affordances, to softly assemble and tune a response device on the basis of this information, and to launch its operation. Following this account *action initiation time* is a more appropriate term for the time between stimulus and response onset.

Affordances are generally defined in terms of a discrete task and scientific investigations have focused on the perception of critical and preferred *action boundaries*. For instance, in Warren's (1984) seminal paper on stair climbing actors were asked to indicate at which height stair risers of different heights were perceived as climbable. Similarly, Pepping and Li (2000) asked participants at which height a ball either started or ceased to be perceived as reachable in the task of overhead reach-and-jumping. At the action boundary, information specifies more ambiguously which actions are permitted by an actor. Using a forced choice paradigm, here the hypothesis was tested that if action initiation time reflects the time it takes to integrate relevant performer and environment information into an adequate action, then near-action boundary's action initiation time will be longer than when initiating well within or well outside the action boundary. In particular it was hypothesized that in the simple task of posting a ball through a hole, action initiation time will be longer when ball and hole are of a similar size (at the action boundary), compared to when ball and hole are of very dissimilar dimensions.

Previously the information specifying affordances has been investigated by carefully manipulating actor and environment properties. In Warren (1984) for instance, participants with different leg lengths were selected. Also, Pepping and

Li (2000) manipulated the participant's weight and the surfaces upon which reaches and jumps were performed. A further aim of the current experiment was to investigate the effect of a manipulation of hole-background on action initiation time in ball posting. Specifically, we were interested in seeing how the presence or absence of texture against which a hole is presented would affect action initiation time. The hypothesis was tested that a textured hole-background provides clearer hole-edge information resulting in superior identification of action boundaries than an un-textured hole-background.

Method

Participants were asked to judge whether a small ball (diameter = 30mm) would fit through a disk-shaped hole presented on a computer screen. Judgments were made by moving a mouse toward the computer screen in the case of a positive response, or away from the screen in the case of a negative response. The diameter of the hole varied in size, ranging from 7mm smaller than the ball, to 7mm larger than the ball, in 2mm steps (note: a hole-size that was exactly the same as the ball-size was not used). Each size was presented 10 times, in a randomized order, on two different backgrounds, viz.: a black background, and a textured background. Action initiation time was recorded in ms as the time between the presentation of a hole on the computer screen and the initiation of a forward or backward mouse movement.

Results and Discussion

Results showed an effect of hole-size on action initiation time, $F(7,112) = 3.38$, $p < .05$, partial $\eta^2 = .17$, and post hoc analysis revealed a quadratic relationship between action initiation time and hole-size (quadratic polynomial contrast: $F(1,16) = 7.96$, $p < .05$, partial $\eta^2 = .33$). In both background conditions, shorter reaction times were associated with holes that would either easily fit or not fit the ball, and longer reaction times were associated with hole-sizes that were near the actual size of the ball (see Figure 1). No effect of background on action initiation time was noted, $F(1,16) = 0.017$, $p = $ ns.

The judged action boundary was estimated by fitting the % positive responses (i.e., forward mouse movements) for different hole-sizes to a psychometric function ($100/(1+e^{-k(c-x)})$, where x denotes the % positive response, c the judged action boundary—the point where 50% of the balls were judged as being able to fit the hole—and k the slope at this point (Bootsma, Bakker, van Snippenberg, & Tdlohreg). An analysis of c and k revealed an effect of background on c, $F(1,16)= 5.55$, $p < .05$, partial $\eta^2 = .26$, but not on k, $F(1,16) = 1.74$, $p = $ ns. In the absence of a textured hole-background participants judged the action boundary (hole-size/ball-size) to be 1.00, compared to 1.05 when there was a textured background. This resulted in significantly more correct positive movement responses (i.e. forward movements) in the textured background condition, $F(1,16) = 9.53$, $p < .05$, partial $\eta^2 = .37$ (see Table 1).

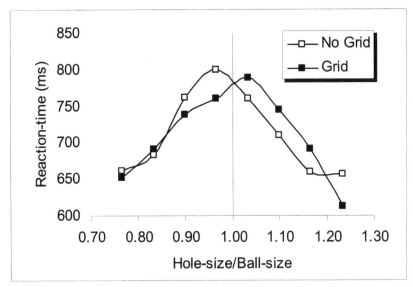

Figure 1. The relationship between hole-size/ball-size and reaction-time (ms) in the two background conditions. The vertical line indicates the ambiguous relationship when hole-size and ball-size are exactly the same.

Response	Correct		Incorrect	
Background	Textured	Un-Textured	Textured	Un-Textured
Positive	60.24	50.65	19.76	11.35
Negative	66.06	68.65	13.94	29.35

Table 1. Average number of correct and incorrect positive (forward mouse movement) and negative (backward mouse movement) responses in the the two background conditions.

In conclusion, the experiment showed that action initiation time when perceiving affordances for ball posting was affected by both hole-size and hole-background. At the action boundary, longer action initiation times were recorded. Following the idea that action initiation time reflects the time taken to find relevant information specifying affordances and to assemble, tune and launch a response device on the basis of this information, these results suggest that at the action boundary information specified more ambiguously which actions were permitted. The hypothesis that near-action boundary's action initiation time is higher than well within or out-with the action boundary was confirmed, introducing the idea that in a forced choice task there is a bell-shaped relationship between action initiation time and adjacent regions of action space. Furthermore, although background texture did not affect action initiation time in the simple case of posting a ball through a hole, when presented with a textured background the action boundary was perceived differently, which resulted in a larger proportion of correct positive movements. The presence or absence of texture against which a hole is presented affected the judged action boundary for ball posting, suggesting that background texture helps the detection of affordances for ball posting. The analysis presented further emphasizes the usefulness of action initiation time for the identification of task relevant information.

References

Bootsma, R. J., Bakker, F. C., van Snippenberg, F. J., & Tdlohreg, C. (1992). The effects of anxiety on perceiving the reachability of passing objects. *Ecological Psychology, 4,* 1-16.

Michaels, C. F. (1988). S-R compatibility between response position and destination of apparent motion: Evidence of the detection of affordances. *Journal of Experimental Psychology-Human Perception and Performance, 14,* 231-240.

Pepping, G. J., & Li, F. X. (2000). Changing action capabilities and the perception of affordances. *Journal of Human Movement Studies, 39,* 115-140.

Warren, W. H. (1984). Perceiving affordances: Visual guidance of stair climbing. *Journal of Experimental Psychology: Human Perception and Performance, 10,* 683-703.

Acknowledgements. We would like to thank Claire Michaels for welcome comments on a very early draft of this paper. The research was sponsored by grants from The University of Edinburgh.

Studies in Perception and Action VIII
H. Heft & K. L. Marsh (Eds.)
© *2005 Lawrence Erlbaum Associates, Inc.*

Comfort as a Determinant of the Location of Critical Boundaries in the Act of Reaching

Sara Stasik & Leonard S. Mark

Miami University, Oxford, Ohio, USA

Previous research (Gardner, Mark, Ward, & Edkins, 2001; Mark et al., 1997) has demonstrated that the distance of the transition between two reach modes (patterns of coordination among the parts of the body) occurs not at the absolute critical boundary for one of the modes, but at a closer distance, what Mark et al (1997) referred to as the *preferred critical boundary* (PCB). While it may be tempting to assume that actors use a reach mode that minimizes the amount of energy expended, it is unlikely that energy expenditure could be monitored and minimized during the brief duration of a single reach. In addition, at distances slightly beyond the PCB between reach modes, it would most likely be more efficient to use the simpler reach action (e.g., leaning forward from a seated position) than one that involves more parts of the body (standing reach). What then precipitates the transition between reach modes that marks the location of the PCB? The current investigation examined the possibility that actors attempt to avoid extreme movements (arm extension, torso lean) and awkward postures that might produce some strain or discomfort.

The current investigation focused on the transition between arm-and-torso (seated) and standing reaches. For an *arm-and-torso reach* the actor remains seated and leans forward with an outstretch arm, usually rotating the torso so as to extend the shoulder of the reach arm toward the target. A *standing reach* involves lifting the buttocks and thigh off of the seat pan (Gardner et al., 2001). The location of participants' preferred critical boundaries was determined by having them reach for objects at placed various distances and observing the reach mode used (Gardner et al., 2001; Mark et al., 1997). In the second part of the study, participants were instructed to reach for objects at the same distances using a seated (arm-and-torso) reach and then rate their level of discomfort or effort experienced during the reach. Our proposal, that in choosing a reach mode, actors attempt to avoid extreme movements, predicts that there should be a marked increase in a participant's discomfort/effort judgments at the location of each participant's PCB.

Method

Subjects. 13 men and 13 women participated in the study as part of a course requirement. All participants were right-handed.

Equipment. Participants were seated on a height-adjustable chair whose seatpan was set to 1.05 of each participant's popliteal height. The chair was placed in front of a table at a distance of 0.75 of the participant's arm length from the chair's backrest. Table surface height was set to a distance halfway between each participant's seated shoulder height and seatpan height. Participants reached for a 3-cm cube. The entire testing session was videotaped so that each reach action could be categorized as one of the following reach modes: (a) arm-only; (b) arm-and-shoulder; (c) arm-and-torso; (d) standing reach. For the purpose of this study we did not distinguish between partial and full standing reaches.

Comfort scale. An 8-point discomfort scale was constructed based on the Borg Scale. A rating of "0" referred to a reach in which they experienced "nothing (discomfort or effort) at all (not effortful, no strain, no discomfort);" a "1" [Very weak (just mentionable, slight amount of effort, wouldn't give it a second thought)]; "2" [Weak (light effort/weak strain)]; "3" [Moderate (requires noticeable effort/some strain)]; and "4" [Somewhat strong (requires near maximum effort for a seated reach/effort would cause some discomfort in order to maintain the reach position for more than a few seconds)]; "8" [Somewhat painful]. Participants were told that the reaches they would be performing should not entail a rating beyond a "4." Half point ratings were included.

Free reach task used to determine the distance of the preferred critical boundary. Participants reached for the 3-cm cube placed at 13 different distances (.50, .60, .70, .75, .80, .85, .90, .95, 1.00, 1.05, 1.10, 1.15) scaled with respect to each person's maximum arm-and-torso reach, which was determined using a procedure devised by Gardner et al. (2001). The order of presentation was randomized. There were three reaches at each distance. Participants were instructed to reach for the object using whatever movements would allow them to pick up the object in the most comfortable or least effortful manner. They were told they could lean forward or stand up. The PCB for seated reaches was calculated by taking for each of the three trials the average of the closest distance at which the participant stood and the next closest distance. The PCB was the average for the three trials.

Determination of the comfort and effort associated with arm-and-torso reaches. After completing the free reach task, participants were introduced to the comfort scale. They were told that they were going to reach for the cube using only a seated reach. This meant that the three distances that exceeded 1.0 could not be achieved using a seated reach. In that case participants were instructed to rate the discomfort/effort of the reach as 4.0. There were two practice trials given at 0.50 and 1.00. Participants were encouraged to use as much of the 4-point scale as possible.

Results

The primary data analysis examined the possibility that actors attempt to avoid extreme movements and awkward postures that might result in discomfort or be effortful. For each participant the PCB between seated and standing reaches was determined. We then examined the discomfort ratings to determine whether there were marked increases in discomfort at the location of each participant's PCB.

Toward this goal we began by comparing the change in ratings between successive reach distances leading up to the critical boundary. (In this analysis we discounted the three closest distances because these were intended to detect a transition between arm-only and arm-and-torso reaches, which we are not reporting in this paper.) For 25 of the 26 participants, the average increase in discomfort for distances closer than the PCB, $M = 0.32$, $SD = 0.05$, was significantly less than the increase at the PCB, $M = 1.21$, $SD = 0.38$. Figure 1 depicts this finding graphically. This graph was constructed by identifying the distance of each participant's PCB and setting the next closest distance to the subject as equal to 1.0 and the next farther distance equal to 1.05. The remaining distances were scaled as 0.95, 0.90, 0.85, 0.80, and 0.75 of the PCB. We then determined the discomfort rating for each of these distances and averaged them over participants. Figure 1 shows that the rate of increase in discomfort ratings increased sharply at the PCB compared to closer distances. It also reveals that significant discomfort was reported only as the distance approached the PCB.

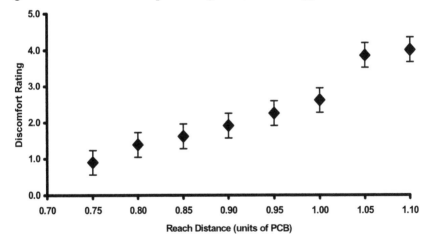

Figure 1. Discomfort ratings expressed as a function of reach distance. Reach distance is expressed in units of each participant's PCB. Thus, 1.05 refers to the shortest distance at which participants consistently stood. 1.00 refers to the farthest distance at which a seated reach was used. Rating of 1.0, just barely noticeable; 2.0, light effort/weak strain; 3.0 noticeable effort/strain; 4.0 near maximum effort for seated reach. Notice the marked increase in discomfort ratings between 1.00 and 1.05 compared to closer distances.

This finding is consistent with our proposal that discomfort or effort may determine the location of the PCB between seated and standing reaches. Although this finding is merely observation because we did not systematically vary discomfort, it suggests that people attempt to maintain a modicum of comfort in their choice of action modes. Interestingly, the data for the transition between arm-only and arm-and-torso reaches, which we did not report here, show that for many participants the discomfort rating actually decreased after the transition, suggesting that a transition to another action mode may result in an increase in comfort, even though the reach distance has increased and more parts of the body are involved in the reach. Finally, the data show the prospective nature of affordances. The choice of reach mode in the free reach task seems to anticipate the relative comfort/effort of two reach modes.

References

Mark, L. S., Nemeth, K., Gardner, D., Dainoff, M. J., Paasche, J., Duffy, M., & Grandt, K. (1997). Postural dynamics and the preferred critical boundary for visually-guided reaching. *Journal of Experimental Psychology: Human Perception and Performance, 23*, 1-15.

Gardner, D. L., Mark, L. S., Ward, J. A., & Edkins, H. (2001). How do task characteristics affect the transitions between seated and standing reaches? *Ecological Psychology, 13*, 245-274.

Studies in Perception and Action VIII
H. Heft & K. L. Marsh (Eds.)
© *2005 Lawrence Erlbaum Associates, Inc.*

Feeling and Seeing to Avoid Tripping

Kona R. Taylor & Jeffrey B. Wagman

Department of Psychology, Illinois State University, USA

In general, individuals perceive the environmental layout in body-scaled terms (Gibson, 1979). For example, affordances for stair climbing are perceived in terms of the relationship between riser height and leg length (Warren, 1984), and affordances for walking through apertures are perceived in terms of the relationship between aperture width and shoulder width (Warren & Whang, 1987). Visually handicapped individuals are faced with perceiving affordances for locomotion without the aid of vision, and research has shown that in many cases touch can be substituted for vision in this respect.

Blind (and blindfolded) individuals can perceive affordances of the environment by using a hand-held object as an extension of the arm (i.e., by means of remote haptic perception). For example, blindfolded participants who probed a gap with a hand-held rod perceived affordances for stepping over that gap in terms of the relationship between the gap width and their leg length (Burton, 1992).

Understanding the perception of affordances by remote haptic perception has implications for theories of perception (Burton, 1993) as well as for the design of hand-held perceptual aids for the visually impaired. Burton (1992) found that although perceivers performed comparably in perceiving whether a gap was crossable by means of vision and by means of haptics, the visually perceived boundary for gap crossing occurred a gap width that was 1.41 times the leg length, and the haptically perceived boundary for gap crossing occurred at a gap width that was 1.25 times the leg length (i.e., more gaps were perceived to be crossable by vision than by haptics).

Furthermore, the only manipulations of the hand-object system that have been shown to influence perception of affordances by remote haptic perception are manipulations that influence the perceived posture of the hand-object system (Burton & McGowen, 1997, see Pagano & Turvey, 1995). For example, Burton & McGowen (1997) asked blindfolded participants to explore a gap with a T-shaped object such that the branches extended vertically from their fist (see Figure 1, left). When gaps were explored with an object weighted on the upper branch, more gaps were perceived as crossable relative to when the rod was equally weighted. When the gap were explored with an object that was weighted on the lower branch, fewer gaps were perceived as crossable relative to when the gap was equally weighted. In two experiments, we investigate these issues and attempt to extend the findings of Burton and colleagues in the perception of whether an object affords stepping over.

Method

In Experiment 1, participants determined whether a horizontal bar could be stepped over in each of two perceptual modalities. In the vision condition, the participant stood 1m from a support frame and viewed the bar placed at one of seven heights (ranging from 30cm to 125cm). They provided a yes or no answer as to whether they could step over the bar (i.e., bring both feet from one side of the bar to the other while keeping one foot on the floor at all times, cf. Hirose & Nishio, 2001). In the haptics condition, the blindfolded participant stood 1m from the support frame and probed the horizontal bar (again placed at one of the seven heights) with a T-shaped object (see Figure 1). They held the T-shaped object such that the branches extended vertically from the fist (cf. Burton & McGowen, 1997). They again provided a yes or no response as to whether they could step over the bar. Each participant completed each modality condition, order of conditions was counterbalanced across participants, and each height was experienced three times in each condition.

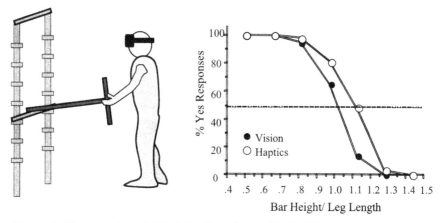

Figure 1. The experimental task for Experiment 1(left). Affordances for stepping over were perceived in body scaled terms. However, different boundaries were perceived by haptics than by vision (right). The perceived boundary for a given condition is the bar height to leg length ratio that generates a response of yes 50% of the time.

In Experiment 2, participants determined whether the bar could be stepped over by probing the bar with a T-shaped object that was weighted so as to alter the orientation of the symmetry axes of the hand-rod system. Except for the added weights, the task was identical to the task in the haptics condition of Experiment 1. In the weighted-up condition, a 164 g mass was placed on the branch that extended "above" their fist, in the weighted down-condition, a 164 g mass was placed on the branch that extended "below" their fist, and in the equal-weight condition, a 82 g mass was placed on each branch of the object. Each participant completed each weight condition, order of conditions was counterbalanced across participants, and each height was experienced three times in each condition.

Results and Discussion

In Experiment 1, a 2 (Modality) x 7 (Bar Height/ Leg Length) ANOVA revealed that the percentage of yes responses decreased as the ratio of bar height to leg length increased, $F(6, 114) = 180.29, p < .05$ (see Figure 1, right). That is, affordances for stepping over were perceived in body-scaled terms. However, the percentage of yes responses differed as a function of modality. Participants were more conservative in the vision condition than in the haptics condition, $F(1, 19) = 11.91, p < .05$ (see Figure 1 right). Probit analysis revealed that this difference created different perceived boundaries in each condition. In the vision condition, the perceived boundary occurred at a bar height to leg length ratio of 0.98, and in the haptics condition, the perceived boundary occurred at a bar height to leg length ratio of 1.07 (see Figure 1, right).

In Experiment 2, a 3 (Mass Placement) x 7 (Bar Height/ Leg Length) ANOVA revealed that participants were more conservative in "mass down" condition than in the "equal mass" condition than in the "mass up" condition, $F(2,12) = 8.07, p < .05$ (see Figure 2, right). Probit analysis revealed that this created different perceived boundaries in each condition. The perceived boundaries in the mass down, equal mass, and mass up conditions were height to leg length ratios of 0.91, 1.00, and 1.04 respectively (see Figure 2, right).

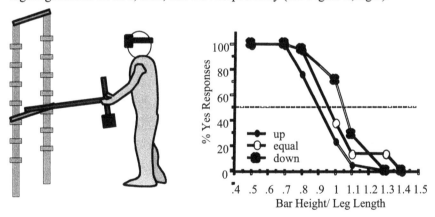

Figure 2. The experimental task for Experiment 2 (left, only the mass down condition is shown here). Different boundaries were perceived in each mass placement condition (right). The perceived boundary for a given condition is the bar height to leg length ratio that generates a response of yes 50% of the time.

The results suggest that affordances for stepping over an obstacle are perceived slightly differently by vision than by remote haptic perception (see Burton, 1992). Furthermore, manipulations that affect the perceive posture of the arm-plus-object system affect perception of affordances of objects probed with that system (see Burton & McGowen, 1997).

References

Burton, G. (1992). Nonvisual judgment of the crossability of path gaps. *Journal of Experimental Psychology, 18*, 698-713.

Burton, G. (1993). Non-neural extensions of haptic sensitivity. *Ecological Psychology, 5, 105-124.*

Burton, G., & McGowan, J. (1997). Contact and posture in nonvisual judgment of gap crossability. *Ecological Psychology, 9*, 323-354.

Gibson, J. J. (1979). *The ecological approach to visual perception.* Boston: Houghton Mifflin.

Hirose, N., & Nishio, A. (2001). The process of adaptation to perceiving new action capabilities. *Ecological Psychology, 13*, 49-69.

Pagano, C. C., & Turvey, M. T. (1995). The inertia tensor as a basis for the perception of limb orientation. *Journal of Experimental Psychology, 21*, 1070-1087.

Warren, W. H. (1984). *Perceiving affordances: Visual guidance of stair climbing.* Journal of Experimental Psychology, 10, 683-703.

Warren, W. H., & Whang S. (1987). Visual guidance of walking through apertures: Body-scaled information for affordances. *Journal of Experimental Psychology: Human Perception and Performance, 13,* 371-383.

Studies in Perception and Action VIII
H. Heft & K. L. Marsh (Eds.)
© *2005 Lawrence Erlbaum Associates, Inc.*

Postural Sway Supports Affordance Perception

Chih-Mei Yang[1], Thomas A. Stoffregen[1], & Benoît G. Bardy[2]

[1]University of Minnesota, Minneapolis, USA
[2]University of Paris XI, France

Recent studies have shown that variations in postural sway (head and torso) often have functional relations to suprapostural activity (e. g., Riley, Mitra, Stoffregen, & Turvey, 1997; Stoffregen, Smart, Bardy, & Pagulayan, 1999; Stoffregen, Pagulayan, Bardy, & Hettinger, 2000). One possibility for this relationship is that body sway can provide information about postural dynamics (Riley et al., 1997) or, more generally, about some of the dynamics of the animal-environment system. We evaluated the hypothesis that body sway can be modulated to facilitate the perception of affordances (Gibson, 1979/1986). We concentrated on actions that can facilitate the perception of affordances. Mark, Balliet, Craver, Douglas, and Fox (1990) found that ordinary body sway was sufficient to permit learning about maximum sitting height, but Mark et al. did not collect quantitative data about body sway. We replicated Mark et al.'s study and collected quantitative data on motion of the head and torso. Several results document functional relations between postural motion and affordance perception.

Method

Experiment 1. We replicated Experiment 2 from Mark et al. (1990). Standing participants (N = 12) made a series of judgments of their own maximum sitting height. From a distance of 10 feet they viewed an experimental chair with a seat pan that was moved up and down by an electric motor with a velocity of 2 cm/s. Participants viewed the moving seat pan and said "stop" when they judged it to be at their maximum sitting height. In the No Block, condition participants stood in their stocking feet, while in the Block condition they stood on 10 cm wooden blocks that were attached to their feet.

Experiment 2. Twenty-four subjects participated. The apparatus and procedure were same as Experiment 1, except that kinematic (sway) data were recorded using a magnetic tracking system. One receiver was placed on the head and one on the torso, with each receiver sampled at 50 Hz. Prior to making any judgments, we recorded quiet stance for 60 s.

Results

Experiment 1. The main effect of viewing condition (Block versus No Block) was not significant, $F(1,22) < 1$, *ns*. The overall main effect of trials was significant, $F(11,242) = 2.928$, $p < .05$, accounting for 11.7% of the variance. The interaction between block and trials was not significant, $F(11,242) = 1.204$, *ns*. As Figure 1 demonstrates, the slope of the regression for the No Block condition was –0.07, which did not differ from 0, $t(142) = -0.35$, *ns*. The slope of the regression for the Block condition was –0.30, which was significantly different from 0, $t(142) = -1.99$, $p < .05$.

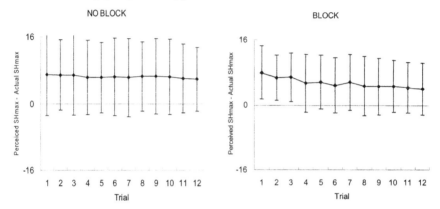

Figure 1. Experiment 1. Mean difference in centimeters between perceived and actual maximum seat height across trials without block and with blocks. Error bars represent one standard deviation above and below the mean.

Experiment 2: Judgment data. The main effect of conditions (Block vs. No block) was not significant, $F(1,46) = 3.624$, ns. The main effect of trials was significant, $F(11,506) = 10.046$, $p < .05$, accounting for 17.9% of the variance, but the interaction was not significant. Post hoc analyses divided participants into those who demonstrated improved performance over trials and those who did not. For the Block condition, the Learning Group comprising 9 subjects had a group slope for judgments of –0.358, which differed from zero, $t(106) = -2.66$, $p < .05$, while the Non Learning group (n = 15) did not differ from 0. In the No Block condition, the Learning Group comprising 11 subjects had a group slope of –0.599, which differed from 0, $t(130) = -4.48$, $p < .05$. The Non-Learning group (n = 13) did not differ from 0.

Experiment 2: *Sway data.* Data on head and torso motion were analyzed separately in the AP and ML axes. Collapsed across participants and trials, there were no differences between No Block and Block conditions. The continuous recordings of head and torso motion were parsed into periods during which subjects were making their judgments, and intervals between judgments. On average, both judgment and inter-judgment intervals were about 15 s long. Across participants and conditions, there was a significant interaction between this factor (judgment intervals vs. inter-judgment intervals) and trials for head motion in the AP axis (Figure 2). We also identified differences in sway between Learning and Non Learning groups. In contrast to the Non Learning group, in the No Block Learning group, sway during the first judgment interval was significantly greater than sway during quiet stance for both AP and ML motion of the head and torso. In contrast to the Non Learning group, in the Block Learning group significant increase in sway during the first judgment interval occurred, albeit only in ML head motion.

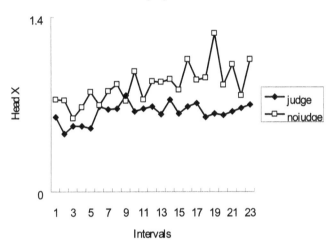

Figure 2. The significant interaction between intervals and trials, for head motion in the AP axis, Experiment 2, collapsed across conditions (No Block and Block) and groups (Learning and Non Learning).

Discussion

Judgments. Unlike Mark et al. (1990), participants in our study tended to begin with overestimates of their maximum sitting height. Aside from this difference, we replicated the learning effects reported by Mark et al. as the main effect of trials in the two experiments reveals. In the absence of practice or feedback, participants generally improved the accuracy of their judgments of maximum sitting height over the course of 12 experimental trials. Moreover, the lack of a significant interaction with viewing condition indicates this improvement was true for both the No Block and Block conditions. However, post hoc analyses suggest that some subgroup of participants did not display detectable learning effects.

Role of sway in perception: We found two types of effects relating sway to affordance judgments. First, there were general effects of the judgment task on sway. Participants tended to sway less when they were engaged in the judgment task than when they were not (between judgments). Moreover, over the course of the experimental sessions participants selectively increased sway between judgments, while maintaining a constant level of sway during judgments (Figure 2). Both these effects mirror previous studies documenting functional integration of postural control with the performance demands of supra-postural visual tasks (Stoffregen et al., 1999, 2000). Second, we found several changes in postural motion that were unique to participants whose judgments of maximum sitting height became more accurate during the experiment. These effects confirm that body sway is related to both perception of and learning about maximum sitting height.

References

Gibson, J. J. (1986). *The ecological approach to visual perception.* Hillsdale, NJ: Lawrence Erlbaum Associates, Inc. [Original work published in 1979]

Mark, L. S., Balliet, J. A., Craver, K. D., Douglas, S. D., & Fox, T. (1990). What an actor must do in order to perceive the affordance for sitting. *Ecological Psychology, 2*, 325-366.

Riley, M. A., Mitra, S., Stoffregen, T. A., & Turvey, M. T. (1997). Influences of body lean and vision on unperturbed postural sway. *Motor Control, 1*, 229-246.

Stoffregen, T. A., Pagulayan, R. J., Bardy, B. G. & Hettinger, L. J. (2000). Modulating postural control to facilitate visual performance. *Human Movement Science, 19*, 203-220.

Stoffregen, T. A., Smart, L. J., Bardy, B. G. & Pagulayan, R. J. (1999). Postural stabilization of looking. *Journal of Experimental Psychology: Human Perception and Performance, 25*, 1641-1658.

Warren, W. H. (1984). Perceiving affordances: Visual guidance of stair climbing. *Journal of Experimental Psychology: Human Perception & Performance, 10*, 683-703.

Acknowledgements. Supported by *Enactive Interfaces*, a network of excellence (IST contract #002114) of the Commission of the European Community, and by the National Science Foundation (BCS-0236627).

Interpersonal Perception & Dynamics

Studies in Perception and Action VIII
H. Heft & K. L. Marsh (Eds.)
© 2005 Lawrence Erlbaum Associates, Inc.

The Salience of Actions over Faces for Young Infants

Lorraine E. Bahrick, Mariana Vaillant-Molina, Melissa A. Shuman, Laura C. Batista, Lisa C. Newell, Irina Castellanos, & Traci S. Williams

Florida International University, Boca Raton, USA

Although faces are salient social stimuli and almost always occur in the context of people engaged in actions, there is little research on infants' perception of faces in the context of dynamic activities. Previously, we (Bahrick, Gogate & Ruiz, 2002) demonstrated that 5-month-old infants were able to discriminate and remember a dynamic activity, but not the face of the individual performing the activity. Following familiarization with a particular woman engaged in a specific activity (e.g., brushing hair, brushing teeth, blowing bubbles), infants showed a preference for a novel activity but not a novel face, and they remembered the action but not the familiar face after a 7-week delay. Further, infants discriminated the faces only in static poses. Prior research has demonstrated exceptional face recognition skills by infants when tested with static displays. Why do 5-month-olds demonstrate such poor face recognition in dynamic activities? We tested an attentional salience explanation for infants' discrimination of actions at the expense of faces. It was hypothesized that the reported failure of face discrimination did not reflect an inability to perceive faces in the context of dynamic events. Rather, it was a result of greater attentional selectivity to the action.

Methods & Results

Stimulus Materials

The events (see Figure 1) consisted of video displays of four different women of different ethnicities (Caucasian, Chinese, Indian, and Hispanic) performing four different repetitive actions: brushing teeth, blowing bubbles, brushing hair, and applying makeup.

Figure 1. Still images of activities

Experiment 1

Experiment 1 assessed whether, with longer exposure time to the events (320 rather than 160 s), infants' interest in the actions would decrease, facilitating attention to the faces. Twenty-four 5.5-month-olds were familiarized to eight 40-s trials of one of three video displays of a woman performing one of the three repetitive actions. One minute later, infants received a novelty preference test consisting of four 30-s trials, two of a novel face performing the familiar action (face test), and two of the familiar face performing a novel action (action test).

Results (see Figure 2) indicated a significant proportion of total looking time (PTLT) to the novel actions, $t(23) = 2.95$, $p < .01$), and a significant PTLT to the novel faces, $t(23) = 2.18$, $p < .05$. These findings demonstrate that when familiarization time was increased twofold, infants discriminated the faces as well as the actions. Thus, infants are able to discriminate faces in the context of actions, but this requires longer exposure time than does discrimination of actions.

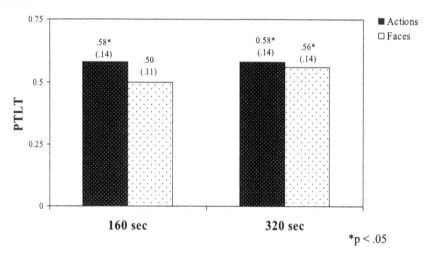

Bahrick, Gogate, & Ruiz (2002)

Figure 2. Proportion of total looking time (PTLT) to novel actions and faces.

Experiment 2

In Experiment 2, 24 5.5-month-old infants were habituated (in an infant control procedure) to videos of the same woman performing three different activities. Because the face was invariant across actions, this should recruit attention to the face and allow generalization across actions. Following habituation, infants received a change in face and action (face test) and a change in action only (control test).

Results (see Figure 3) indicate that infants showed visual recovery to the face/action change, $t(23) = 2.99$, $p < .01$, but not the action change alone, $t(23) = .19$, $p = .85$, and visual recovery to the face/action change was significantly greater than to the action change alone, $t(23) = 2.72$, $p < .05$. The results demonstrate that faces are discriminated when they are invariant across different activities.

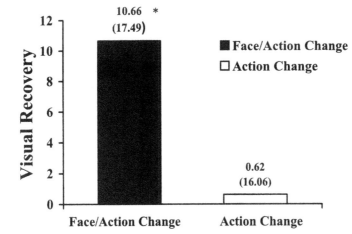

*p < .05, groups are significantly different from each other

Figure 3. Mean visual recovery (and SD) to a change in face and action vs. a change in action alone

Experiment 3

Experiment 3 was a replication of the original study (Bahrick et al., 2002) with 7-month-old infants, investigating whether with age and experience infants are able to detect both actions and faces in the context of dynamic actions. Twenty-four 7-month-olds were familiarized during four 40-s trials to one of three displays of a woman performing a repetitive activity. Face and action test trials were presented one minute after familiarization, identical to the procedure for Experiment 1.

Results (see Figure 4) indicated a significant PTLT to both the novel action, $t(23) = 2.5$, $p < 0.05$, and the novel face, $t(23) = 2.77$, $p < 0.05$.

Discussion

Results indicate that for young infants, actions are more salient than the faces of people engaged in the actions. Three experiments demonstrated that perception of faces in the context of dynamic activities was enhanced when infants received additional exposure time to the events (Experiment 1), when one face was invariant across several activities (Experiment 2), and when infants were older and more experienced (Experiment 3). These findings are consistent with an attentional salience hypothesis. During early infancy actions are highly salient, drawing attention away from the face of the individual who performs the activity. However, with additional exposure time, training with one woman engaging in several activities, or additional experience in the world, the salience of actions over faces diminishes, allowing faces to be discriminated in the context of actions. These findings of infant perception of dynamic face events contrast with those of static face displays and highlight the importance of limiting research generalizations to the domain under study.

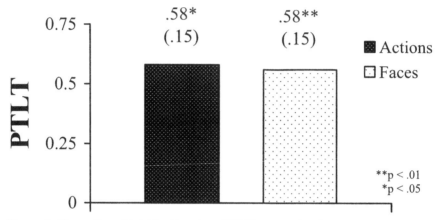

Figure 4. Proportion of total looking time (PTLT) to novel actions and faces.

References

Bahrick, L.E., Gogate, L.J., & Ruiz, I. (2002). Attention and memory for faces and actions in infancy: The salience of actions over faces in dynamic events. *Child Development, 73,* 1629-1643.

Acknowledgements. This research was supported by grants from NIMH (R01MH62226, "Intersensory Redundancy and the Development of Perception") and NSF (SBE - 0350201, "South Florida Research Consortium on the Development of Attention, Perception, Learning, and Memory").

Studies in Perception and Action VIII
H. Heft & K. L. Marsh (Eds.)
© *2005 Lawrence Erlbaum Associates, Inc.*

Verbal Constraints on Interpersonal Postural Coordination

Aimee A. Baker[1], Kevin Shockley[1], Michael J. Richardson[2], & Carol A. Fowler[2,3]

[1]University of Cincinnati, Cincinnati, OH, USA
[2]Center for the Ecological Study of Perception and Action,
University of Connecticut, Storrs, CT, USA
[3]Haskins Laboratories, New Haven, CT, USA

Clark (1996) has suggested that language serves to coordinate "joint actions" allowing two or more people to achieve a mutual goal. Verbal inter-actions among conversers are known to produce a natural, rhythmic patterning, having related-content, similar stress patterns, and compatible rhythms (Couper-Kuhlen, 1993). Furthermore, listeners to a speaker have also been observed to move in time with the rhythms of a speaker's speech (Condon & Ogston, 1971; Newtson, 1994). Speech necessarily has postural consequences by virtue of the mechanical linkage of the speech apparatus (e.g., Dault, Yardley, & Frank, 2003). Findings of postural entrainment among two people are, therefore, interesting because they appear to index the interpersonal coordination that must occur if the joint activities are to be completed.

Shockley, Santana, and Fowler (2003) used an objective measure, known as cross recurrence quantification (CRQ), to quantify the degree to which cooperative conversation influences interpersonal coordination. They found that participant-pairs had greater shared postural activity when cooperatively conversing with one another than when conversing with others. In addition, the postural trajectories of the participant-pairs showed less divergence when conversing with each other versus conversing with others. The present study investigated the nature of the coordination observed by Shockley et al. (2003) with three experiments testing what aspects of speaking may mediate interpersonal postural coordination in the context of conversation. In all experiments, the proportion of shared postural locations visited relative to the total postural locations visited in reconstructed phase space (*%REC*) and the length of time postural trajectories remained adjacent (*MAXLINE*) served as indices of postural coordination (see Shockley, et al., 2003, for detailed explanation of measures and computation methods).

Experiment 1

The first experiment manipulated turn-taking (*Phase*), speaking rate (*Pace*), and degree of *Word Similarity* for speaking participant-pairs.

Method

Participant-pairs stood side-by-side and read words aloud as they appeared on a computer screen positioned directly in front of each participant. The participants could not see each other's words. There were twelve participant-pairs in each of three *Word Similarity* groups, for a total of 36 pairs. A magnetic motion capture sensor (Polhemus, Inc., Colchester, VT), attached at the waist of each participant was used to measure postural sway in the anterior-posterior direction at a sampling rate of 60 Hz. There were three trials per condition for a total of 18 trials for each participant-pair in a given group. Each trial lasted two minutes.

Each participant-pair was shown words at either the same time (in-phase), or in an alternating fashion (anti-phase). There were three *Pace* conditions—fast (ISI = 1.2 sec), slow (ISI = 2 sec), and natural. In the latter condition, words were presented as a list, and participants were instructed to read the words—one down the columns and one across the rows—at their own naturally chosen tempo. In each of the above conditions, *Word Similarity* was manipulated using two-syllable words for which the stress is naturally on the first syllable (e.g., wonder) or on the second syllable (e.g., return). In the different-word, different-stress (DD) condition, for a given word-pair different words were presented to each participant in the pair—each word emphasizing a different syllable. In the different-word, same-stress (DS) condition, for a given word-pair the words presented to each participant emphasized the same syllable. In the same words (S) condition, for a given word-pair the same words were presented to each person.

Results and Discussion

A 3 (*Word Similarity*) × 3 (*Pace*) × 2 (*Phase*) mixed ANOVA revealed that speaking words faster yields greater shared postural locations (greater *%REC*; $F(2, 56) = 4.66$, $p < .05$; Figure 1A) and postural trajectories that stayed adjacent longer (greater *MAXLINE*; $F(2, 56) = 5.20$, $p < .05$; Figure 1B) than speaking slowly or at a self-selected pace. This suggests that the more time within a trial participants were required to speak, the greater the shared postural activity and the greater similarity in the evolution of postural trajectories.

Experiment 2

A non-significant trend in Experiment 1 (Figure 2A) suggested that *%REC* increases with degree of word similarity. Experiment 2, therefore, involved the

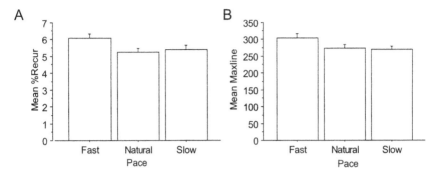

Figure 1. Influence of Speaking Rate on (A) %RECUR and (B) Maxline in Experiment 1.

manipulation of *Word Similarity* in the same manner as in Experiment 1, though as a within-subjects factor (in-phase with ISI = 1.5 sec). The goal was to determine whether the influence of *Word Similarity* on shared postural activity in Experiment 1 may have been undetected statistically due to individual variations in %*REC* magnitudes across the three groups. Seventeen pairs of participants each underwent nine total trials (three trials for each *Word Similarity* condition) of two minutes each.

Results and Discussion

A one-way repeated measures ANOVA revealed a main effect of *Word Similarity* on %*REC* ($F(2, 30) = 5.22, p < .05$). Shared postural activity (%*REC*) increased with the similarity of the words spoken (Figure 2B), suggesting that the postural trajectories of different speakers uttering similar words are influenced in similar ways.

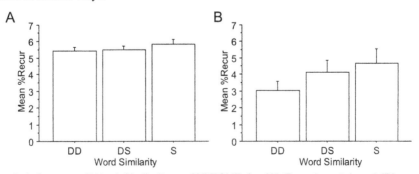

Figure 2. Influence of Word Similarity on %RECUR for (A) Experiment 1 and (B) Experiment 2.

Experiment 3

Experiment 3 investigated the influence of listening on the shared postural activity of participant-pairs. The same manipulations of *Pace* and *Word*

Similarity of Experiment 1 were used for the acoustic presentation of words to determine whether these variables have a similar effect on shared postural activity as speaking. Each member of a participant-pair listened to previously recorded two-syllable words. Words were simultaneously projected onto computer monitors in front of the participants, and they were instructed to silently read the words on the monitor while listening to the same words. There were 18, two-minute trials for each of twelve pairs of participants—three trials for each condition. The same apparatus and measurements as in the previous two experiments were used.

Results and Discussion

A 3 × 2 repeated measures ANOVA found no effect of *Pace* nor of *Word Similarity* on *%REC* ($Fs < 1$) or on *MAXLINE* ($Fs < 1$), suggesting that listening does not influence postural activity between two individuals in the same manner as when two individuals are speaking to one another.

Conclusions

The findings from the first two experiments suggest that the interpersonal postural coordination observed by Shockley, et al (2003), may be at least partially mediated by convergent speech patterns observed in previous studies. Although we found no effect of listening on shared postural activity, the nature of the task in Experiment 3 was not inherently cooperative unlike that of Shockley et al., (2003). The extent to which listening may influence shared postural activity in a more cooperative setting remains to be seen.

References

Clark, H. H. (1996). *Using language.* New York: Cambridge University Press.

Condon, W., & Ogston, W. (1971). Speech and body motion synchrony of the speaker-hearer. In D. Horton & J. Jenkins (Eds.), *The perception of language* (pp.150-184). Columbus, OH: Charles E. Merrill.

Couper-Kuhlen, E. (1993). *English speech rhythms.* Amsterdam: John Benjamins.

Dault, M.C., Yardley, L. & Frank, J.S. (2003). Can articulation explain modifications in postural control during dual-task paradigms? *Cognitive Brain Research, 16*, 434-440

Newtson, D. (1994). The perception and coupling of behavior waves. In R. R. Vallacher & A. Nowak (Eds.), *Dynamical systems in social psychology* (pp. 139-167). San Diego, CA: Academic Press.

Shockley, K., Santana, M., & Fowler, C. (2003). Mutual interpersonal postural constraints are involved in cooperative conversation. *Journal of Experimental Psychology, 29(2)*, 326-332.

Acknowledgements. This research was supported by National Science Foundation Grant BSC-0240277.

Studies in Perception and Action VIII
H. Heft & K. L. Marsh (Eds.)
© 2005 Lawrence Erlbaum Associates, Inc.

Inter-Personal Coordination among Articulations, Gesticulations, and Breathing Movements—A Case of Articulation of /a/ and Flexion of the Wrist

Nobuhiro Furuyama[1], Koji Hayashi[2], Hiroyuki Mishima[3]

[1]National Institute of Informatics, Japan
[2]The University of Tokyo, Japan [3]University of Fukui, Japan

The present study was designed to explore the dynamics underlying inter-personal coordination of speech articulation and hand gesture movements and their relationship with breathing movements. It was conducted from the viewpoint of a dynamical systems approach, and the experimental parameters manipulated were the relative phase mode (2 levels) and oscillatory frequency (10 levels) of the coordination between articulation and gesticulation. The results will be discussed in relation to an intra-personal version of the experiment that shows very similar results (Furuyama, Takase and Hayashi, 2002) and in terms of their implications for emerging interests in an ecological approach to communication.

Method

Twenty right-handed students participated in this experiment. The subjects were tested in same-gender pairs, resulting in five male pairs and five female pairs. They were each asked to synchronize the articulation of the vowel /a/ by one of the subjects with the action of extending/bending the wrist by the other subject in either mode A or B of oscillation, at the rate specified by PC-generated sound pulses. The rate of the sound pulses was set to increase in increments of approximately 0.2 Hz, covering ten frequencies in the range shown in Table 1, and there were ten pulses for each frequency. In mode A, when the gesturer subject bent the wrist, the articulator subject was to articulate the vowel; but when the gesturer subject extended the wrist, no speech sound was to be produced. In mode B, when the gesturer subject extended the wrist, the articulator subject was to produce the vowel; but when the gesturer subject

Frequency level	F1	F2	F3	F4	F5
Frequency (Hz)	0.59	0.78	0.98	1.17	1.36
Frequency level	F6	F7	F8	F9	F10
Frequency (Hz)	1.54	1.73	1.91	2.09	2.28

Table 1. Frequency of PC-generated sound pulses.

bent the wrist, no speech sound was to be produced. In both modes, the articulator subject was allowed to look at her/his partner, but the gesturer subject was not. The latter subject was only allowed to listen to the articulator's speech sound conveyed through a headphone set. The means and the standard deviations of phase lags between the wrist movements and the vowel articulation were calculated, and they were used as indices of the degree of equilibrium of coordination at different frequencies in the two modes of synchronization.

Results

In general, relative phase φ was very high, and we categorized such cases as "preferred mode." If the subjects followed the instructions exactly, however, mean φ would be expected to come close to 0 rad regardless of the relative phase mode. There were unignorable numbers of such cases and they were categorized as "instructed mode." Although we did not observe a so-called "phase transition" between the two relative phase modes (e.g., from mode B to mode A), we observed cases in which a relative phase φ abruptly jumped from the instructed mode to the preferred mode, as defined above, and remained there. We categorized such cases as "phase shift." We also observed cases in which the articulation became increasingly delayed with respect to the gesticulation and the phase lag became more than one cycle (i.e., more than 2π rad). We categorized such cases as "negative asynchrony." There were two cases in which the speech-hand coordination never became stabilized.

Because our goal was to compare samples from a homogeneous rather than heterogeneous population for each frequency level, the data affected by the phase shifts and other cases of unstable coordination were excluded from the data set. (By this operation, data for two subjects had to be excluded.). The remaining data for each subject, across five trials for each relative phase mode, were averaged for each given frequency level. In other words, the factor of trial was collapsed for each subject. The result of this operation is the target of the analyses below.

SD φ. Figure 1a shows SD φ as a function of frequency, arranged by the two modes of coordination. As shown in the figure, SD φ increases as the oscillatory frequency increases, regardless of the relative phase mode. ANOVA conducted for SD φ (mode x frequency) revealed that while there was no significant main effect of mode, $F(1,7) = 1.88$, *ns*, there was a main effect of frequency, $F(9,63) = 5.63$, $p < .01$. Polynomial contrasts applied to frequency showed a significant linear trend, suggesting that SD φ increases as frequency increases, $F(1,7) = 64.89$, $p < .01$. This confirms the observation above that SD φ increases as the oscillatory frequency increases, regardless of the relative phase mode (Figure 1a). It suggests that there is an equal likelihood in either mode that coordination will become more unstable as frequency increases. This result is consistent with findings obtained in our investigation of intra-personal coordination of articulation and gesticulation (Furuyama et al., 2002).

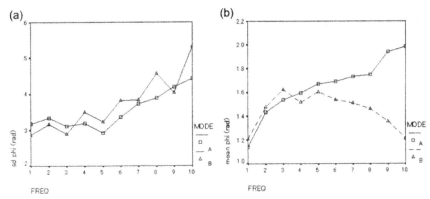

Figure 1. (a) SD φ and (b) mean φ as a function of frequency for inter-personal speech-gesture coordination.

Mean φ. In either mode, when frequency level is below F4, mean φ tends to increase as frequency increases (Figure 1b). Beyond F4, while mean φ in mode A maintains the tendency to increase as frequency increases (albeit with a slower rate of increase), in mode B it tends to decrease as frequency increases. ANOVA conducted for mean φ (mode x frequency) showed no main effect of frequency, $F(9,63) = .831$, n.s., but it showed a main effect of mode, $F(1,7) = 5.909, p < .05$), and an interaction between mode and frequency, $F(9,63) = 5.02, p < .01$). Polynomial contrast applied to this interaction confirmed a significant linear trend, suggesting that the difference of mean φ between the two modes increases linearly as frequency increases, $F(1,7) = 13.98, p < .01$). This means that the impact of frequency on coordination is different for the two relative phase modes. Furuyama et al. (2002) showed that mean φ for intra-personal coordination of articulation and gesticulation is higher in mode B than in mode A when frequency is below F4, and higher in mode A than in mode B when frequency is above F4. Comparing this with the present data analysis of inter-personal coordination, the behavior of mean φ seems similar for intra- and inter-personal coordination when frequency level is above F4, but different when frequency level is below F4.

Figure 1b also shows that at frequency level F10, mean φ is approximately 1.8 rad in mode A and 1.3 rad in mode B. To understand the physical position of the hand when the vowel articulation begins, we converted the figure in mode A and found that 1.8 rad in mode A corresponds well to 1.3 rad in mode B. Meanwhile, as we saw above, there is no significant difference in SD φ between the two modes. Taking all this into consideration, we can say that when the frequency level is F10, articulation of the vowel starts when the hand is in the neighborhood of 1.8 rad in mode A (or 1.3 rad in mode B), regardless of the direction in which the hand is moving. This marks a striking similarity be-tween the present data and the intra-personal coordination data (Furuyama et al., 2002).

Breathing movements. How are chest movements of breathing for the articulator subjects related to inter-personal speech-hand coordination between the two subjects? There were several qualitatively different breathing movement patterns identifiable by two independent coders, whom we kept uninformed not only of the purpose of the experiment, but also of what the waveforms represented. To see where the major pattern shift could most readily be located, we further asked the same coders to divide each waveform into two parts based purely on the shape of the graph. The results are given in Figure 2. It shows that the distribution of the scoring is almost normal with F4 as its peak. This suggests that the major pattern shift in breathing movements is located at around F4.

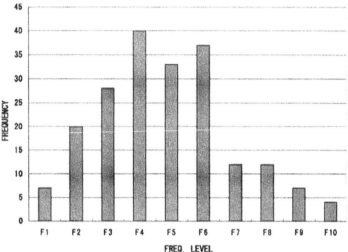

Figure 2. Histogram of frequency level locations, indicating where two naive coders considered the major shift in pattern to occur, based on data from the breathing patterns of the articulating subjects in the inter-personal coordination data.

These results suggest the following: (1) A comparison of the present results with those for intra-personal coordination experiment (Furuyama et al., 2002) showed certain similarities when oscillatory frequency was in the range between F4 and F10 ($\approx$ 1.2 Hz and 2.4 Hz), and certain differences when oscillatory frequency was in the range between F1 and F4 ($\approx$ 0.6 Hz and 1.2 Hz), suggesting that some of the underlying dynamics in the two types of coordination are the same, while others are different. (2) There are several patterns in breathing movements. The major pattern shift occurs at around F4 ($\approx$ 1.2 Hz), suggesting that breathing movement patterns undergo reorganization as speech-gesture coordination is reorganized. These results have notable implications for an ecological approach to communication.

Reference

Furuyama, N., Takase, H., & Hayashi, K. (2002). *Coordination among articulations, gesticulations and breathing movements—A case of articulation of /a/ and flexion at the wrist.* A paper read at the 12th International Conference on Perception and Action held in Gold Coast, Australia.

Acknowledgement. We gratefully acknowledge the support of the Japan Society for the Promotion of Science to the first author (Contract number: 16016290).

Studies in Perception and Action VIII
H. Heft & K. L. Marsh (Eds.)
© *2005 Lawrence Erlbaum Associates, Inc.*

The Interpersonal Phase Entrainment of Rocking Chair Movements

Justin R. L. Goodman[1], Robert W. Isenhower[1], Kerry L. Marsh[1,3], R. C. Schmidt[1,2], & Michael J. Richardson[1]

[1]Center for the Ecological Study of Perception and Action, University of Connecticut; [2]College of the Holy Cross, Worcester, MA [3]Department of Psychology, University of Connecticut, Storrs, CT, USA

Most research on interpersonal coordination has employed the wrist-pendulum paradigm to demonstrate that visual information is sufficient to couple the rhythmic movements of co-actors (Schmidt & Turvey, 1994, Schmidt & O'Brien, 1997; Schmidt, Bienvenu, Fitzpatrick & Amazeen, 1998). Despite the clarity of this work, questions about the ecological validity of this methodology for the study of interpersonal coordination have been raised (Richardson, Marsh, & Schmidt, 2005). As a result, a new methodology was developed which employs a more commonplace, everyday task; namely, having individuals sit side-by-side in rocking chairs. Two experiments reported here examined the validity of this paradigm for the study of interpersonal coordination.

Experiment 1

Experiment 1 examined the validity of the rocking chair paradigm for the study of intentional coordination by having participants coordinate rocking chairs inphase ($\phi = 0°$) or antiphase ($\phi = 180°$) under three different magnitudes of detuning ($\Delta\omega$). It was expected that the patterns of interpersonal coordination would be consistent with a coupled oscillator dynamic, such that: (1) inphase would be more stable (less variable) than antiphase; (2) $\Delta\omega \neq 0$ would result in a phase shift that would be (3) more pronounced for antiphase than for inphase, and (4) the variability of relative phase would be greater for $\Delta\omega \neq 0$ than for $\Delta\omega = 0$ (Schmidt & Turvey, 1994; Schmidt et al., 1998).

Method

Seven pairs participated in the experiment and coordinated wooden rocking chairs (52 cm apart) at a self-selected tempo (Figure 1). $\Delta\omega$ was manipulated by placing 60lb (27.2 kg) lead weights in a wooden cradle beneath the seat of each chair resulting in three levels of $\Delta\omega$ (near 0, ±1 rad). Movements were recorded at 60 Hz using a magnetic Polhemus motion capture sensor. Two 60 s trials were performed for each phase mode (ψ: inphase, antiphase) by $\Delta\omega$ (-1, 0, 1) condition, yielding a total of 12 trials. The movement time series were converted to phase angles (θ_i) so the relative phase time series ($\phi = \theta_{chair1} - \theta_{chair2}$) could be calculated for each trial. From these time series, the phase-shift (PS = $\langle \phi \rangle$ - ψ, where $\langle \phi \rangle$ is mean relative phase and ψ is intended phase) and SDϕ were computed as the dependent measures of coordination.

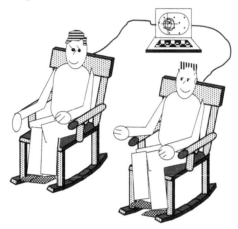

Figure 1. Experimental setup for the interpersonal coordination of rocking chair movements.

Results and Discussion

PS and SDϕ (averaged across trial) were submitted to separate 2 (ψ) × 3($\Delta\omega$) repeated measures ANOVAs. Confirming expectations (2) and (3), the results for PS yielded a significant ψ by $\Delta\omega$ interaction, $F(2,12) = 4.785$, $p < .05$, and a main effect of $\Delta\omega$, $F(2,12) = 16.35$, $p < .01$. As seen in Figure 2a, participants were able to maintain both inphase and antiphase coordination and were phase shifted when $\Delta\omega \neq 0$, by an average of ± 4.6° for inphase and ± 7.7° for antiphase coordination. Consistent with expectation (1), the SDϕ was significantly less for inphase than antiphase coordination, $F(1,6) = 14.99$, $p < .01$; and while the magnitude of SDϕ for $\Delta\omega \neq 0$ was not significantly different from $\Delta\omega = 0$, the trends were consistent with expectation (4) (see Figure 2b).

Experiment 2

Experiment 2 examined the validity of the rocking chair paradigm for the study of unintentional coordination. Two participants were instructed to rock *independently* and at their *own* preferred tempo while in presence of each other. In addition to the three magnitudes of $\Delta\omega$ used in Experiment 1, the amount of visual information (coupling) about a co-actor's movement was manipulated. Participants were expected to (1) exhibit relative coordination (tend toward $\phi = 0°$ and 180°) when visual information was available. Moreover, the amount of unintentional coordination was expected to be (2) greater as the amount of visual information increased and (3) less for $\Delta\omega \neq 0$ than for $\Delta\omega = 0$ (Schmidt & O'Brien, 1997; Richardson et al., 2005).

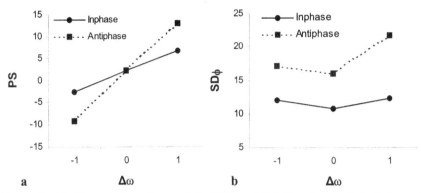

Figure 2. (a) The relative phase shift (PS) and (b) the standard deviation of relative phase (SD) for Experiment 1, as a function of intended phase mode (inphase, antiphase) and detuning ($\Delta\omega$).

Method

Twelve individuals (six pairs) participated in the experiment. The materials and apparatus were the same as in Experiment 1. The amount of visual information was manipulated by having each participant fix their gaze on a target, which was located in the opposite direction from the co-actor (v1, no visual information), directly in front of themselves (v2, peripheral information), or on the armrest of their co-actor's chair (v3, focal information). Two 60 s trials were performed for each visual information (v1, v2, v3) by $\Delta\omega$ (-1, 0, 1) condition, yielding a total of 24 trials.

Results and Discussion

The magnitude of unintentional phase entrainment (coordination) was identified from the frequency of occurrence of relative phase angles across nine regions of relative phase between 0° and 180°. These counts were averaged across trial and submitted to 3(visual information) × 3($\Delta\omega$) × 9 (phase regions) repeated measures ANOVA. This analysis yielded a significant three-way interaction, $F(32,160) = 2.731$, $p < .001$, significant two-way interactions between phase region and $\Delta\omega$, $F(16,80) = 4.763$, $p < .001$, and between phase-region and visual information, $F(16,80) = 12.351$, $p < .001$, and a significant main effect of phase region, $F(8,40) = 21.335$, $p < .001$. As can be seen from Figure 3, these results are consistent with (1), (2) and (3), with participants exhibiting an increased tendency towards relative phase angles near 0° when more visual information was available and when $\Delta\omega = 0$.

Conclusions

Overall, the results are consistent with previous research using a wrist-pendulum paradigm to study interpersonal coordination (Schmidt & Turvey, 1994, Schmidt & O'Brien, 1997; Schmidt et al., 1998) and provide further evi-

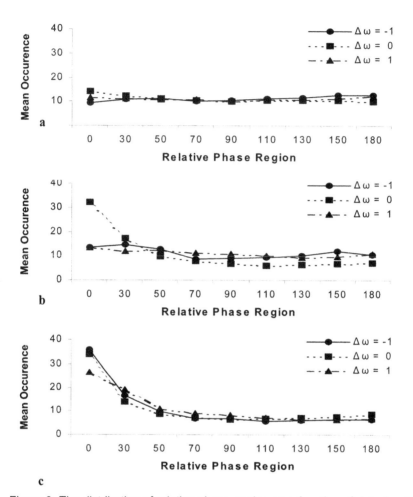

Figure 3. The distribution of relative phase angles as a function of detuning (Δω) for the three visual information conditions ((a) = v1: no visual information, (b) = v2: peripheral information, (c) = v3: focal information) of Experiment 2.

dence that such coordination is constrained in accordance with a coupled oscillator dynamic. Moreover, the data establish the efficacy and ecological validity of the rocking chair paradigm for the study of interpersonal coordination.

References

Richardson, M. J. Marsh, K. L., & Schmidt, R. C. (2005). Effects of visual and verbal interaction on unintentional interpersonal coordination. *Journal of Experimental Psychology: Human Perception and Performance, 31,* 62-79.

Schmidt, R. C., Bienvenu, M., Fitzpatrick, P. A., & Amazeen, P. G. (1998). A comparison of within- and between-person coordination: Coordination breakdowns and coupling strength. *Journal of Experimental Psychology: Human Perception and Performance, 24,* 884-900.

Schmidt, R. C., & O' Brien, B. (1997). Evaluating the dynamics of unintended interpersonal coordination. *Ecological Psychology, 9,* 189-206.

Schmidt, R. C., & Turvey, M. T. (1994). Phase-entrainment dynamics of visually coupled rhythmic movements. *Biological Cybernetics, 70,* 369-376.

Acknowledgements. This research was supported by NSF Grants SES-9728970 BSC-0240277 awarded to Schmidt, Fowler, Marsh, and Richardson.

Studies in Perception and Action VIII
H. Heft & K. L. Marsh (Eds.)
© 2005 Lawrence Erlbaum Associates, Inc.

The Specificity of Intrapersonal and Interpersonal Affordance Boundaries: Intrinsic vs. Extrinsic Metrics

Robert W. Isenhower, Kerry L. Marsh, Claudia Carello, Reuben M. Baron, & Michael J. Richardson

Department of Psychology & Center for the Ecological Study of Perception and Action, University of Connecticut, Storrs, CT, USA

An affordance is an opportunity for action that is scaled to the capabilities of an organism. For example, whether or not an object is graspable scales to an individual's hand size (Chan, Carello, & Turvey, 1990). Recent research has extended the framework of intrinsic or body-scaled perception to interpersonal situations as well. The transition from one-hand (1H) to two-hand (2H), and two-hand (2H) to two-person (2P) grasping behavior is also scaled intrinsically (Richardson, Marsh, & Baron, 2005). The present study controls for effector size (e.g., hand-span or arm-span) in order to focus on the particular intrinsic scaling of the transition points as individuals were instructed to grasp and move wooden planks of various lengths either alone, or together with another individual.

Experiment 1

The transition from 1H to 2H grasping was examined for participants with small and large hand-spans. It was expected that participants with large hand-spans would make the transition from 1H to 2H at a larger plank length than participants with small hand-spans, but that this point of transition would correspond to an invariant ratio of hand-span to plank length (Cesari, & Newell, 2000; Newell, Scully, Tenenbaum, & Hardiman, 1989; van der Kamp, Savelsbergh, & Davis, 1988). This experiment also provided a task baseline for 2H to 2P transitions investigated in Experiment 2.

Method

Twenty-four participants with hand-spans ranging from 17.5 cm to 25.5 cm were assigned to one of two groups according to a median split: The small hand-span group averaged 18.9 cm (SD = 1.09); the large hand-span group averaged 22.2 cm (SD = 1.50). Forty-one planks ranging in length from 4.5 to 24.5 cm in 0.5 cm intervals were cut from 2.5 cm × 7.5 cm lumber. The last 0.5 cm at each end was painted red, and the rest was painted matte black (Figure 1a). The planks were presented on a table one at a time. Each participant was instructed to grasp and move the planks from point *a* to point *b* (Figure 1b) by touching only their red ends, and to do so using either one or two hands. Participants completed three sets of trials, during which the planks were presented in ascending, descending, or random order. The point of transition was determined for each presentation order as the mean plank length (PL_t) at which a participant changed from 1H to 2H or from 2H to 1H grasping. The PL_t was divided by each participant's hand-span to obtain the point of transition as a body-scaled ratio, BSr_t (Richardson et al., 2005; van der Kamp et al., 1998).

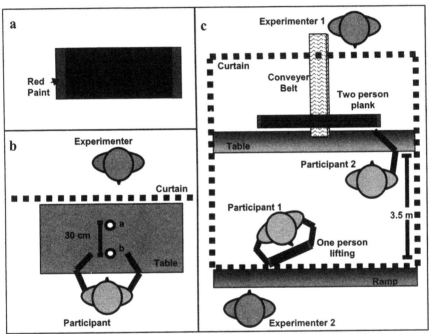

Figure 1. (a) Example of a plank used in the experiments. (b) Set up for Experiment 1. (c) Set up for Experiment 2.

Results and Discussion

Separate 2 (small hand-span vs large hand-span) × 3 (ascending, random, descending sequence) ANOVAs were conducted on PL_t and BSr_t. As expected, the analysis of PL_t revealed a significant effect of hand-span, $F(1, 22) = 4.33$, $p < .05$, with participants in the small hand-span group making the transition at a smaller plank-length than participants in the large hand-span group (Figure 2a). In contrast, the analysis of the BSr_t revealed no effect of hand-span, $F < 1$: Participants in both groups made the transition from 1H to 2H at the same body-scaled ratio (Figure 2b). Consistent with previous research, the analysis also yielded a significant effect for presentation sequence, $F(2, 44) = 12.82$, $p < .05$. Participants exhibited hysteresis—the transition from 1H to 2H tended to occur at a smaller BSr_t in the descending sequence than in the ascending sequence (Richardson et al., 2005; van der Kamp et al., 1998).

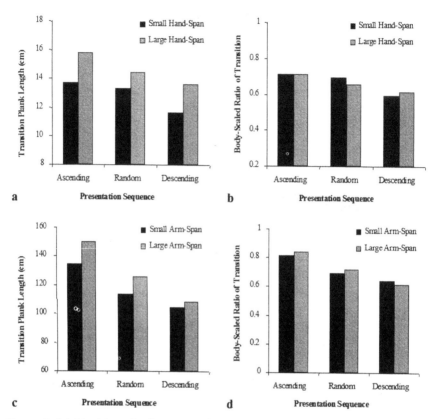

Figure 2. (a) Plank length of transition for small and large hand-span participants for the three sequences in Experiment 1. (b) Body-scaled ratio of transition for small and large hand-span participants for the three sequences in Experiment 1. (c) Plank length of transition for small and large arm-span participants (with covariate included) for the three sequences in Experiment 2. (d) Body-scaled ratio of transition for small and large arm-span participants (with covariate included) for the three sequences in Experiment 2.

Experiment 2

In Experiment 2, the transition from 2H to 2P grasping was examined for participant pairs with small and large arm-spans. Similar to the expectations of Experiment 1, pairs with large arm-spans were expected to make the transition from 2H to 2P at a larger plank length than pairs with small arm-spans, but that this group difference would be eliminated with plank scaled to arm-span (Richardson et al., 2005).

Method

Thirteen same-sex pairs were recruited and matched by height in order to obtain pairs with small and large arm-spans. The participants' arm-spans ranged from 151.3 cm to 184.5 cm. The mean arm-span was calculated for each pair and a median split (median = 169.6 cm) was used to create a short arm-span group (mean = 162.7 cm, SD = 6.11 cm) and a long arm-span group (mean = 177.5 cm, SD = 5.99 cm). The wooden planks ranged in length from 80 to 220 cm in 2 cm intervals and were cut from the same lumber as in Experiment 1; the last 2.5 cm of each end was painted red, and the rest was painted matte black. Participants were instructed to grasp and move the planks either alone or together by touching only the red ends. Planks traveled down a conveyer belt and were moved one at a time to a ramp located opposite the conveyer belt (Fig. 1c). Each participant pair completed an ascending, random, and descending order. PL_t and BSr_t were recorded as before, with the exception that BSr_t was equal to the plank-length divided by the mean arm-span of a participant pair.

Results and Discussion

As in Experiment 1, separate 2 (small arm-span vs. large arm-span) × 3 (ascending, random, descending sequence) ANOVAs were conducted on PL_t and BSr_t. The lack of a group effect for BSr_t, $F < 1$, was anticlimactic because, contrary to expectations, the effect of group did not reach significance for PL_t either, $F(1, 11) = 2.13$, $p = .17$. This was due, in part, to the small sample size. There was also a tendency for pairs that contained participants with a large difference in arm-span to make the transition at a body-scaled ratio consistent with the short arm-span participant. Thus, the 2 × 3 ANOVAs were repeated with the difference in the arm-span of participants in a pair as a covariate. Confirming our conjecture, this analysis yielded an effect of arm-span group on PL_t, $F(1, 10) = 4.15$, $p = .06$, but not on BSr_t, $F < 1$ (Figure 2c and d). As in Experiment 1, there was also a significant effect of presentation sequence, $F(2, 20) = 7.48$, $p < .05$, again showing hysteresis.

Conclusions

Confirming the findings of Richardson et al. (2005), these results demonstrate that both interpersonal and intrapersonal affordance boundaries are body-scaled. Moreover, individuals not only actualize affordances by recruiting bodily degrees of freedom, but also extend their perception-action capabilities by cooperating with other individuals. The current study provides further evidence that the transition between action modes is a dynamical process. In particular, (1) body-scaled ratios can be viewed as a control parameter for phase transitions, and (2) hysteresis was obtained (cf. Fitzpatrick, Carello, Schmidt, & Corey, 1994).

References

Cesari, P., & Newell, K. M. (2000). Body scaling of grip configurations in children aged 6-12 years. *Developmental Psychobiology, 36*, 301-310.

Chan, T-C., Carello, C., & Turvey, M. T. (1990). Perceiving object size by grasping. *Ecological Psychology, 2*, 1-35.

Fitzpatrick, P., Carello, C., Schmidt, R. C., & Corey, D. (1994). Haptic and visual perception of an affordance for upright posture. *Ecological Psychology, 6*(4), 265-287.

Newell, K. M., Scully, D. M., Tenenbaum, F., & Hardiman, S. (1989). Body scale and the development of prehension. *Developmental Psychobiology, 22*(1), 1-13.

Richardson, M. J., Marsh, K. L., Baron, R. M., (2005). *One-effector and two-effector lifting: The mutually nested structure of affordances and perception-action systems.* Manuscript in preparation.

Van der Kamp, J., Savelsbergh, G. J. P., & Davis, W. E. (1998). Body-scaled ratio as a control parameter for prehension in 5- to 9-year-old children. *Developmental Psychobiology, 33*(4), 351-361.

Acknowledgments. This research was supported by NSF Grant BCS-0342802 awarded to Marsh, Baron, Carello, and Richardson and a University of Connecticut Outstanding Scholar Fellowship awarded to Isenhower.

Studies in Perception and Action VIII
H. Heft & K. L. Marsh (Eds.)
© *2005 Lawrence Erlbaum Associates, Inc.*

Coordination of Self-Disclosure and Gossip in Adolescent Conversations

S. Stavros Valenti, Morgan Anderson, Karen Chin, & Jocelyn Schwartz

Hofstra University, Hempstead, NY, USA

Reciprocity is a commonly observed form of social of coordination, seen in verbal and nonverbal behavior of humans across the life span. We reason that reciprocity at both shorter and longer time scales (e.g., postural matching; gift exchange) can provide an informational support for the perception of relationship type and rapport (Bernieri & Rosenthal, 1991; Valenti & Good, 1991; Valenti, Wagner, & Sobel, 1997).

For example, our studies of face-to-face interactions of adolescent friends have revealed a tendency to reciprocate disclosures about emotional states. For example, if Bill said "...I started cursing my mom out ..." Bob may reply "Yeah ... me and my father got into an actual fist fight once ...". We reported a surprising finding that adolescent males show a greater tendency to reciprocate verbalized affect compared to adolescent females, when autocorrelation (consistency of a speaker across time) is controlled (Valenti, Bhagavathula, Goldstein, Follari, Mitchell, & Wagner, 1999).

Verbalized affect is only one form of self-disclosure. A more recent study from our laboratory showed that disclosures of intimate thoughts are also reciprocated. Once again, the tendency to reciprocate disclosure was stronger for male adolescents than for female adolescents when autocorrelation is controlled (Valenti & Cox, 2001).

Our first goal was to examine disclosure reciprocity in adolescent conversations using a more direct and exhaustive coding system than previously used (event coding from transcripts with videotape, rather than interval coding from videotape alone). A second goal was to examine the sequential relation between gossip and self-disclosure. Previous authors have suggested that the function of gossip changes throughout childhood. In middle childhood, gossip is a vehicle for exploring social norms about inclusion/exclusion and building solidarity ('we against them'). In adolescence, " . . . gossip is only the appetizer on the menu; the main course is psychological exploration of the self." (Gottman & Mettetal, 1986, p. 216).

Method

We transcribed videotaped conversations of high-school students (10 male and 10 female) on the topic of "something interesting that happened" or "the worst fight with family." After being trained to a reliability criterion (Kappa > .80) coders classified 4,345 conversational turns (roughly 200 per dyad) into 13 categories. Codes were then collapsed into 3 global categories: Disclosure, Gossip and Other. Conversations were represented as a time series of alternating turns, then transformed into Time 1 x Time 2 x Time 3 contingency tables. Hierarchical log-linear analysis was used to estimate each dyad's model parameters (lambda) for base rate distribution of codes (T3), autocorrelation (e.g., self consistency; T1 x T3), actor-partner reciprocity (T2 x T3), and the interaction of T1 with reciprocity (T1 x T2 x T3). Code proportions, transitional probabilities, and log-linear lambda values were then compared across the male and female groups.

Results and Discussion

As expected, analysis of mean code proportions revealed significantly more disclosure for adolescent women (.28) compared to men (.12). Mean gossip proportion, however, did not show a reliable sex difference (female = .16; male = .11).

An analysis of gossip-disclosure transition probabilities did not reveal temporal associations between these two codes, nor did it indicate a sex difference in sequential dependency of disclosure on gossip. The observed transition probabilities for males and females were not different from the expected values as indicated by the magnitude of the adjusted residuals, and the gossip-to-disclosure transition was not different from the disclosure-to-gossip transition. These data suggest that while gossip is a substantial component of adolescent conversations, gossip does not appear to prime one's partner to self-disclose on a turn-to-turn basis. This does not rule out the possibility of sequential dependencies between gossip and disclosure at longer time-scales.

Figure 1 displays the mean log-linear parameters for the analysis of disclosure reciprocity. As anticipated, there was a reliable sex difference, where adolescent men showed higher disclosure reciprocity; none of the other parameters showed a significant sex difference. We must emphasize that our analysis is focused on the tendency to reciprocate *immediately*. The absence of a T2 x T3 interaction for women may result from the expectation that adolescent women's disclosures span several turns, and female partners postpone their own disclosures while listening. Current studies in our laboratory are using more global coding systems to study disclosure across longer series of turns in an effort to understand this sex difference in disclosure reciprocity.

Face-to-face encounters, such as these ordinary conversations among adolescent friends, create interaction possibilities—social affordances—that can be perceived and acted upon. From an early age, girls and boys develop distinct

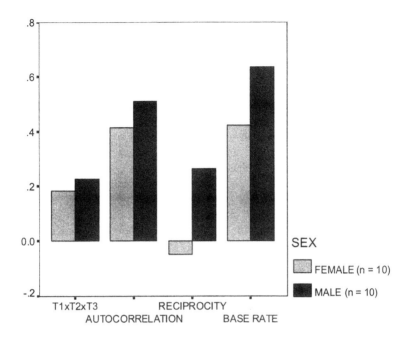

LOG-LINEAR PARAMETER

Figure 1. Mean log-linear parameters as a function of sex.

patterns of social coordination, and show increasing preference for same-sex play partners (Maccoby, 1998). We suspect humans are particularly sensitive to variations in the quality of social coordination, and develop expectations about the structure of conversational patterns that will predict who approaches whom for assistance and for the comfort of a friendly exchange.

References

Bernieri, F., & Rosenthal, R. (1991).   Interpersonal coordination: Behavior matching and interpersonal synchrony. In R. S. Feldman & B. Rime (Eds.), *Fundamentals of nonverbal behavior* (pp. 401-432).   Cambridge, MA: Cambridge University Press.

Gottman, J., & Mettetal, G. (1986). Speculations about social and affective development: Friendship and acquaintanceship through adolescence. In J. M. Gottman & J. G. Parker (Eds.), *Conversations of friends: Speculations on affective development* (pp. 192-237). Cambridge: Cambridge University Press.

Maccoby, E. E. (1998). *The two sexes: Growing up apart, coming together*. Cambridge, MA: Belknap Press of Harvard University Press.

Valenti, S. S., Bhagavathula, S., Goldstein, J., Follari, G., Mitchell, C., & Wagner, K. (1999). Modeling reciprocity (coordination) in adolescent conversations: A log-linear approach (pp. 187-190). In M. A. Grealy & J. A. Thomson (Eds.), *Studies in Perception and Action V: Tenth International Conference on Perception and Action, Edinburgh, Scotland.* Mahwah, New Jersey: Lawrence Erlbaum Associates, Publishers.

Valenti, S. S., & Cox, B. D. (2001). Reciprocity and coordination of self-disclosure by adolescents (pp. 129-132). In G. Burton & R. Schmidt (Eds.), *Studies in Perception and Action VI: Eleventh International Conference on Perception and Action, Storrs, CT.* Mahwah, New Jersey: Lawrence Erlbaum Associates, Publishers.

Valenti, S. S., & Good, J. M. M. (1991). Social affordances and interaction I: Introduction. *Ecological Psychology, 3,* 77-98.

Valenti, S. S., Wagner, K., & Sobel, M. (1997). Possible informational bases for the percepton of rapport. In M. A. Schmuckler & J. M. Kennedy (Eds.), *Studies in Perception and Action IV: Ninth International Conference on Perception and Action, University of Toronto, Canada* (pp. 165-168). Mahwah, New Jersey: Lawrence Erlbaum Associates, Publishers.

Control of Locomotion

Studies in Perception and Action VIII
H. Heft & K. L. Marsh (Eds.)
© 2005 Lawrence Erlbaum Associates, Inc.

Integrating Target Interception and Obstacle Avoidance

Hugo Bruggeman & William H. Warren

Dept. of Cognitive and Linguistic Sciences, Brown University,
Providence, RI, USA

Introduction. Fajen & Warren (2003) modelled locomotor behavior as a dynamical system in which stationary targets and obstacles function as attractors and repellers of an agent's target-heading angle. Subsequent work extended this model to the case of a moving target (Warren & Fajen, 2002) or a moving obstacle (Warren, Di, & Fajen, 2003). Our purpose is to test whether these four components can be integrated into general model of locomotor behavior. The present study examines intercepting a moving target in the presence of a stationary obstacle.

Research Question. Participants are asked to intercept a moving target when a stationary obstacle is placed in the vicinity of their interception path. We test model predictions about (1) under what conditions participants pass on the inside or outside of the obstacle, and (2) when and where participants start to avoid the obstacle. This is a strong test of the model as its components were developed separately for target interception and obstacle avoidance.

Method

Participants. Twelve students, 4 women and 8 men who ranged in age from 18 to 28 years, participated in the experiment. They were compensated with $8 for their participation.

Apparatus & Displays. Testing was done in the Virtual Environment Navigation Laboratory (VENLab) at Brown University. Participants walked freely in a 40 x 40 ft room while viewing a virtual environment through a head-mounted display with a resolution of 640x480 and with a 60deg horizontal x 40deg vertical field of view (Proview 80, Kaiser Electro-optics, Inc, Carlsbad, CA). The participant's head position and orientation was recorded at 30Hz by a hybrid inertial-ultrasonic tracking system (IS-900, Intersense, Burlington, MA). The environment was a textured ground plane with colored poles that serve as obstacles and targets. See Fajen & Warren (2003) for further details.

Procedure. Prior to the experiment, the placement of the eye-pieces of the HMD was calibrated to each participant's interocular distance. A subsequent test assured that the participant could fuse a stereo image. Participants familiarized themselves to walking in a virtual environment of many stationary posts, until they reached a somewhat firm walking pace—they were encouraged to walk as if they going to class. Next, participants completed a series of 5 practice trials to comply with the experimental procedure and to learn the task.

Design. The task of the participant was to intercept a moving goal pole and to avoid a stationary obstacle pillar if present. There were 20 conditions in a 5 (obstacle placement) x 2 (goal speed) x 2 (side) design with 3 trials per condition, for a total of 60 trials. Trials were symmetrical for each side (to the left or right from the midline of the participant's starting position). The goal pole moved at .6 or .9m/s at a 90deg trajectory (frontal plane) and its starting location was at a distance of 7.25m from the participant and at a direction of 15deg to the side with respect to midline. The obstacle was positioned at one of four possible locations (opposite in side to the starting point of the target) or was not present. The four locations were at a direction of 0deg, 6deg, 12deg, or 18deg with respect to the midline and at a distance of respectively 5, 5.03, 5.11 and 5.26m from the starting point. All the above variables were within-subject, and trials were presented in a random order.

Results and Discussion

Human behavior. Participants passed the obstacle on both the inside and outside, even when the situation was kept identical (Figure 1). Participants were more likely to pass the obstacle on the inside when the target was moving slower and when the obstacle was placed further towards the side (Figure 2, left panel).

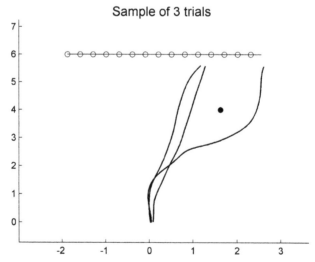

Figure 1. Sample of three trials; the thick lines are the paths of the participant (all starting at the origin). For two of the three trials the participant passes the obstacle on the inside. For a third trial she passes it on the outside. The goal pole, moving from left to right, is represented as the open circles (rendered at 2Hz) and the stationary obstacle is the solid black dot. (Axis units are in meters.)

Model simulations. The model was built of two separate components; an 'attractor' component of target interception and a 'repeller' component of obstacle avoidance. Unlike humans, model simulations reproduced a consistent and identical path for a given situation of target speed and obstacle placement. Thus, for a given situation the model predicted the side of all passes at either the inside or at the outside of the obstacle (Figure 2, right panel). When the human data is bisected at the 50% point, the model did fit six out of the eight conditions.

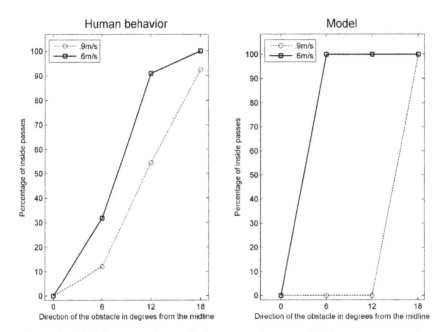

Figure 2. Model comparison of the percentage of inside passes of the stationary obstacle when intercepting a moving target pole. Each panel displays two lines (the fast and the slow moving target); each line connects the data points of the four different placements of the obstacle.

Future analysis will include walking speed as a covariate in the model (in the current model the walking speed is kept constant at 1.4m/s). For example, for a slower walking speed the model will predict fewer inside passes. Adjustment for walking speed could make the model more refined in predicting the side of obstacle passes.

Implications. This study is part of a research program to develop a general model of locomotor behavior that can predict human paths through complex environments. Such a model demonstrates that locomotor paths may emerge on-line from the interaction between an agent and a structured environment, rather than being explicitly planned.

References

Fajen, B. R., & Warren, W. H. (2003). Behavioral dynamics of steering, obstable avoidance, and route selection. *Journal of Experimental Psychology: Human Perception and Performance, 29*(2), 343-362.

Warren, W. H., Di, S., & Fajen, B. R. (2003). Behavioral dynamics of avoiding a moving obstacle. *Journal of Vision, 3*(9), 134a.

Acknowledgements. Supported by NIH EY10923, NSF LIS IRI-9720327.

Studies in Perception and Action VIII
H. Heft & K. L. Marsh (Eds.)
© 2005 Lawrence Erlbaum Associates, Inc.

Estimating TTC (Time-To-Collision) Of Non-Rigid Approaching Objects

Hirokazu Doi & Kazuhiro Ueda

Department of General System Studies, University of Tokyo, Japan

Recent research has shown that the information used in TTC (time-to-collision) estimation is situation-dependent and influenced by many parameters (Tresilian, 1999) such as binocular vision. Though many parameters that influence TTC estimation were identified in previous research (Gray & Regan, 1998; Heuser, 1993), the collisions studied previously were exclusively with rigid objects. Little attention has been paid to collision with non-rigid objects. Because the strategy of TTC estimation is situation-dependent, it is possible that a different strategy is adopted in the TTC estimation of non-rigid approaching objects. Thus, in this study, we examined the strategy of TTC estimation of non-rigid approaching object, specifically, human walkers.

Experiment 1

Because there is a correspondence between walking velocity and body movement (Jacobs et al, 2004), body movement can serve as an effective cue for estimating walking velocity. Smeets et al (1996) found that TTC was estimated based on the apparent velocity of the object. Thus we hypothesized that the judgment of TTC with human-walker is based on the apparent walking velocity and, at the same time, that the walking velocity is estimated on the basis of the walker's body movement.

To test this hypothesis, we compared the measurements of TTC for displays of stick-figure walkers who were walking at the same velocity but using different body movements. One was that of a walker who moved with a small walk ratio, which means shorter stride amplitude and larger stride frequency, and the other was that of a walker with a large walk ratio. In our previous unpublished experiments, we found that apparent walking velocity was systematically affected by the walk ratio even if the walkers were walking at the same velocity: The walking velocity of a walker with larger walk ratio was judged to be significantly faster. Thus if the above mentioned hypothesis is correct, the TTC estimation should be systematically affected by walk ratio.

Method

We used stick-figures of a walker as stimuli, which were created from data acquired through Vicon 3D motion-capture system. When a trial began, the stick figure walker traveled toward the goal which was placed on the floor for two steps, and then disappeared. The four versions of the stick-figure walker were created for the two types of the walk ratio (small and large) and the two types of the walking velocity (fast and slow). Our subjects were instructed to press a mouse button when they thought that the walker reached the goal, assuming that the walker continued on its path after the goal's disappearance. Reaction time (RT) was recorded in msec: RT was defined by the interval between the walker's disappearance and the subject's response. We emphasized that they should estimate intuitively. The experiment was run with sixty stimuli, i.e., 4 versions of walker × 15 stimuli, which were presented in random order.

Five males and two females participated in the experiment. The average age was 22.43 years old (SD = 2.77). They all had normal or corrected to normal vision.

Results and Discussion

The RT data were analyzed in terms of either absolute value of TTC in msec (hereafter, we call this variable "TTC"), or error as a proportion of actual TTC (hereafter, we call this variable "Relative error"). The relative error was calculated by dividing the RT by the actual TTC. These two dependent variables were tested by a two-way analysis of variance (ANOVA), whose independent variables were the walk ratio (2) and the velocity (2).

TTC. The walk ratio significantly effected the TTC, $F_{(1,6)}$ = 20.38, $p <$ 0.05. There was also a significant main effect of velocity, $F_{(1,6)}$ = 24.49, $p <$ 0.05, and a significant interaction between velocity and walk ratio, $F_{(1,6)}$ = 2,95, $p < 0.05$.

Relative error. The result of relative error is shown in Figure 1. The main effect of walk ratio was significant, $F_{(1,6)}$ = 21.39, $p < 0.05$. There was also a significant interaction between walk ratio and velocity, $F_{(1,6)}$ = 7.99, $p < 0.05$. The main effect of walking velocity was marginally significant, $F_{(1,6)}$ = 5.49, $p < 0.1$.

Experiment 2

It has been suggested that the stored representation of the body movement of a biological object is necessary to construct a meaningful representation of the movement (Thornton et al, 2002; Pinto, 1994). Thus if body movement information is utilized in TTC estimation, it is possible that the less familiar body movements, whose representation is thought not to exist in the representation system of the participants, will lead to greater error in TTC estimation. To test this hypothesis, in Experiment 2, the subjects were shown three different types of walkers: a hexapod, which is thought to be an unfamiliar biological object; a human "Hakobi" walker, which is a familiar biological object with an unfamiliar gait pattern; and a normal walker, which is a familiar biological object with familiar body movement.

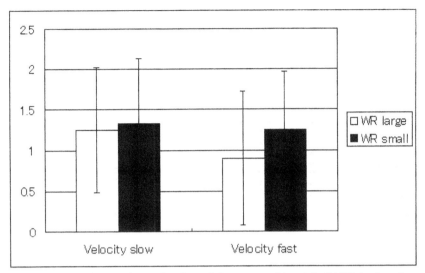

Figure 1. Experiment 1 results for relative error (Y axis). "WR" in the figure means "walk ratio" and "Velocity" means "walking velocity".

Method

The experimental procedure of Experiment 2 was essentially the same as in Experiment 1. The six versions of the stick-picture walker were created by the three types of the walkers (hexapod, hakobi walker, and normal walker) and the two types of the walking velocity. The experiment was run with ninety stimuli, i.e., 6 versions of walker × 15 stimuli, which were sectioned by the types of the walker. The stimuli within each section were presented in random order.

Four males and two females participated in the experiment. The average age was 21.3 years old ($SD = 3.45$). They all had normal or corrected to normal vision.

Results and Discussion

The RT data were analyzed as in Experiment 1.

TTC. The main effect of velocity was significant, $F(2,5) = 37.1558$, $p < 0.05$. There were also a marginally significant main effect of type of walkers, $F(2,10) = 3.32$, $p < 0.1$, and a marginally significant interaction between velocity and types of walker, $F(2,10) = 2.98$, $p < 0.1$.

Relative error. None of the main effects or the interaction was significant.

Conclusions

The results of Experiment 1 show that the TTC of a walker with a small walk ratio was estimated to be significantly shorter than that of a walker with a large one, even if the actual walking velocity and TTC were the same in the two conditions of walk ratio. That is, if the actual TTC was held constant, the faster the apparent walking velocity was, the shorter the TTC estimation was. And the results of Experiment 2 showed that the stored representation of the objects marginally influenced the TTC estimation.

These results indicate that the TTC of a non-rigid approaching object was judged on the basis of cognitive operation, which was suggested by Smeets et al (1996) and DeLucia et al (2000): The strategy of TTC estimation is task and situation dependent. More importantly, the subtle difference of body movement systematically affected the apparent walking velocity and TTC estimation, which implies that the non-rigid body movement is exploited as an effective cue to estimate TTC with human-walkers.

References

DeLucia, P. R., Tresilian, J. R., and Meyer, L. E. (2000). Geometrical illusions can affect time-to-contact estimation and mimed prehension. *Journal of Experimental Psychology: Human Perception and Performance, 26,*552-567.

Gray, R. and Regan, D. (1998). Accuracy of estimating the time to collision using binocular and monocular information. *Vision Research, 36,* 499-512.

Heuser, H. (1993). Estimates of time to contact based on changing size and changing target vergence. *Perception, 22,* 549-563.

Jacobs, A., Pinto, J., & Shiffrar, M. (2004). Experience, context and the visual perception of human movement. *Journal of Experimental Psychology: Human Perception and Performance, 30,* 822-35.

Pinto, J. (1994). Human infants' sensitivity to biological motion in point-light cats. *Infant Behavior & Development, 17,* 871.

Smeets, J. B., & Brenner, E. (1996). Is Judging time-to-contact based on 'tau'?. *Perception, 25,* 583-590.

Thornton, I. M., Rensink, R. A., and Shiffrar, M. (2002). Active versus passive processing of biological motion. *Perception, 31,* 837-53.

Tresilian, J. R. (1999). Visually timed action: time-out for 'tau'? *Trends in Cognitive Sciences, 3,* 301-10.

Studies in Perception and Action VIII
H. Heft & K. L. Marsh (Eds.)
© 2005 Lawrence Erlbaum Associates, Inc.

The Role of Calibration in Visually Guided Braking

Brett R. Fajen

Rensselaer Polytechnic Institute, Troy, NY, USA

The limitations of our action capabilities impose a critical constraint on successful performance. When braking to avoid a collision, for example, the rate of deceleration that would bring the actor to a stop at the intended location (the "ideal deceleration") must be kept below the maximum possible deceleration. Ideal deceleration is optically specified, but maximum decelera-tion is a property of the actor's body or vehicle. Hence, adaptation to changes in maximum deceleration must involve calibration. Calibration may be understood in terms of scaling information about ideal deceleration in intrinsic units of maximum deceleration, such that 1.0 separates situations in which it is still possible to stop from situations in which it is no longer possible to stop.

Participants in this study viewed computer generated displays simulating approaches to a stop sign, and used a joystick as a brake to stop as closely as possible to the sign. Brake strength was manipulated by varying the slope of the linear function mapping joystick position to simulated deceleration. If participants calibrate to the strength of the brake by scaling information about ideal deceleration in intrinsic units of maximum deceleration, then the ratio of ideal deceleration at brake onset to maximum deceleration should be the same across different brake strength conditions. This prediction was tested in Experiment 1 by manipulating brake strength as a between-subjects variable. In Experiment 2, the rate of recalibration was investigated by manipulating brake strength as a randomly presented within-subjects variable.

Method

Thirty students (10 per group) participated in Experiment 1 and twelve students participated in Experiment 2. In Experiment 1, brake strength was manipulated between subjects with three levels of maximum deceleration (5, 7, or 9 m/s^2). In Experiment 2, brake strength was manipulated as a randomly presented within-subjects variable with the same three levels of maximum deceleration. Initial distance and time-to-contact were also varied within subjects in both experiments. Ideal deceleration at onset was calculated using the following equation: $v_{onset}^2/2z_{onset}$, where v_{onset} and z_{onset} are the speed and distance at the onset of braking, respectively.

Results

In Experiment 1, ideal deceleration at the onset of braking (expressed in extrinsic units of m/s^2) increased with brake strength as expected, $F(2, 27) = 58.85, p < .01$ (Figure 1A). When ideal deceleration was scaled in intrinsic units as a percentage of maximum deceleration for all three groups, braking was initiated at the same mean value, $F(2, 27) = 1.44, p = .26$ (Figure 1B). These results provide support for the hypothesis that people calibrate to changes in brake strength by scaling information about ideal deceleration in intrinsic units of maximum deceleration.

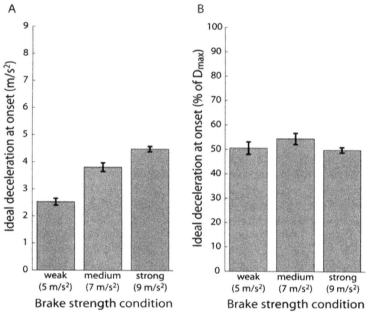

Figure 1. Mean ideal deceleration at the onset of the initial brake adjustment (A) in extrinsic units (m/s^2), and in intrinsic units (B, % of maximum deceleration) for all three brake strength conditions in Experiment 1.

In Experiment 2, brake strength was manipulated as a randomly presented within-subjects variable. Separate analyses were performed on the initial brake adjustment and subsequent brake adjustments made on the same trial. If participants were able to rapidly recalibrate within a single trial, then the effect of brake strength on subsequent brake adjustments should be weaker than it was for the initial brake adjustment. An analysis of brake adjustment magnitude revealed no significant differences between the initial and subsequent brake adjustments, $F < 1$ (Figure 2), indicating that participants were unable to recalibrate within a single trial. However, a post-hoc analysis indicated that performance was affected by brake strength on the previous trial, $F(2, 20) = 17.50, p < .01$. Braking was initiated earlier when brake strength was weak on the previous trial, and later when brake strength was strong on the previous trial

(Figure 3A). Although participants partially recalibrated after just one trial, they did not fully recalibrate. When the same data are expressed as a percentage of maximum deceleration on the previous trial (Figure 3B), the main effect of brake strength was significant, $F(2, 20) = 198.52$, $p < .01$. Taken together, the results suggest that participants were unable to recalibrate based on the initial brake adjustment alone, but that additional adjustments executed during the same trial provided sufficient information for partial recalibration that affected performance on the next trial.

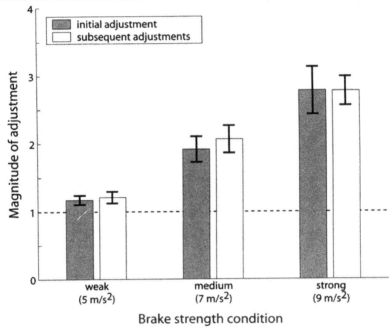

Figure 2. Mean magnitude of initial (gray bars) and subsequent brake adjustments (white bars) for all three brake strength conditions in Experiment 2.

Discussion

These findings cannot be explained by the Tau-dot model of braking (Lee, 1976; Yilmaz & Warren, 1995) because tau-dot is independent of maximum deceleration. However, the findings can be easily understood from the perspective that braking is controlled by making adjustments to keep ideal deceleration between zero and maximum deceleration (Fajen, in press-a, in press-b). Within this framework, people adapt to changes in brake strength by learning to adjust the metric in which information about ideal deceleration is detected. The scaling of information to action provides a parsimonious alternative to theories that explain calibration in terms of the formation of an internal model of the body or vehicle dynamics.

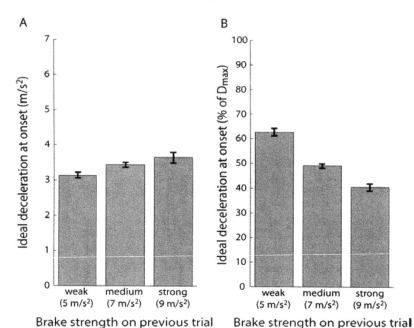

Figure 3. Mean ideal deceleration at the onset of the initial brake adjustment (A) in extrinsic units (m/s²), and (B) in intrinsic units (% of maximum deceleration) as a function of brake strength on the previous trial in Experiment 2.

References

Fajen, B. R. (in press-a). Calibration, information, and control strategies for braking to avoid a collision. *Journal of Experimental Psychology: Human Perception and Performance.*

Fajen, B. R. (in press-b). Perceiving possibilities for action: On the sufficiency of perceptual learning and calibration for the visual guidance of action. *Perception.*

Lee, D. N. (1976). A theory of visual control of braking based on information about time-to-collision. *Perception, 5,* 437-459.

Yilmaz, E. H., & Warren, W. H., Jr. (1995). Visual control of braking: a test of the tau hypothesis. *Journal of Experimental Psychology: Human Perception and Performance, 21,* 996-1014.

Acknowledgements. This research was supported by a grant from the National Science Foundation (BCS 0236734).

Studies in Perception and Action VIII
H. Heft & K. L. Marsh (Eds.)
© 2005 Lawrence Erlbaum Associates, Inc.

Velocity Control of Harbor Porpoise (*Phocoena phocoena*): A Case Study

Kiyohide Ito[1], Takashi Matsuishi[2], Ayumi Ito[1], Yuji Kojima[1], Atsuko Miyashita[2] & Mamoru Aoyama[3]

[1]School of Systems Information Science, Future University-Hakodate
[2]Graduate School of Fisheries Sciences, Hokkaido University, Japan
[3]Otaru Aquarium, Japan

In the reported study we demonstrated how a harbor porpoise controls its velocity to catch fish. This behavior has been little studied among porpoises; specifically, there is no knowledge about the feeding process. This experiment was conducted in a controlled setting because of the difficulty of observing a porpoise's behavior in the natural environment. Consider the case as an animal approaches a surface. The ratio of the distance between the animal and the surface to its velocity provides a first-order estimate of its time-to-contact with the surface. This ratio picked up in perceptual flows is defined as tau (τ) obtained by Equation 1:

$$\tau(x) = \frac{x}{\dot{x}} \qquad (1)$$

where x is a distance of an animal to a surface, $\dot{x}$ is the rate of change of x, and $\tau(x)$ is a value of tau at x. By differentiating it with respect to time, the rate of change of $\tau(x)$ ($\dot{\tau}(x)$) provides sufficient information for controlling velocity; hence, calculations of distance, velocity and deceleration/acceleration are not necessary. It was hypothesized that, as in the cases of flying hummingbirds and pigeons, a harbor porpoise will follow the controlled-collision procedure if it can pick up τ and $\dot{\tau}$.

Method

Our subject was a female harbor porpoise (*Phocoena phocoena*), caught off Usujiri Port of Hokkaido, Japan, in April 2004. For the purpose of rehabilitation, the subject was moved to Otaru Aquarium. Figure 1 illustrates the experimental setting. We recorded swimming trajectories via four video cameras. Three data series were computed from 44 trials each.

(1) Time-to-contact: The time it took the subject to swim from each location to a fish in the feeder's hand.

(2) Velocity ($\dot{x}$): We calculated inter-location distance per frame. The inter-

location distance was divided by inter-frame time (0.03 s). It was a measure of velocity of passing each location.

(3) Tau: The distance (x) from each location to a fish was divided by the velocity ($\dot{x}$) of each location.

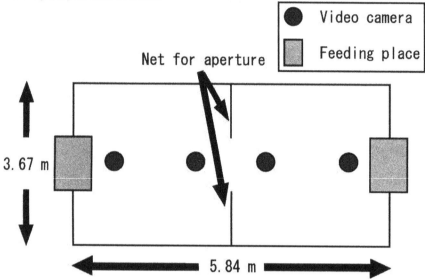

Figure 1: *Experimental setting.* Four video cameras with the sampling frequency of 30 Hz recorded her swimming behavior approaching a feeder to catch a fish. The video cameras were suspended from the ceiling and their optic axes were placed perpendicular to the water surface. The data recorded were loaded in the personal computer and analyzed frame-by-frame by using the Videopoint software. On each trial, we transferred the relative locations of tip of her mouth into the values of x-y coordinates.

Results and Discussion

Figure 2(a) represented mean τ as a function of time-to-contact. We performed linear regression analyses between time-to-contact and τ, as well as between time-to-contact and velocity. As for τ against time-to-contact, the linear regression coefficient ($\dot{\tau}$) was 0.772, and R^2 was 0.986 ($p < 0.001$). As for velocity against time-to-contact, the linear regression coefficient was -0.178, R^2 was 0.446 ($p < 0.001$). These values indicate that the subject decelerated overall. Figure 2(b) represents standard deviations (SD) of τ as a function of time-to-contact. The dispersion of the porpoise's spatial position tended to converge as it reached the target fish.

As seen in Figure 2(a) there were two inflection points. Thereupon we used maximum likelihood estimation to fit the three best lines to data and get two crossing points between two lines out of the three. The first and second inflection points were respectively -0.835 s and -2.003 s. Time duration of phases were designated as follows: from -2.870 s to -2.003 s as the first phase, from -2.003 s to -0.835 s as the second phase, and from -0.835 s to 0 s as the third phase. We carried out linear regression analyses on all three phases each.

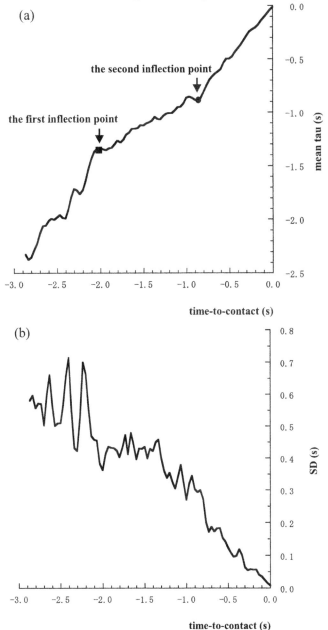

Figure 2: *Tau against time-to-contact*. (a) Mean tau as a function of time-to-contact. The figure showed that as time-to-contact approached zero, mean tau became smaller. (b) Standard deviations of tau as a function of time-to-contact. This figure also illustrated that the smaller time-to-contact became, the smaller SD became.

$\dot{\tau}$ s for the first, second, and third phases were 1.058, 0.567, and 1.008 respectively. This result showed that $\dot{\tau}$ was the closest to 1 in the third phase. R^2s were 0.954, 0.972, and 0.992 for the first, second, and third phase respectively. R^2 in the third phase did not significantly differ from 1, while R^2s were significantly lower than 1 in the first and second phases ($p < 0.01$, t-test). $\dot{\tau}$ in the third phase only had the perfect linearity. This meant that the subject kept $\dot{\tau}$ constant in the third phase. Consequently, it was evident that the third phase was qualitatively distinctive from the other two.

Here we should consider which variable, $\dot{\tau}$ or decelerating rate, is more effective in catching fish by the harbor porpoise. The porpoise should make accurate estimation of time-to-contact if variables are constant. $\dot{\tau}$ or velocity constancy is expressed as perfect linearity of regression slope. According to the analyses of the whole course, R^2s were 0.986 for $\dot{\tau}$ and 0.446 for velocity, respectively. A t-test showed that R^2 for $\dot{\tau}$ was significantly higher than velocity ($p < 0.01$). This means that $\dot{\tau}$ was more constant than velocity. It indicates that the harbor porpoise took the $\dot{\tau}$ constancy strategy to approach fish overall, rather than the strategy of maintaining the constant deceleration.

The mean τ at contact-time (time-to-contact = 0) was -0.012 s, and the mean velocity at the time was 0.402 m/s. These values significantly differed from 0, as shown by a t-test ($p < 0.01$). This indicates that the harbor porpoise maintained braking but tried not to stop short of fish. Additionally, $\dot{\tau}$ of the whole swimming course was 0.772, which significantly differed from 1 and 0.5 ($p < 0.01$ by t-test). It reveals that the subject took a controlled-collision procedure. This finding is consistent with previous studies by Lee and colleagues who found that $\dot{\tau}$ was 0.721 in Lee, Reddish, and Rand (1991), 0.775 in Lee, Davies, Green, and van der Weel (1993, $\dot{\tau}_{(feet-lp)}$ normal condition).

Furthermore, the whole approach can be divided into three phases according to the regression analyses:

(1) Exploratory approach: In this phase the subject swam exploring fish, but she did not yet make any decisions of catching fish. In our data, the 'exploratory approach' ranged from -2.87 s to -2.003 s to the contact time. During the 'exploratory approach', $\dot{\tau}$ did not keep perfectly constant (R^2 = 0.954, significantly less than 1) and the velocity is slightly increased.

(2) Deceleration approach: In this phase the subject appeared to control the collision and swam to the fish. 'Deceleration approach' occurred from -2.003 s to -0.835 s in our data. The subject took a decelerating strategy in this approach. $\dot{\tau}$ ranged from 0.5 to 1 and remained more constant (R^2 = 0.974) in this approach than 'exploratory approach' though not completely. The difference between τ and actual time was generally reduced to the minimum until she entered the 'final approach'.

(3) Final approach: The subject swam straight toward fish and caught it in this phase, during which the difference between τ and time-to-contact

maintains a minimum. When the subject enters 'final approach', she has no choice but catching fish regardless of its consequence. This approach was designated from -.835 s to 0 s in our data. In 'final approach', the subject took a strategy to keep $\dot{\tau}$ 1 and the most linear ($R^2 = 0.992$, non-significantly less than 1). In other words, she swam to reach the fish by maintaining her velocity and $\dot{\tau}$ constant.

Unfortunately the present study did not determine variables from which harbor porpoise picked up τ. Here, possible alternative variables that we propose are acoustic flow, and optic flow based on the videotaped behaviors. A harbor porpoise registers τ by echolocating sounds (clicks) approaching a fish from afar. At the end of the 'deceleration approach' she switches over from acoustic τ to optic τ. This does not mean that a harbor porpoise follows this process exactly in the natural environment. It should be noted that the present findings only demonstrate the capability that a harbor porpoise can pick up both of acoustic and optic τ.

We conclude that a harbor porpoise can follow the controlled-collision procedure by using acoustic and optic τ potentially. Another possibility of coupling τ in different (multi) modalities will be investigated in the near future.

References

Lee, D. N., Davies, M. N. O., Green, P. R., and van der Weel, F. R. (1993). Visual control of velocity of approach by pigeons when landing. *The Journal of Experimental Biology, 180*, 85-99.

Lee, D. N., Reddish, P. E., and Rand, D. T. (1991). Aerial docking by hummingbirds. *Naturwissenschaften, 78*, 526-527.

Studies in Perception and Action VIII
H. Heft & K. L. Marsh (Eds.)
© 2005 Lawrence Erlbaum Associates, Inc.

Basic Strategies of Target Search by Smell

E. E. Kadar, P. Fisher, & G. S. Virk

University of Portsmouth, UK

Navigation by smell is perhaps the most fundamental form of perceptual control of locomotion. Even the simplest species such as bacteria use chemical substances and associated gradient fields for navigation. Although navigation by smell seems to be simpler than similar tasks based on other perceptual modalities (e.g., vision, hearing, etc.), search patterns in navigation towards a source of a chemical diffusion field are still not fully understood.

It is commonly assumed that bisensory chemotaxis is the fundamental search strategy in chemical field. According to this method, the animal moves forward whilst the direction of motion is modified based on the detected field intensity values at the two sensors. Since the animal turns in the direction of higher intensity values whilst moving forward, the generated search pattern is expected to be a smooth trajectory toward the target in a stable and smooth diffusion field. But this is in contrast with empirical observations, which show that animals (dogs, cats, etc.) typically exhibit strange meandering patterns by moving slowly, often stopping and changing direction but gradually drifting toward the target.

Chemotaxis can, in principle, be used in a stable smooth diffusion field, but it cannot fully account for meandering search patterns in intrinsic instable and naturally weak diffusion fields. Chemotaxis seems unreliable when chemical gradients are weak and easily disturbed by other processes (e.g., wind, fluid current) (Kadar & Virk, 1998). Also, for chemotaxis two distinct but simultaneous measurements are needed, but it has been shown that animals are usually successful with one sensor only (Hangartner, 1967). These difficulties suggest that perhaps chemotaxis is not the basic search strategy in chemical diffusion fields.

And indeed, a pioneering study on bacteria navigation paved the way toward a new understanding of basic principles of chemical search strategies. Berg and Brown (1972) observed Escherichia coli (E. coli) bacteria and noticed that the movement trajectory is shaped by two different modes of motion, moving straight ahead (translation) or tumbling (rotation). Bacteria switch between these two fundamental modes of motion creating a zig-zag shaped trajectory. In a homogeneous medium the motion is an aimless random walk process. In the presence of a chemical gradient field, the random walk process is modified by a drift toward the preferred level of concentration. This movement pattern is a biased random walk process, a seemingly inefficient but robust search strategy.

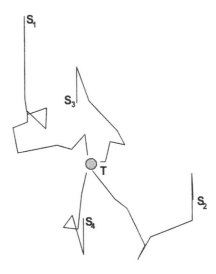

a   b

Figure 1. a) The robot used in the experiment with BRW search strategy. b) Four successful trials from the calibrated unisensory (BRW) search strategy. $S_1 - S_4$ are the starting positions and T is the target.

Since the late 1990s, we have been trying to demonstrate that unisensory search patterns are feasible solutions not only at the scale of E coli but in larger species such as insects, dogs and cats. In early simulation studies, we have successfully tested several biased random walk [BRW] strategies (Kadar & Virk, 1998). But simulation studies have their limitations because the complex disturbances in the chemical field caused by animal movement are nearly impossible to model accurately. It has been argued recently, however, that robotics research can help us testing biological methods (Webb, 2000). In our effort to clarify navigational principles in diffusion fields, we have implemented BRW strategies on robotic platforms. Preliminary studies in relatively stable and strong diffusion fields have already been conducted, but the present study provides the first demonstration of the feasibility of a unisensory BRW strategy in a weak and highly unstable diffusion field.

Method

The robot is circular, 150 mm in diameter, with the configuration shown in Figure 1a. Whilst four TGS2620 odor sensors can be seen mounted on the robot's antennae, only the front central sensor was used in this experiment.

The experiment was conducted in an arena measuring 2.5 m^2 with a slowly developing acetone diffusion field. The search trials started at a range of distances from the target, at random angles from the target.

Since TGS2620 odor sensors have relatively slow response times (about 10 seconds), and particularly slow recovery time (30 seconds), six second settling time was allowed after each movement (run or turn). The unisensory BRW search algorithm was also calibrated to scale it to the size of the robot and the search area.

Results and Discussion

Four successful BRW search trials are presented in Figure 1b. The four starting positions are 112, 85, 45, 32 cm from the target. The search patterns are similar to those observed in simulation studies (Kadar & Virk, 1998) with more meandering patterns at far range and a stronger drift towards the target at a closer range. All trials were successful demonstrating the feasibility of unisensory BRW strategy at a large scale in a weak diffusion field. Although the distance of the starting positions in these trials was constrained by the narrow sensitivity range of the robots, we hope that the fast developing sensor technology will allow us to test long-range BRW strategies in the near future.

References

Berg, H. C. & Brown, D. A. (1972). Chemotaxis in *E Coli* analysed by three dimensional tracking, *Nature, 239*, 500-504.

Hangartner, W. (1967). Spezifitat und Inactivirung des Spurpheromons von Lasius fuliginosus Latr. und Orientierung der Arbeiterinnen im Duftfeld. *Z. verl. Physiol. 57*, 103-136.

Kadar, E. E., & Virk, G. S. (1998). Field theory based navigation for autonomous mobile machines. In A. Ollero (Ed.), *Proceedings of the IFAC Workshop on Intelligent Components for Vehicles (ICV '98)* (pp. 137-142). Amsterdam: Elsevier Sciences

Webb, B. (2000). What does robotics offer animal behaviour? *Animal Behaviour, 2000*, 60, 545-558.

Dynamic Touch

Studies in Perception and Action XIII
H. Heft & K. L. Marsh (Eds.)
© 2005 Lawrence Erlbaum Associates, Inc.

CyARM: Direct Perception Device by Dynamic Touch

Junichi Akita[1], Kiyohide Ito[2], Takanori Komatsu[2], Tetsuo Ono[2], & Makoto Okamoto[2]

[1]Kanazawa University, [2]Future University-Hakodate, Japan

Under the rubric of `ecological human-machine' interface, especially for visually impaired persons, we have developed an electric aid for guiding their perception and action. The device, named CyARM, measures with an ultrasonic sensor the distance between its holder and certain object that holder points to, and transmits the distance information to her/his haptic sense (Akita et al., 2004, Okamoto et al., 2004).

Concept

Figure 1 shows the concept of CyARM. The user holds CyARM in the hand, and explores her/his environment of interest. CyARM is tied to the user's body by a wire, and its tension is controlled according to the measured distance to the object. If the object is located at a short distance, CyARM pulls the wire

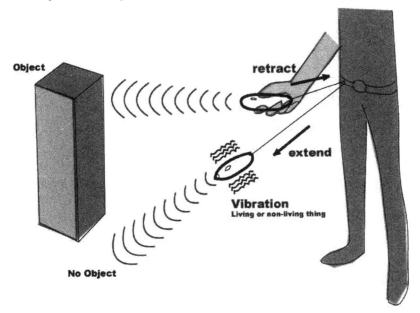

Figure 1. Concept of CyARM and its operation.

tightly so that the user feels as if s/he is touching an object by bending the arm. If the object is located at a far distance, CyARM pulls the wire loosely so that the user feels as if s/he is not touching the object by extending the arm, as shown in Figure 2.

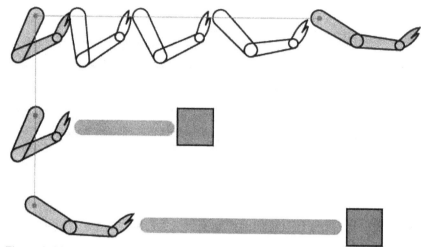

Figure 2. Metaphor of arm's motion and recognizing objects.

The user can explore the environment of interest by pointing in any direction, and when an object is detected, the CyARM will give the user a feeling as if the user's hand is extended and reaching out to the object. In this case, the user experiences a novel feeling that we call the "future body." This method offers a new type of interface for the user, who can recognize the environment as if walking by groping around. In this way it may be experienced as a natural interface for user. This coupling of tensor perception and explora-tory action provides opportunities for the pickup of affordances through action.

Implementation

CyARM has a sensor module with the capability of range measurement and the actuator module that has a motor with a wheel to rewind the wire. The wire is tied to the user's body (e.g., to a belt on the waist), and the user holds CyARM in her/his hand for operation. The motor is controlled with reference to the measured distance so as to implement the operation for stretching or bending the user's arm. Figure 3 shows the developed CyARM device.

Experiments – Recognizing the Presence of an Object

We carried out an experiment to evaluate the function of the CyARM, especially to assess whether a user of the CyARM can recognize the presence of an object. A white board (2m in height) was randomly placed in front of blinded-folded participants, and they were asked to report if they felt the presence of the object using the CyARM. Five participants (four sighted and one blind) took part in the experiment.

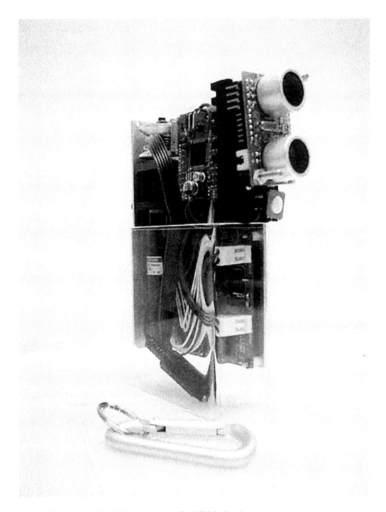

Figure 3. Photograph of developed CyARM device.

The results are summarized in Table 1. The subjects correctly reported the presence of the object on 90% of the trials in which it was present, and the absence of the objects for 96% of the trials in which it was not present. This obtained values differed significantly from expected values ($\chi^2 = 61.9$, $p < 0.001$). The results indicate that CyARM can be an effective means for recognizing the presence of an object.

Expansion for Collaborative Action

We are next planning to attach another sensing device on CyARM so that one person can detect an object that another person is pointing to. This method can be implemented by means of a visible spot of light with a special frequency modulation as well as spot photo detector with demodulator. If two users have

	Recognized as 'exist'	recognized as 'not exist'
object exists	90% (17.3%)	10% (17.3%)
object doesn't exist	4% (8.9%)	96% (8.9%)

Table 1. Results of experiment for recognizing the existence of the object, listing averages of subjects' answers (standard deviations in parentheses).

these new CyARMs individually, and one can know that an object being detected is also being pointed to by the other person, these two users can eventually perceive that they are pointing the same object simultaneously. This procedure offers a new methodology for judging the other's attentions or intentions without information about gaze direction. For example, although the reference terms such as "this" or "that" are usually visually-grounded, this new CyARM could permit users to share each other's "this" or "that" by CyARM's output. Such 'joint haptic attention' can be applied in collaborative work with a human and a robot, especially on a task in which a robot needs to detect the object of a human's attention, and vice versa. Furthermore, usefulness of CyARMs could be employed to guide blind infants' development of pointing and reaching, and in turn provide the basis for a triadic relationship between an infant, an object, and a mother.

References

Akita, J., Takagi, T., Okamoto, M. (2004). CyARM: Environment Sensing Device using Non-Visual Modality. *CSUN2004 International Conference on Technology and Persons with Disabilities.*

Okamoto, M., Akita, J., Ito, K., Ono, T., Takagi, T.(2004).CyARM: Interactive Device for Environment Recognition Using a Non-Visual Modality. *Proceedings of International Conference Computers Helping People with Special Needs (ICCHP2004),* 462-467.

Acknowledgements. This work was supported by Northern Advancement Center for Science & Technology, Japan.

Studies in Perception and Action VIII
H. Heft & K. L. Marsh (Eds.)
© *2005 Lawrence Erlbaum Associates, Inc.*

Peripheral Neuropathy and Length Perception by Dynamic Touch

Claudia Carello[1], Jeffrey Kinsella-Shaw [1,2], & Eric Amazeen[3]

[1]Center for the Ecological Study of Perception and Action,
University of Connecticut, Storrs, CT, USA
[2]Department of Physical Therapy, University of Connecticut, Storrs, CT
[3]Department of Psychology, Arizona State University, Tempe, AZ, USA

Dynamic touch is involved whenever an object is grasped and forces are imposed in order to move, stabilize, or carry it. Given its role in manipulating commonplace tools and utensils such as forks and hammers and coffee cups, dynamic touch can be considered critical to everyday function. A good deal of research suggests that time-invariant moments of the mass distribution of hand-held objects, extracted by the nervous system during movement, constrain perception of object properties by dynamic touch. Nonvisual perception of object length, for example, is easily accomplished without practice or feedback and is constrained by the object's resistance to being moved—quantified by its inertia tensor, I_k (Figure 1). One particularly robust finding is that the maximum principal moment of inertia I_1 is the primary constraint on muscle-based perception of the length of a wielded object.

The sensory disorder of *peripheral neuropathy* poses an interesting challenge for muscle-based perception. In extreme cases of the condition, individuals cannot feel anything touching their limbs, cannot feel anything their limbs are touching, and cannot feel the limbs themselves. Although full neuropathy is rare, partial neuropathy (typically affecting the extremities) is a

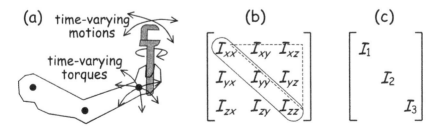

Figure 1. (a) The motions of a wielded object vary over time as do the torques used to produce the movements. (b) The inertia tensor couples the motions and torques, quantifying the resistance to being moved in different directions. (c) When the tensor is transformed relative to symmetry axes, the principal moments of inertia remain.

fairly common consequence of aging and diabetes. Clearly, older adults and individuals with partial neuropathies continue to engage in behaviors that require them to manipulate objects. But to what extent is their everyday functioning compromised? Insight into this question was provided by an evaluation of dynamic touch in a patient with pronounced neuropathy in one arm.

Method

CA, a 40 year-old right-handed female, experienced complete insensitivity in the left arm, extending from the hand through the elbow with some involvement of the shoulder. The condition was due to a growth on the sensory tract at the top of the spine that was detected two months before testing. The loss of sensation was confirmed by a haptic identification task. Small 3-D numbers (approximately 2 cm × 2 cm × 1 cm) were placed in one hand singly, in random order. While blindfolded, she correctly identified every number immediately using the unaffected hand but none using the numb hand. (She declined to continue after dropping the first three, noting that she could not feel anything.)

Length perception by dynamic touch was evaluated using the typical methodology (Figure 2a). Wooden dowels were cut into three sets of three lengths (L = 45, 60, and 80 cm). In order to manipulate I_k, one member of each length set was presented with a metal disk at 1/3 L, one with the disk at 2/3 L, and one without a disk. Each of the nine rod configurations was presented three times in random order. Perceived length was evaluated for the numb hand in the first block of 27 trials and for the intact hand in the second block of 27 trials. (CA wielded the rods in the affected hand without objection. She could not use that hand to grip the string of the report apparatus, however, so the experimenter made the back-and-forth adjustments for her; Figure 2b.)

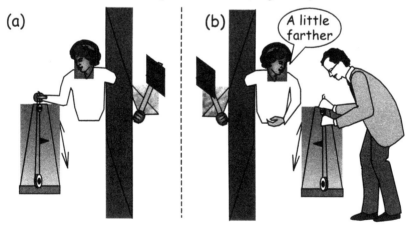

Figure 2. (a) When rods were wielded by the numb hand, the intact hand adjusted a marker to indicate felt length. (b) CA was unable to control the pulley system with her numb hand. Therefore, when the rods were wielded by the unaffected hand, she instructed the experimenter where to place the marker to indicate felt length.

Results and Discussion

Standard findings for these kinds of experiments were replicated: Perceived length increased with rod length; rods with attached masses were felt to be longer than rods without attached masses; and perceived length increased the farther the attached disk was from the hand. All of these reflect the influence of the maximum principal moment of inertia I_1 on perceived length. In particular, the 1/3 scaling of log perceived length on log I_1 emerged—the slope of the regression was .35 for both the intact and the numb hand.

A Discrimination Index was used to evaluate whether the two hands were comparable in discriminating the rods:

$DI = a/\text{s.d.}$

where a is the slope of the regression of perceived length on actual length. $DI = 5.5$ for the intact hand and 5.8 for the numb hand. These numbers are comparable to those found for the right (5.7) and left hands (5.9) of right-handers without neuropathy (Carello, Adams, Starski, Salaman, & Wagman, 2002).

A difference between the two hands was found with respect to the intercept of the regressions, indicating that perceived length using the numb hand was rods whose actual lengths varied from 45–80 cm, perceived lengths varied from 41–80 cm (mean = 60.1 cm) for the intact hand and from 28–65 cm (mean = 47.4 cm) for the numb hand. For normal right-handers, in contrast, neither the slopes nor the intercepts of the two regressions differed, $p > .50$ (Figure 3b). The latter result indicates that the shorter perceived lengths associated with CA's numb hand were not simply a consequence of being wielded by the non-dominant hand.

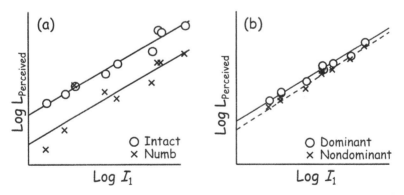

Figure 3. Regressions of perceived length on the maximum principal moment of inertia (I_1) in log-log coordinates. (a) The functions for the affected and unaffected hands of a right-handed woman with unilateral neuropathy are parallel but with distinct intercepts. (b) Comparable functions for the right and left hands of normal right-handers show the same slope and single intercept.

How is CA able to perceive length at all with such severely compromised neuromuscular contact? More pointedly, given that the scaling to I_1 is appropriate, why are perceived lengths in a shorter range? For insight, we appeal to experiments in which tissue contact with a target rod is varied. Perceived rod length is comparable whether a rod is grasped in one hand or contact is distributed over two hands, one hand and one knee (Carello et al., 1992), or even supported by an axle at one end and lifted with a probe rod at the other end (Peck, Jeffers, Carello & Turvey., 1996). In all cases, perceived length is constrained by rotational dynamics. Most notably, shorter perceived lengths accompany a wider separation between rod supports, a manipulation that has the effect of reducing the resistance to rotation (Carello et al.., 1992). The success of the insensate limb suggests that the subsystem of dynamic touch can exploit the field-like structure of the mechanoreceptor support for haptic perception— wielding an object deforms the tissues of the body not just of the hand. The reduced magnitudes arise because the proximal field structure is reduced where the deformation is registered (presumably, at or beyond the shoulder). Thus, the detection of invariants revealed through movement is a major mechanism in kinesthetic perception involving intact limbs, neuropathic or anesthetized limbs, prosthetic devices, and hand-held-tools and implements (Pagano & Turvey, 1998).

References

Carello, C., Adams, C., Starski, J., Salaman, A., & Wagman, J. B. (2002). Handedness effects in haptic perception. Presented at the Spring Meeting of the International Society for Ecological Psychology, Oxford, OH.

Carello, C., Fitzpatrick, P., Domaniewicz, I., Chan, T-C., & Turvey, M. T. (1992). Effortful touch with minimal movement. *Journal of Experimental Psychology: Human Perception and Performance, 18*, 290-302.

Pagano, C., & Turvey, M. T. (1998). Eigenvectors of the inertia tensor and perceiving the orientations of limbs and objects. *Journal of Applied Biomechanics, 14*, 331-359.

Peck, A., Jeffers, R. G., Carello, C., & Turvey, M. T. (1996). Haptically perceiving the length of one rod by means of another. *Ecological Psychology, 8*, 237-258.

Acknowledgments. This research was supported by NSF Grant SBR 00-04097 and a grant from the Provost's Office at the University of Connecticut.

Studies in Perception and Action VIII
H. Heft & K. L. Marsh (Eds.)
© 2005 Lawrence Erlbaum Associates, Inc.

Haptic Perception of Rod Length in Force

Tin-cheung Chan

The Chinese University of Hong Kong

Perception starts with information pick up. For Gibson, information is the discoverable "flowing array of energy at the sense organs of an animal" (1959, p. 457). More specifically, for haptic perception, "the stimulus information from wielding can only be an invariant of the changing flux of stimulation in the muscle and the tendons: an exteroceptive invariant in the play of forces" (Gibson, 1966, p. 127). Thus, what specifies haptic perception of object properties in dynamic touch has to be force pattern.

Yet, there are difficulties in reckoning the invariant force pattern. First, the force is ever changing in a sinusoidal manner as a rod is wielded. Second, Solomon, and Turvey (1988) showed that the rate of wielding does not affect perceived rod length. Instead, inertia tensor is regarded as the coordinate-independent description that is relevant to dynamic touch (Turvey, Carello, Fitzpatrick, Pagano, & Kada.,1996).

In this short report, I want to show that, in wielding a rod, force does affect perceived length. Yet, in the continuous cycle of wielding, where is the force that is relevant to length perception? In fact, we exert force mostly at the two extreme points of the swing where the direction of motion is reversed. Force for specifying perceived length may be sampled at these extreme points. To show that force sampled at these positions affects length perception, therefore, we need only to alter the force at these two critical points to observe a change in perceived length.

Method

Participants. Sixteen male baseball players participated in the experiment. The 8 expert participants played for a college baseball team affiliated with the National Junior College Athletic Association (NJCAA). The 8 novice participants varied in baseball experience, but were not currently playing college baseball. Participants were between the ages of 18 and 31.

Apparatus. Five homogeneous, thin hollow steel rods (1 cm dia) of 70, 80, 90, 100, 110 cm with respective masses of 143.4, 164.6, 183.45, 206, and 225.6 g were used. The force exerted at the extreme points of the swing was modified in three conditions: free swinging, force reduced by rebounding rods between two horizontal strings, and force further reduced by rebounding rods between two rubber bands. The strings or rubber bands were 15 cm apart fixed on a frame of 25 cm wide placed 30 cm in front of the wielding hand.

To occlude the hand and the grasped rods, a curtain, 3 m wide and 2 m high, with a slit for getting the hand through was used (Figure 1). A chair back, 0.8 m high, was placed below the slit as an armrest. A self-fabricated measurer was used to capture the perceived length of the rod. A bright line made up of LED lights could be produced along a horizontal, plastic, rectangular block (length indicator) with its length adjustable by pressing a foot paddle to match the perceived length of a rod wielded in the hand. The number of lit LED units measures the length of the bright line and thus the perceived length of the rod.

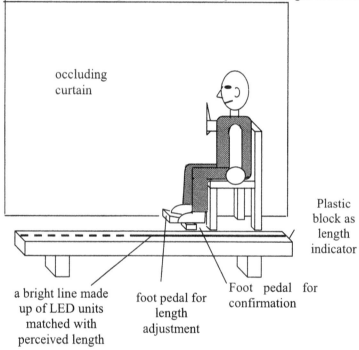

Figure 1. The set up of the experiment.

Procedure. Participants positioned their right arm on the armrest occluded by the curtain. At the beginning of each trial, a rod was placed by the experimenter horizontally onto their occluded right hand with a grip 10 cm from the rear end. For the rebound conditions, the far end of rods was placed between two strings or rubber bands, and when wielded, rods were rebounded from the strings or rubber bands at the two extreme positions of the swing. The assignment of the 15 rod-rebound configurations was in random order in a block of trials. There was a total of four blocks of trials. In each trial, participants wielded each rod for at least 5 cycles before making length judgment with the measurer. Before the experimental trials, each participant was given a practice trial with a rod of similar material that was not used in the experiment. There was a rest of 3 minutes between blocks of trials. Perceived whole length was recorded.

Results and Discussion

Of the five rods used, for rebounding with rubber bands, perceived lengths were 71.8 (17.2), 81.61(19.8), 93.69 (19.12), 102.62 (20.41), and 110.54 (17.58) cm for rebound with rubber bands. For rebounding with strings, perceived lengths were 72.4 (18.39), 82.46 (20.29), 98.58 (17.96), 108.97 (21.01), and 115.69 (19.48) cm. For free wielding, perceived lengths were 72.85 (16.2), 87.45 (13.9), 102.21 (20.96), 110.75 (20.25), and 117.24 (18.53) cm. Analysis of variance (ANOVA) showed that length was significant, $F(4, 28) = 10.73, p < .05$. Post hoc pairwise comparison with Tukey test showed that all five levels were different from one another ($p < .05$). This showed that relative length could be discriminated. Also, the effect of rebound was significant, $F(2, 14) = 5.30, p < .05$, (Figure 2). Post hoc pairwise comparisons with Tukey test showed that rods rebounded by rubber bands were perceived shorter than rods in free wielding and string-rebound condition ($p < .05$).

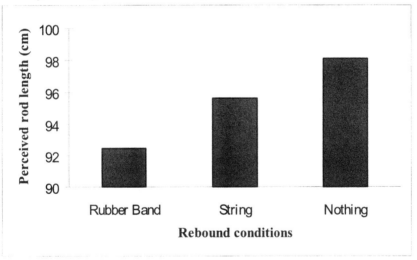

Figure 2. The effect of rebound on perceived length (via reduced force exertion).

Between different lengths of rods, longer rods were perceived as longer. The results did not discriminate between the inertia tensor hypothesis and the force hypothesis. Between different rebound conditions, perceived length were shortened with rebound. As inertia remains the same in all conditions, and force was reduced in the rebound conditions, results support the force hypothesis.

There are inadequacies in the inertia hypothesis. First, it falls short of Gibson's notion of information (Gibson, 1959, 1966). Information involves an array of energy. In visual perception, it is an optical array, and in haptic perception, it must be a force array. Moreover, energy distribution is at the sense organs. Haptic perception must relate to sensory stimulation in the skin, muscle and tendons. Finally, the information invariant is produced as a result of "changing flux". Although inertia tensor can produce force with angular acceleration, it is not a force itself. The force produced by inertia tensor on the hand depends also on a number of factors. In addition, first moment can produce force with gravitational acceleration.

Second, as Turvey, Solomon, and Burton (1989) rightly pointed out, "Perception is specific to information and information is specific to the environment and to one's movement" (p. 387). Inertia tensor is only an environmental property (Lerner & Trigg, 1991) without the involvement of any movement of the observer. Force, on the other hand, involves both the mass and movement of the observer. Even keeping a rod stationary requires muscular effort.

Third, strictly speaking, the wrist is not a point of free rotation. It has only two degree of freedom. Euler's equation of motion cannot be applied. Moreover, inertia tensor is not an invariant. It changes with orientation of a hand-held object.

References

Gibson, J. J. (1966). *The senses considered as perceptual systems.* Boston, MA: Houghton Mifflin.

Gibson, J. J. (1959). Perception as a function of stimulation. In S. Koch (Ed.), *Psychology: A study of science: Vol. 1* (pp. 456-501). New York, NY: McGraw-Hill.

Lerner, R. G. & Trigg, G. L. (1991). *Encyclopedia of Physics* (2nd ed.). New York: VCH.

Solomon, H.Y., & Turvey, M.T. (1988). Haptically perceiving the distances reachable with hand-held objects. *Journal of Experimental Psychology: Human Perception and Performance, 14,* 404-427.

Turvey, M. T., Carello, C., Fitzpatrick, P., Pagano, C., & Kada, E. (1996). Spinors and selective dynamic touch. *Journal of Experimental Psychology: Human Perception and Performance, 22,* 1113-1126.

Turvey, M. T., Solomon, H. Y., & Burton, G. (1989). An ecological analysis of knowing by wielding. *Journal of the Experimental Analysis of Behavior, 52,* 387-407

Acknowledgements. This research is funded by a UGC grant from The Hong Kong Government (CUHK4230/02H).

Studies in Perception and Action XIII
H. Heft & K. L. Marsh (Eds.)
© 2005 Lawrence Erlbaum Associates, Inc.

Do Children And Adults Use Haptic Information When Selecting Tools For Simple Power And Precision Tasks?

S. E. Cummins-Sebree[1], A. M. Tollner[2], & K. Shockley[2]

[1]Raymond Walters College, Cincinnati, OH, USA
[2]Department of Psychology, University of Cincinnati, Cincinnati, OH

Young children (ages 1 – 5 years) show increased sensitivity to properties of objects that make good tools; however, developmental studies have focused on properties that are detected visually. For example, Brown (1990) showed that older infants and toddlers (ages 1 – 3 years) can learn to select which objects make more appropriate tools to pull in target items (e.g. a hook to pull in a toy), and van Leeuwen, Smitsman, and van Leeuwen (1994) showed that children (9 months – 4 years) change in their abilities to select tools based on the position of the tools relative to the target items (e.g. selecting a cane that contains the target item within the crook instead of a cane that does not contain the target item within the crook).

Adults, on the other hand, also rely on haptic information when choosing objects for tool use. Wagman and Carello (2001) showed that adults are able to distinguish between objects that would make good "hammers" from objects that would make good "pokers", simply by wielding the objects in the hand and *without* visual information. When adults select tools to solve problems, they often select objects based on the properties they can see *and* feel; when a tennis player selects a racket for play, he/she chooses it based on not only how it looks, but also on how it feels in the hand (e.g., detecting the racket's sweet spot: Carello, Thuot, Anderson, & Turvey, 1999; Carello, Thuot, & Turvey, 2000).

This study investigated: (a) whether young children rely on haptic information to choose tools in simple tasks, and (b) if adults' ratings of the task-appropriateness of tools correspond with tool selection in the same tasks. Children (4- and 5-years-old) and adults were asked to choose one of two objects identical in appearance and mass, but with different mass configurations, and to perform a precision task and a power task. We hypothesized that the adults would distinguish between the two tools and select the tool with the additional mass at the grip end for the precision task and the tool with the additional mass at the distal end for the power task. Though young children can be sensitive to the size-weight illusion (e.g. Kloos & Amazeen, 2002), the relationship between their sensitivity to haptic information and tool selection has not been thoroughly investigated; thus, we did not predict that young children would perform similarly to the adults in selecting the more "appropriate" tool. We did, however, predict that adults would perform better at these tasks (i.e.

require fewer trials to reach a success criterion, require fewer attempts per trial) than young children.

Method

We presented 14 4-year-olds, 15 5-year-olds, and 16 adults with two sticks that were visually identical but that differed in mass configuration. The precision stick ("poker") contained mass concentrated near the grip, and the power stick ("hammer") contained mass concentrated near the distal end. To manipulate the mass concentration, we added 50 g of metal beads to the appropriate end per stick. Both sticks were also stuffed with cotton to keep the additional mass in place and eliminate sound as a potential source of information. We placed the sticks in front of each participant; we then asked him/her to pick up both sticks simultaneously and choose which one he/she wanted to use as a tool for one of two tasks. For the precision task, each participant was required to use the tool to poke a stuffed animal off a stand so that it fell into a basket (knock-the-monkey-off game). For the power task, each participant was required to use the tool to hammer a peg into a board until the peg was flush with the base of the table containing the board (hammering game). Participants were required to successfully complete 10 trials per task (i.e. getting the monkey in the basket, hammering the peg flush with the table). For each task and tool, we measured initial tool selection, overall tool preference, average number of attempts per trial (strikes or pokes), and the number of trials required. We also asked the adults and a subset of children to rate each tool's appropriateness as a "hammer" and a "poker".

Results

Children's Performance

Children did not reliably select the power tool for the hammering task (4-year-olds: $t(13) = .000$, $p > .05$; 5-year-olds: $t(14) = 1.031$, $p > .05$) or the precision tool for the monkey task (4-year-olds: $t(13) = .748$, $p > .05$; 5-year-olds: $t(14) = 1.061$, $p > .05$) (see Table 1 for descriptive statistics for all performance variables). A subset of children indicated that the tools were "the same" (4 of 4 4-year-olds and 3 of 6 5-year-olds). This did not affect the number of attempts per trial for the 5-year-olds in either task, $t(14) = .176$, $p > .05$; 4-year-olds required more strikes with the precision tool compared to the power tool in the hammering task, $t(13) = 2.759$, $p = .016$.

Adults' Performance

Adults did not exhibit a preference across testing for the power tool for hammering, $t(15) = 1.564$, $p > .05$, though they initially selected the power tool for that task (11 of 16) and indicated that the power tool made the "better hammer" (13 of 16 adults). Adults also did not prefer the precision tool for the monkey task, $t(15) = .451$, $p > .05$, either across testing or as their initial selection (7 of 16 adults), and only approximately half (7 of 16) indicated that

	4-Year-Olds *Mean, SD*	**5-Year-Olds** *Mean, SD*	**Adults** *Mean, SD*
Tool Selection			
Precision Task			
Precision Tool	.475, .125	.446, .197	.464, .316
Power Tool	.525, .125	.554, .197	.536, .316
Power Task			
Precision Tool	.500, .147	.460, .150	.381, .304
Power Tool	.500, .147	.540, .150	.619, .304
Attempts			
Precision Task			
Precision Tool	1.230, .400	1.130, .141	.920, .367
Power Tool	1.320, .340	1.175, .183	1.098, .250
Power Task			
Precision Tool	10.879, 6.956	6.585, 2.968	2.863, 1.526
Power Tool	7.680, 3.550	6.730, 5.178	3.450, 2.571
Trials To Criterion			
Precision Task	11.640, 1.692	11.60, 1.844	13.69, 3.459
Power Task	10.000, .000	10.000, .000	10.000, .000

Table 1. Values for the means and standard deviations for each age group and performance variable are presented. Those values for tool selection are given as proportions; values for attempts and trials to criterion are given as average frequency counts.

the precision tool would make the "better poker". In any case, this lack of preference did not affect performance in either task (monkey task: $t(15) = .451$, $p > .05$; hammering task: $t(15) = 1.564, p > .05$).

Across Age Groups

The three age groups did not differ in their tool selections for either task (monkey task: $F(2,42) = .059$, $p > .05$; hammering task: $F(2,42) = 1.174$, $p > .05$). However, an interaction for age and tool type was significant when comparing the average number of strikes required in the hammering task, $F(2,42) = 4.921$, $p = .012$. Four-year-olds required more attempts at hammering than 5-year-olds when using the precision tool, $t(27) = 2.668$, $p = .032$, and adults when using either tool (precision: $t(28) = 5.060$, $p < .001$; power: $t(28) =$

2.965, p = .015). No differences in performance occurred between the 5-year-olds and adults when comparing attempts. Interestingly, adults needed more trials to reach criterion on the precision task than 4-year-olds, $t(28)$ = 2.228, p = .031, or 5-year-olds, $t(29)$ = 2.317, p = .026.

Discussion

Our results suggest that young children do not use haptic information when selecting tools for precision and power tasks, but performance can be affected when they do not use this information, as evidenced by the performance of the 4-year-olds in this study. When asked if the two sticks were the same or different, most of the subset of children simply looked at both sticks and replied that they were the same. It may be the case that young children focus on the properties of objects to be used as tools that can be detected visually and not haptically, and that the ability to use both sources of information develops during mid-childhood.

Our results also suggest that although adults can identify tools that make good hammers, they may not select tools based on haptic information for a simple tool-using task such as ours, as evidenced by the lack of preference for either tool for either task. With more difficult tasks, however, adults may rely more on the properties of the tools that can be detected haptically, as observed by Carello et al. (1999; 2000).

In future investigations, we plan to study the developmental timeline for the use of haptic information in tool selection and the thresholds of sensitivity for this information in children. We also plan to study how task difficulty may promote the use of haptic information when adults select tools.

References

Brown, A. L. (1990). Domain-specific principles affect learning and transfer in children. *Cognitive Science, 14*, 107-133.

Carello, C., Thuot, S., Anderson, K. L., & Turvey, M. T. (1999). Perceiving the sweet spot. *Perception, 28*, 307-320.

Carello, C., Thuot, S., & Turvey, M. T. (2000). Aging and the perception of a racket's sweet spot. *Human Movement Science, 19*, 325-336.

Kloos, H., & Amazeen, E. L. (2002). Perceiving heaviness by dynamic touch: An investigation of the size-weight illusion in preschoolers. *British Journal of Developmental Psychology, 20*, 171-183.

van Leeuwen, L., Smitsman, A., & van Leeuwen, C. (1994). Affordances, perceptual complexity, and the development of tool use. *Journal of Experimental Psychology: Human Perception & Performance, 20*, 174-191.

Wagman, J. B., & Carello, C. (2001). Affordances and intertial constraints on tool use. *Ecological Psychology, 13*, 173-195.

Acknowledgements. We would like to thank the parents and children of the YMCA Childcare Center at Raymond Walters College in Cincinnati, OH, as well as those of Lincoln Elementary Preschool Program at Dayton Independent Schools in Dayton, KY, for their participation in this project.

Studies in Perception and Action VIII
H. Heft & K. L. Marsh (Eds.)
© *2005 Lawrence Erlbaum Associates, Inc.*

Perceived Heaviness with Variation in Rotational Inertia or Static Moment

Steven J. Harrison[1], Stacy Lopresti-Goodman[1], Robert W. Isenhower[1], Alen Hajnal[1], & Jeffrey Kinsella-Shaw[1, 2]

[1]Center for the Ecological Study of Perception and Action [2]Department of Physical Therapy, University of Connecticut, Storrs, CT, USA

A good deal of research has shown that perceiving heaviness by dynamic touch is dependent on the moments of the mass distribution of a wielded object, in particular, mass and rotational inertia (e.g., Amazeen, 1998). These are, respectively, the zeroth moment and the second moment of the mass distribution. It has been suggested recently that the dependencies on mass and rotational inertia are due, instead, to the first or static moment, which often differs along with the second moment (Kingma, Beek & van Dieen, 2002). Although mass and rotational inertia have been implicated in experiments in which all three moments have been manipulated independently (Shockley, Carello, & Turvey, 2004), first moment also emerges in experiments in which the moments have been similarly disentangled (Kingma et al., 2004).

Independent manipulation of the moments can be achieved with specially constructed objects. So-called tensor objects (Amazeen & Turvey, 1996) were designed to allow a wide range of variation in the variables. Weights can be affixed to a stem as well as to each branch of an attached cross whose own position can also be altered along the stem. These objects allow variation in mass (M), static moment (SM), the maximum principal moment of inertia (I_1) as well as the minimum (I_3) and intermediate (I_2) principal moments of inertia. Objects that are restricted to a central stem and weights attached to it are less successful in producing wide variation in I_3. The experiments that find a stronger role for M and I_k have tended to use tensor objects whereas experiments that find a stronger role for SM use rod-like objects. In addition, there is some ambiguity as to whether I_1 was actually held constant when intended with the rod-like objects. Kingma and his colleagues calculate moments relative to the end of the rod rather than a rotation point in the wrist as has been conventional for proponents of I_k.

In the present experiments, the issue of rotation point was made moot by restricting the objects' rotation to the coronal plane about an axle. I_1 and SM were manipulated by means of rods and attached weights; M was held constant throughout. In Experiment 1, I_1 was fixed and SM varied; in Experiment 2, SM was fixed and I_1 varied. Two additional manipulations assessed the malleability of heaviness perception in different movement contexts. Wielding was restricted within either a small (45°) or large (135°) range of motion. Object orientation was either vertical, with the attached weights primarily below the hand to exploit the pendulum-like nature of the objects, or horizontal, with the attached weights primarily away from the thumb side, to enhance the torque needed to maintain the required orientation.

Method

Sixteen participants took part in one of two experiments. Orientation (vertical or horizontal) was manipulated between participants; movement amplitude (small, 45°, and large, 135°) and moment variation (SM, in Experiment 1, and I_1 in Experiment 2) were manipulated within participants. Heaviness was reported as a magnitude estimation relative to a standard, designated 100, which was presented on every trial. In Experiment 1, SM values of 40, 83, 125, 160 and 185 $\times$ 10^2 g•cm were compared to a standard of 83 $\times$ 10^2 g•cm. All objects weighed 500 g with I_1 fixed at 1000 $\times$ 10^3 g•cm². In Experiment 2, I_1 values of 452, 580, 748, 972, and 1229 $\times$ 10^3 g•cm² were compared to a standard of 748 $\times$ 10^3 g•cm². All objects weighed 500 g with SM fixed at 100 $\times$ 10^2 g•cm.

Results and Discussion

Parallel 2 (horizontal or vertical orientation) $\times$ 2 (small or large amplitude movement) $\times$ 5 (moment variation) ANOVAs on magnitude estimations of heaviness were conducted for the two experiments. For the SM variation of Experiment 1, the main effect of SM, $F(4, 40) = 78.84$, $p < .0001$, $\eta_p = 0.89$, indicates that perceived heaviness increases with increases in the first moment even when I_1 is held constant. However, SM interacted with orientation, $F(4, 40) = 6.14$, $p < .001$, $\eta_p = 0.38$, and together they interacted with movement amplitude, $F(4, 40) = 11.06$, $p < .0001$, $\eta_p = 0.52$. The effect of SM was reduced in the vertical orientation but only for small amplitude movements (Figure 1). An additional interaction of amplitude and orientation, $F(4, 10)=34.17$, $p <.0002$,

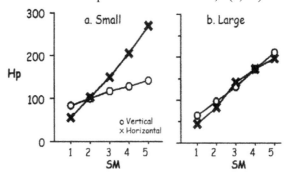

Figure 1. Perceived heaviness Hp increased with increases in SM but this influence was reduced when vertically oriented objects were moved through (a) a small amplitude but not (b) a large amplitude.

$\eta_p = 0.77$, reveals an orientation effect for small movement amplitudes only. For the I_1 variation of Experiment 2, the main effect of I_1, $F(4, 48) = 13.07$, $p < .0001$, indicates that perceived heaviness increases with increases in I_1, $p < .05$, and together they interacted with orientation, $F(4, 48) = 5.03, p < .002$. The effect of I_1 was, eliminated in the vertical orientation but only for large amplitude movements (Figure 2).

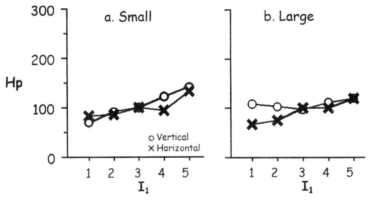

Figure 2. Perceived heaviness Hp increased with increases in *I* but this influence was eliminated when vertically oriented objects were moved through a large amplitude (b) but not a small amplitude (a).

Although it might appear that the rods were more distinct with variation in *SM* than variation in I_1 (Figure 1 vs. 2), the appearance is due to the relationship that the objects bore to their respective standards. When each object is normalized by the standard, perceived heaviness falls on the same function for variation in *SM* and variation in I_1 (Figure 3a). It should also be noted that converting each object to its equivalent pendulum length and calculating the frequency for each (normalized to the frequency of the appropriate standard object) does not capture the combined data from the two experiments (Figure 3b).

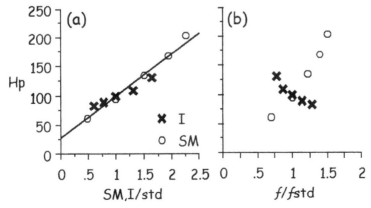

Figure 3. (a) When objects were scaled to their respective standards, the increase in Hp was comparable. (b) Pendulum frequency was not the constraining variable.

Discussion

At first blush, it appears that variation in either the first or the second moment can bring about changes in perceived heaviness. Such a conclusion is premature, given the restrictions on this experiment. Not only was the mass held constant but it was essentially eliminated as any kind of influence, given that the weight of the object was born by the axle. Clearly, the objects felt different but whether perceived heaviness was what distinguished them remains to be seen. It has been shown, for example, that perceived heaviness can more usefully be understood as perceived moveable-ness (Shockley et al., 2004) and that would be a legitimate interpretation of the present data. Although this distinction is orthogonal to the issue with which we began—what variables constrain perceived heaviness—it raises a concern that may be relevant to the resolution of this debate. When evaluating perceptual responses, we must pay heed to the functional constraints of the experimental setting. In the present case, does a large swinging movement constitute the same behavior as a small twisting movement? If these behaviors are, in fact, different, then heaviness (or moveable-ness) may well not be the same property in those two circumstances (cf. Carello, 2004). Whether the style of movement, object orientation, and object properties combine to alter the implicit affordances of the perception-action setting remains to be seen.

References

Amazeen, E.L., & Turvey, M.T. (1996). Weight perception and the haptic size-weight illusion are functions of the inertia tensor. *Journal of Experimental Psychology: Human Perception & Performance, 22,* 213-232

Amazeen, E., & Turvey, M. T. (1996). Weight perception and the haptic size-weight illusion are functions of the inertia tensor. *Journal of Experimental Psychology: Human Perception and Performance, 22,* 213-232.

Carello, C. (2004). Perceiving affordances by dynamic touch: hints from the control of movement. *Ecological Psychology, 16,* 31-36.

Kingma, I., Beek, P., & van Dieen, J. H. (2002). The inertia tensor versus static moment and mass in perceiving length and heaviness of hand-wielded rods. *Journal of Experimental Psychology: Human Perception and Performance, 28,* 180-191.

Kingma, I., van de Langenberg, R., & Beek, P. (2004). Which mechanical invariants are associated with the perception of length and heaviness of a nonvisible handheld rod? Testing the inertia tensor hypothesis. *Journal of Experimental Psychology: Human Perception & Performance, 30,* 346-354.

Shockley, K., Carello, C., & Turvey, M. T. (2004). Metamers in the haptic perception of heaviness and moveable–ness. *Perception & Psychophysics, 66,* 731-742.

Acknowledgment. This research was supported by NSF Grant SBR 00-04097.

Studies in Perception and Action VIII
H. Heft & K. L. Marsh (Eds.)
© *2005 Lawrence Erlbaum Associates, Inc.*

The Orientation of T-Shaped Objects Cannot be Perceived by Dynamic Touch

Christopher C. Pagano

Clemson University, Clemson, SC, USA

A kind of kinesthesis that is prominent in everyday manipulatory activity involves the hand supporting a manipulated object, such as a racquet, hammer, cup, or pencil. When one grasps and rotates an occluded object there is conjointly perception of aspects of the object and perception of how the object is oriented relative to the body. Such perception of object properties by 'dynamic touch' is a prominent example of exteroception through the muscle sense. Recent research has identified the inertia tensor as the relevant mechanical quantity to which such perception is tied (see Carello & Turvey, 2000, for a review). The inertia tensor I_{ij} quantifies an object's resistances to angular rotation in various directions. The eigenvalues of I_{ij} (or principal moments of inertia, I_1, I_2, I_3) are the object's resistances to rotation about the respective directions of the eigenvectors (or principal axes of inertia, e_1, e_2, e_3). The eigenvectors include the axes of maximal (e_1) and minimal (e_3) resistance to rotational acceleration. A useful summary is that I_{ij} provides the domains for two sets of functions, one consisting of the eigenvalues, that map onto perceived object magnitudes, such as object length and shape, and one consisting of the direction of e_3, that maps onto perceived direction such as the orientation of an object in the hand (e.g., Pagano & Turvey, 1992).

The perceived orientation of hand-held objects has been studied by asking subjects to wield an occluded L-shaped rod and adjust a visible pointer to coincide with the felt direction of the branch of the L relative to the hand. Under a variety of conditions subjects' perception of branch direction closely matched its actual direction, and it was shown that the principal axis of inertia e_3 provides a basis for this perception (Turvey et al., 1992). For L-shaped objects, e_3 points from the location of grasp at the proximal end of the stem through the branch at the distal end of the object (see Figure 1, Top). Additional experiments broke the covariation between e_3 and the object's geometric orientation, and it was found that perception of orientation was a function of e_3 rather than of geometric orientation (Pagano & Turvey, 1992).

We report two additional experiments that demonstrate that the orientation of the crosspiece of a T-shaped object, held at the base of the T, cannot be apprehended by dynamic touch. This is because the orientation of e_3 does not change as the crosspiece is rotated about a fixed stem (See Figure 1, Bottom). The crosspiece is, in effect, rotating about e_3, leaving e_3 unchanged. Put differently, the orientation of the T-shaped object is not specified by the inertia tensor, thus it may be expected that the orientation of a T-shaped object my not be apprehended by dynamic touch.

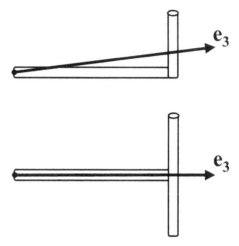

Figure 1. For L-shaped objects, e_3 extends from the point of rotation O located near the proximal end of the stem through the branch, thus providing a basis for perceived orientation by dynamic touch (Top). For T-shaped objects e_3 extends through the center of the crosspiece and remains unaltered by rotations of the crosspiece (Bottom).

Method

In Experiment 1 six subjects wielded a T-shaped object eight times in each of four different orientations corresponding to the crosspiece oriented horizontally, vertically, 45 degrees angling from the subject's upper left to lower right, and 45 degrees angling from upper right to the lower left. The subjects were not informed that these four orientations would be used. They were instructed that the crosspiece could be positioned in any orientation. The object was constructed of 1.2 cm diameter oak dowels with the stem and crosspiece each 30.0 cm in length. Subjects in the experiments of Turvey et al. (1992) reliably apprehended the orientation of L-shaped objects constructed from oak rods with branches as small as 6.0 cm. In the present experiments the subjects' task was to wield the occluded T-shaped rod and adjust a visible pointer to coincide with the felt direction of the crosspiece (see Figure 2). During each trial the object was placed in the subject's hand, with the thumb on top, aligned with the stem, and parallel to the ground. After wielding, the subject returned the hand and object to this configuration before adjusting the report device. Experiment 2 was identical to Experiment 1, except that six new subjects wielded an object with a much heavier crosspiece designed to raise the salience of the object's orientation. Turvey et al. (1992) found that orientation was perceived more accurately when the size of an oak branch was increased from 6.0 to 16.25 cm. The crosspiece for the new object consisted of a 1.0 cm diameter aluminum rod that was 40.0 cm in length. The crosspiece was attached to the end of a 2.5 cm diameter oak rod that was 20 cm in length. The stem was wrapped with sports tape to facilitate its grip and to keep the objects from rotating in the hand.

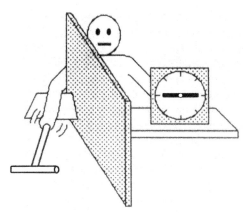

Figure 2. Subjects indicated the perceived orientation of a T-Shaped object by rotating a marker on a visible report device.

Results and Discussion

None of the twelve subjects who participated in the two experiments were able to perceive the orientation of the T-shaped objects. Their performance did not differ from what would be expected from chance. Performance was not improved by the used of a much heavier object in Experiment 2.

Given that the stimulus for dynamic touch is force-based rather than geometric, the perception of hand-held objects via dynamic touch should be expected to differ from how the objects are perceived via vision. However, the nature of these differences are likely to be non-arbitrary, and they should be predictable from I_{ij}. Perception by dynamic touch, for example, appears to be governed by the shape and orientation of the ellipsoid of inertia (e.g., Pagano & Turvey, 1993). Future work should be directed at the possibility that the orientation of roughly 'T-shaped' or otherwise symmetrical tools and implements, like paddles and racquets, might be apprehended on the basis of resistances to rotation caused by air resistance rather than inertia. Similarly, it seems likely that the orientation of T-shaped objects can be apprehended when wielding occurs in water rather than in air. Such a result would complement the finding that the perception of rod length remains unchanged when wielding occurs in air or water (Pagano & Cabe, 2003).

References

Carello, C., & Turvey, M. T. (2000). Rotational invariants and dynamic touch. In M. A. Heller (Ed.), *Touch, representation, and blindness* (pp. 27-66). Oxford: Oxford University Press.

Pagano, C. C., & Cabe, P. A. (2003). Constancy in dynamic touch: Length perceived by dynamic touch is invariant over changes in media. *Ecological Psychology, 15*, 1-17.

Pagano, C. C., & Turvey, M. T. (1992). Eigenvectors of the inertia tensor and perceiving the orientation of a hand-held object by dynamic touch. *Perception & Psychophysics, 52*, 617-624.

Pagano, C. C., & Turvey, M. T. (1993). Perceiving by dynamic touch the distances reachable with irregular objects. *Ecological Psychology, 5*, 125-151.

Turvey, M. T., Burton, G., Pagano, C. C., Solomon, H. Y., & Runeson, S. (1992). Role of the inertia tensor in perceiving object orientation by dynamic touch. *Journal of Experimental Psychology: Human Perception and Performance, 18*, 714-727.

Acknowledgements. I would like to thank Aaron Glidden for running the subjects. This work was supported by the Clemson University Research Grant Committee.

Studies in Perception and Action VIII
H. Heft & K. L. Marsh (Eds.)
© *2005 Lawrence Erlbaum Associates, Inc.*

Spatial Distortions in Active Tactile Exploration

W. L. Ben Sachtler[1], Philip M. Grove[1], Thomas E. von Wiegand[2], & S. James Biggs[3]

[1] School of Psychology, The University of New South Wales
Sydney, Australia
[2] Sensimetrics Corporation, Somerville, MA, USA
[3] Research Laboratory of Electronics
Massachusetts Institute of Technology, Cambridge, MA, USA

Encoding the location of tactile features during active exploration poses at least two problems for a perceptual system. First, as the hand is moved through space, processing delays may displace the perceived locations of features. Second, due to the sequential nature of the process, some form of memory, which itself may be subject to spatial distortions, is required for integration of spatial samples.

We investigated these issues using a task involving active haptic exploration with a stylus swept back and forth in the horizontal plane by flexing and extending the wrist. The simplicity of the task improved upon various shortcomings encountered with other methods. For example, spatial properties of manual localization are commonly studied by reaching for visually presented targets (e.g., Chieffi, Allport & Woodin, 1999), which introduces the complexity of cross-modal transformations. Studies of kinesthesia often involve matching position or movement of one limb with the other corresponding limb (e.g., Clark & Horch, 1986), which raises issues of hemifield asymmetries. Rod-bisection tasks inherently involve encoding of two well-separated features (the ends of the rod), which again introduces issues regarding the inhomogeneity of peri-personal space, and are affected by a bewildering plethora of idiosyncratic factors (Jewell & McCourt, 2000). On the other hand, studies on the perceived length of repeated movements can be elegantly simple (e.g., Woodworth, 1899) but do not generally involve localization of external features.

Here, we measured the perceived location of a force pulse encountered during a simple sweeping movement with a second pulse encountered during a subsequent sweep.

Method

In conditions LL and RR (see Figure 1) participants returned the stylus to the starting position after the first sweep and repeated the movement. Participants indicated with a key press using the left hand whether the force pulse during the second sweep was to the left or right of the first one. Probe pulses were presented at any of several relative offsets with respect to the first pulse using the method of constant stimuli. In conditions LR and RL, the probe pulse was applied during the return sweep immediately following the first.

Figure 1. Sweep pairs used to compare the locations of two force pulses (examples of pulse locations shown as dots on the arrows). Participants indicated whether the second pulse was to the right or left of the first one.

Targets were randomly placed within the range +/- 20^0 from straight ahead, defined as the medial axis of the forearm. A computer display indicated when the stylus had entered the start and end zones located at +/- 30^0 as well as beginning and end of a trial. Results were only recorded if the velocity was between 90^0 and 180^0/sec at the time a force pulse was applied. Upward force pulses of 1 Newton were applied for 5 milliseconds by a Phantom force-feedback device (Sensable Devices, Inc.) attached to the stylus tip.

An opaque panel occluded the participants' view of their right hand, and auditory cues were masked with a pink noise source played through head-phones. All four participants were right-handed. Two participants (KB and NS) were naïve regarding the purpose of the experiment.

One experimental session consisted of four blocks, one for each of the sweep conditions, completed within one day. The order of the four blocks was counterbalanced across six sessions distributed across several days.

Results and Discussion

The data were grouped into three sectors according to the location of the first target in each trial, as indicated at the top of Figure 2. For a given sector, results for various offsets between the first and second force pulse were used to derive a psychometric function, and probit analysis was used to determine the point of subjective equality (PSE), that is, the amount by which the second pulse had to be offset with respect to the first to appear coincident with it.

PSEs for LL and RR sweeps are shown in the top row of graphs in Figure 2. Small symbols show individual results for participants indicated on the left, while the large symbols at the top of each graph show the mean of the four participants' PSEs. Error bars indicate 95% confidence intervals.

An ANOVA with one repeated measure showed a significant difference among PSEs of the three sectors, $F(2, 18) = 58.77$, $p < 0.01$. Contrast analysis showed that PSEs differed across all three sectors ($p < 0.01$). There was no significant difference between LL and RR sweeps.

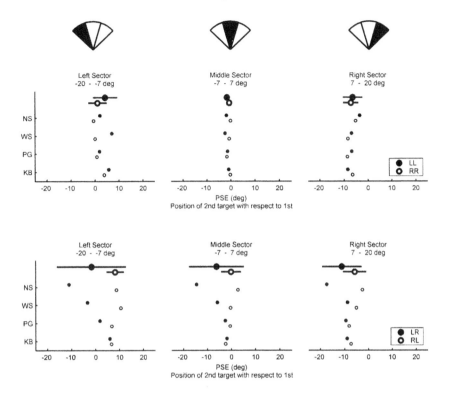

Figure 2. Points of subjective equality (PSEs) for the location of the second pulse with respect to the first.

PSEs were shifted leftward for targets located to the right of the medial axis, and rightward for targets on the left. These shifts cannot be accounted for by the direction of motion since they were positive on one side of the medial axis and negative on the other, and were similar for leftward and rightward sweeps. Instead, these results indicate a distortion of tactile space. This spatial distortion is also apparent for LR and RL sweeps shown in the bottom row of graphs, $F(2, 18) = 13.72, p < 0.01$.

PSEs for LR sweeps were significantly different from RL sweeps, $F(1, 18) = 15.17, p < 0.01$, indicating a displacement of perceived pulse locations in the direction of sweep motion. We hypothesize that these displacements are due to a delay in the processing of the force pulse while the hand is in motion by assigning a spatial location to it after it is processed without correcting appropriately for the distance travelled in that time.

Summary

Locations of features encountered during tactile exploration may be subject to a central tendency in haptic spatial memory resulting in a distortion of haptic space. Difficulties of encoding during movement can lead to further spatial distortions.

References

Chieffi, S., Allport, D.A. and Woodin, M. (1999). Hand-centred coding of target location in visuo-spatial working memory. *Neuropsychologia, 37,* 495-502.

Clark, F.J. and Horch, K.W. (1986) Kinesthesia. In: Boff, KR., Kaufman, L. and Thomas, J.P (Eds.) *Handbook of Perception and Human Performance v.1 Sensory Processes and Perception* (pp. 13-1—13-62) Wiley, New York.

Jewell, G. and McCourt, M. E. (2000). Pseudoneglect: a review and meta-analysis of performance factors in line bisection tasks. *Neuropsychologia,* 38, 93-110.

Woodworth, R.S. (1899). The accuracy of voluntary movement. *The Psychological Review, (Monograph) Vol 3, No. 2 (Whole No. 13).*

Acknowledgement. This work was supported by NIH grant 5 R03 EY014177.

Studies in Perception and Action VIII
H. Heft & K. L. Marsh (Eds.)
© 2005 Lawrence Erlbaum Associates, Inc.

Perceiving Affordances of Hockey Sticks

Alison M. Tollner[1], Philip Hove[1,2], & Michael A. Riley[1]

[1]Department of Psychology, University of Cincinnati, USA
[2]Whirlpool Corporation, Benton Harbor, MI, USA

People can use the haptic subsystem of dynamic touch to perceive a multitude of object properties, including properties that contribute to an object's utility as a tool. An object's utility as a tool may depend, among other factors, upon physical properties such as mass distribution. Haptic perception of a tool's utility seems to be accordingly constrained by the object's distribution of mass (e.g., Wagman & Carello, 2001, 2003), reflecting perceiver sensitivity to both the physical constraints and informational variables that distinguish tools as being more or less well suited for performing a given task.

We examined the use of dynamic touch in perceiving the utility of hockey sticks for power and precision actions. The sticks were modified by adding weights at different locations relative to the points of grasp. Hove (2004) previously found that experienced hockey players (17+ years experience) preferred a top-weighted stick for both power and precision tasks, and gave verbal reports indicating a preference for lighter sticks. Novices also exhibited a preference for top-weighted sticks for both tasks, but only after performing power and precision actions with the sticks.

Manipulating the mass distributions of hockey sticks makes the sticks more or less well suited for power and precision actions—bottom-heavy sticks allow for greater force transfer, but are less controllable, whereas top-heavy sticks are controllable but afford less forceful hitting. Participants wielded the sticks in the absence of vision and haptically gauged the suitability of the sticks for power and precision tasks. We were interested in determining whether experienced hockey players would actually prefer a lighter stick, or one that was heavier but felt more maneuverable by virtue of its distribution of mass (Shockley, Grocki, Carello, & Turvey, 2001; Turvey, Shockley, & Carello, 1999).

Method

Participants

Five male University of Cincinnati club-level ice-hockey players with an average of 13.4 years of experience participated in this study. They had an average age of 20.2 years, and an average height of 177.29 cm. They were compensated $10 for their participation.

Apparatus

Hockey Sticks. Participants held and wielded three differently weighted, right-handed Nike Quest 2 hockey sticks. The sticks were 162 cm long and were composed of fiberglass-wrapped solid aspen. Metal weights were attached to the shaft of each stick at different locations, yielding three unique mass-distribution conditions (added masses: 200 g at bottom, 200 g at top, or 300 g at top). To mask the weight location, low-density foam blocks were taped around all three potential weight locations (regardless of the actual weight location, so that the sticks were visually identical).

Action-Phase Materials. For the power task, participants used the sticks to strike a street-hockey puck (111.9 g, 8 cm diameter × 2.2 cm tall) into a block of foam padding (142 cm wide × 181 cm tall). The foam pad was located approximately 125 cm in front of the puck and served to absorb the puck's impact after a shot. For the precision task, participants had to intercept an object attached to a pendulum. The pendulum consisted of a pulley that was fixed to the laboratory ceiling. The swinging arm of the pendulum was a rigid wooden dowel (174 cm long) that was attached to the center groove of the pulley so as to hang 73 cm from the ground when hanging perpendicular to the ground. A small rubber ball (4 cm diameter) was attached to the end of the dowel and constituted the target to be intercepted with the center of the blade of the hockey stick.

Procedure

Participants engaged in three separate experiment phases for each of the two experimental conditions: *pre-action* ratings, the action phase, and *post-action* ratings. Participants were instructed in the *pre-* and *post-action* phases to wield each of the hockey sticks with their eyes closed and to verbally rate each of the sticks according to its suitability for power or precision actions using a 1-7 scale (1: "not at all suited to the task"; 7: "ideally suited to the task"; c.f. Wagman & Carello, 2003). For the action phase, participants used each of the sticks to hit a puck as hard as possible into the foam pad (power condition) or intercept the ball swinging on the pendulum when the ball reached the midpoint of its movement cycle after falling from a fixed location (precision condition). Because the action phase required visual guidance, participants completed it with the eyes open.

Results

Precision. The mean (*M*) and standard deviation (*SD*) of the pre-action ratings for the bottom 200 g, top 200 g, and top 300 g mass locations were, respectively, $M (SD) = 2.70 (0.57)$, $6.00 (0.61)$, and $4.30 (0.57)$; M and SD of the post-action ratings in those respective conditions were, $2.60 (0.65)$, $5.85 (0.55)$, $4.30 (0.27)$ (see Figure 1). Repeated-measures ANOVA showed a statistically significant effect of mass location, $F(2,8) = 43.85$, $p < .001$, but no experiment

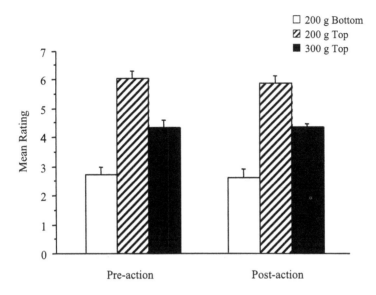

Precision Condition

Figure 1. Mean hockey stick ratings (error bars indicate 1 standard error) for the precision condition in the pre- and post-action phases

interaction effects (p > .05). Pairwise comparisons revealed significant differences between the bottom 200 g and top 200 g locations, $t(9)$= 11.45, the bottom 200 g and top 300 g locations, $t(9) = 6.48$, and the bottom 200 g and top 200 g locations, $t(9) = 5.91$ (all $p < .01$).

Power. The mean (M) and standard deviation (SD) of the pre-action ratings for the bottom 200 g, top 200 g, and top 300 g mass locations were, respectively, $M (SD) = 5.0$ (1.28), 4.5 (1.00), and 4.3(1.26), and of the post-action ratings in those respective conditions were, 5.20 (1.64), 4.20 (1.15), and 4.55 (0.94) (see Figure 2). A repeated-measures ANOVA did not reveal any significant effects (all $p > .05$).

Discussion

The hockey players were remarkably consistent in how they rated the three hockey sticks and were generally uninfluenced by performing the power and precision tasks. For both *pre-* and *post-action* ratings for the precision condition, the hockey players preferred the top-weighted 200 g stick, followed by the top-weighted 300 g stick and then the bottom-weighted 200 g stick. However, hockey players did not prefer a lighter stick for the power task (the mass configuration effect was not significant). The results support our contention that hockey players do not necessarily prefer a stick that, above all else, is lighter. Rather than absolute mass, the distribution of the sticks' mass played a role in determining the perceived utility of the sticks for performing a power task. That

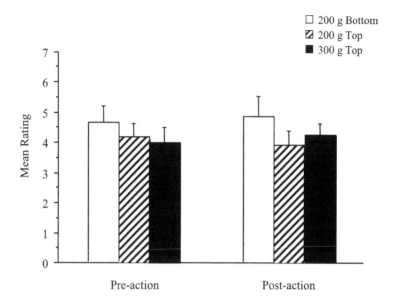

Power Condition

Figure 2. Mean hockey stick ratings (error bars indicate 1 standard error) for the *power* condition in the pre- and post-action phases

is, the sticks' perceived maneuverability, not absolute mass, seems to have influenced the hockey players' ratings of the sticks for power and precision tasks. From a human factors standpoint, the results are important with respect to identifying the aspects of tools that contribute to the way people perceive and use them, which may have implications for increasing product acceptance and usability.

References

Hove, P. (2004). *Haptic perception of affordances of a sport implement: Choosing hockey sticks for power versus precision actions on the basis of "feel".* Unpublished doctoral dissertation, University of Cincinnati, Cincinnati, Ohio.

Shockley, K., Grocki, M., Carello, C., & Turvey, M. T. (2001). Somatosensory attunement to the rigid body laws. *Experimental Brain Research, 136,* 133-137.

Turvey, M. T., Shockley, K., & Carello, C. (1999). Affordance, proper function, and the physical basis of perceived heaviness. *Cognition, 73,* B17-B26.

Wagman, J. B., & Carello, C. (2001). Affordances and inertial constraints on tool use. *Ecological Psychology, 13,* 173-195.

Wagman, J. B., & Carello, C. (2003). Haptically creating affordances: The user-tool interface. *Journal of Experimental Psychology: Applied, 9,* 175-186.

Studies in Perception and Action VIII
H. Heft & K. L. Marsh (Eds.)
© *2005 Lawrence Erlbaum Associates, Inc.*

"How Heavy?" Does Not Depend on Which Hand

Jeffrey B. Wagman & Students in Psychology 331.04

Department of Psychology, Illinois State University, USA

One of the explicit goals of the ecological approach to perception-action is to uncover stimulation patterns that are specific to perception of behaviorally relevant environmental properties (i.e., affordances, Gibson, 1979). To a large extent, research on dynamic touch has been successful in this respect (see Carello, 2004). The affordances of a hand-held object are determined by how easy or difficult it is to move that object in particular directions about the wrist. Such resistance to movement about the wrist can be quantified by the inertia tensor (I_{ij}). A large body of research has shown that I_{ij} and variables derived from I_{ij} constrain perception of both geometric and functional properties of wielded hand-held objects (see Carello, 2004; Carello & Turvey, 2004).

For example, perception of heaviness is constrained by the volume of the inertial ellipsoid (V, which describes the mean level of rotational force required to move an object), the symmetry of the inertial ellipsoid (S, which describes how that force should be directed), and the mass of the object (M) (Shockley, Grocki, Carello, & Turvey, 2001, see Figure 1). Such variables describe how much force needs to be applied and in which directions this force needs to be applied to control a hand-held object. Perception of heaviness is better understood as perception of moveability, controllability, or steerability (Shockley et al., 2001).

Another explicit goal of the ecological approach is to uncover how perception of affordances scale to the perceiver's action capabilities (Gibson, 1979). Perceivers who differ in their ability to raise their leg to a particular height differ in their perception of stairs that can be easily climbed (Konczak, Meeuwsen, & Crees, 1992). Importantly, differences in action capabilities are not limited to differences between different perceivers. The same perceiver can possess different action capabilities at different points in time depending on constraints such as posture. Accordingly, seated perceivers perceive different affordances for reaching for leaning reaches and for non-leaning reaches (Carello, Grosofsky, Reichel, Solomon, & Turvey, 1989).

Along these lines, perceivers seem to possess different action capabilities in controlling objects with their preferred and non-preferred hands (Guiard, 1987). If (a) perception of heaviness is perception of moveability, controllability, or steerability, and (b) the ability to move, control, or steer objects differs in the preferred and non-preferred hands, then perceivers may show differences in the perception of heaviness in the preferred and non-preferred hands. This experiment investigates this possibility.

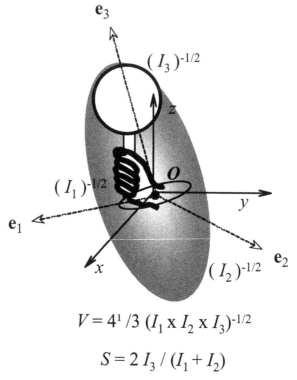

$$V = 4^1/3\ (I_1 \times I_2 \times I_3)^{-1/2}$$

$$S = 2\,I_3\,/\,(I_1 + I_2)$$

Figure 1. The inertial ellipsoid for a hand-held object. The formulae for the volume of the inertial ellipsoid (V) and the symmetry of the inertial ellipsoid (S) are also provided.

Method

Blindfolded participants wielded wooden dowels with attached plastic masses and were asked to estimate the heaviness of each of these objects relative to a similar object that was designated as the "standard" (cf. Shockley et al., 2001). The standard object was a 60cm wooden dowel with a 163g mass attached at 30cm from the bottom of the rod. The objects to be compared to the standard were also 60cm wooden dowels with masses of 82g, 163g, or 245g placed at either 20cm or 40cm from the bottom of the rod.

Blindfolded participants grasped the standard object such that the bottom of the rod was flush with the bottom of their hand and wielded it about their wrist. They were told that the standard object weighed 100 units. One of the comparison objects was then exchanged with the standard. The participant grasped and wielded the comparison object in the same manner. They then estimated the heaviness of this object relative to the standard (by providing a number relative to 100). This procedure was repeated for each of the experimental objects. Each experimental object was wielded three times, and order of presentation of the experimental object was randomized. Participants performed this task with both their preferred hand and their non-preferred hand. The order of this condition was counterbalanced across participants.

Results and Discussion

A 2 (hand) x 2 (mass placement) x 3 (mass) ANOVA was conducted on heaviness ratings. There was a significant interaction of mass placement and mass on perceived heaviness, $F(4,22) = 24.421$, $p < .001$, suggesting that perceived heaviness increased as mass increased and that this effect was more salient as mass placement was located further from the hand (see Figure 2). However, there were no significant effects (main effects or interactions) of hand on perceived heaviness (see Figure 2). That is, the preferred and non-preferred

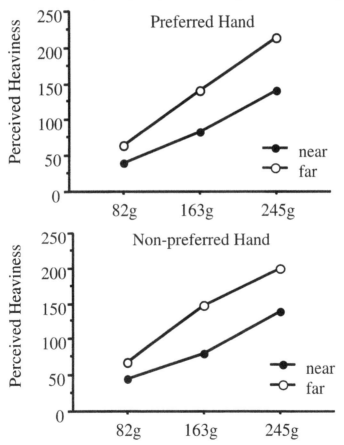

Figure 2. Perceived heaviness for the preferred hand (top) and the non-preferred hand (bottom) for the three object masses and the two mass placements (20cm from rotation point and 40cm from rotation point) for the objects used in the experiment.

hands seem to perceive heaviness in the same way. An additional 2 (hand) x 2 (mass placement) x 3 (mass) ANOVA was conducted on the variability of perceived heaviness rating (as quantified by variable error, *VE*). *VE* increased as mass increased, $F\,(4,22) = 10.83, p < .001$, and as a mass placement was located further from the hand, $F\,(4,22) = 27.31, p < .05$. There were no significant effects (main effects or interactions) of hand on variability of perceived heaviness.

Multiple and stepwise regression revealed that together *V*, *S*, and *M* account for all of the variance in perceived heaviness with the preferred hand ($R^2 = 1.0$, with each variable accounting for significant portions of variance). These same analyses revealed that *V* and *M* account for almost all of the variance in perceived heaviness in the non-preferred hand ($R^2 = .99$, with *S* not accounting for a significant portion of variance).

These results suggest that any differences in action capabilities between the preferred and non-preferred hand do not create differences in perception of heaviness or in the variability of these perceptual reports. The two hands seem to experience the size-weight illusion in the same way (cf. Shockley et al., 2001). If we consider the preferred hand to be the "expert" hand and the non-preferred hand to be the "novice" hand (at least in some action tasks), such findings are comparable with those of Carello, Thout, Anderson, and Turvey (1999) who found that expert tennis players were no better than novices at perceiving the location of the sweet spot of a tennis racket. However, the fact that the two hands seem to be sensitive to slightly different aspects of an object's resistance to movement suggest that the differential action capabilities of the two hands may influence perception in terms of how attention is directed toward a given property without influencing perception of that property itself.

References

Carello, C. (2004). Perceiving affordances by dynamic touch: Hints from the control of movement. *Ecological Psychology, 16*, 31-36.

Carello, C., Grosofsky, A., Reichel, F. D., Solomon, J., & Turvey, M. T. (1989). Visually perceiving what is reachable. *Ecological Psychology, 1*, 27-54.

Carello, C., Thout, S., Anderson, K., & Turvey, M. T. (1999). Perceiving the sweet spot. *Perception, 28*, 307-320.

Carello, C. & Turvey, M. T. (2004). Physics and the psychology of the muscle sense. *Current Directions in Psychological Science, 13*, 25-28.

Gibson, J. J. (1979). *The ecological approach to visual perception*. Boston: Houghton Mifflin.

Guiard, Y. (1987). Asymmetric division of labor in human skilled bimanual action: The kinematic chain as a model. *Journal of Motor Behavior, 19*, 486-517.

Koncazk, J., Meeuwsen, H. J., & Crees, M. E. (1992). Changing affordances in stair climbing: The perception of maximum climbability in young and older adults. *Journal of Experimental Psychology: Human Perception & Performance, 18*, 691-697.

Shockley, K., Grocki, M., Carello, C., & Turvey, M. T. (2001). Somatosensory attunement to the rigid body laws. *Experimental Brain Research, 136*, 133-137.

Perception and Interception of Moving Objects

Studies in Perception and Action VIII
H. Heft & K. L. Marsh (Eds.)
© 2005 Lawrence Erlbaum Associates, Inc.

Hand Trajectories for Catching Balls on Horizontal, Linear Trajectories

Ryan Arzamarski, Steven J. Harrison, & Claire F. Michaels

Center for the Ecological Study of Perception and Action,
University of Connecticut, Storrs, CT, USA

Catching a sideward-passing ball requires that one be attuned to an informational variable that will guide the hand to the interception point. Jacobs and Michaels (2004) showed that when participants caught balls swinging down from the ceiling on a thin line, the course of the hand's movement could be predicted by the ratio of lateral angular optical velocity to rate of expansion. However, support for this variable has been complicated by empirical inconsistencies concerning hand movement reversals (i.e., moving the hand left then right, or vice-versa, over the course of intercepting the ball). Montagne, Laurent, Durey, & Bootsma (1999) reported movement reversals for balls approaching on a flat surface in conditions where the ball's final position coincides with the hand's initial position (Figure 1). The optical ratio used by

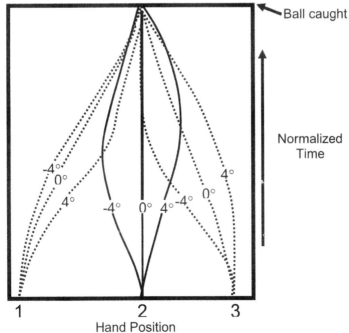

Figure 1. Characterization of hand trajectories from an "exemplary" participant, redrawn after Montagne et al., (1999).

Jacobs and Michaels (2004), on the other hand, while it predicts unilateral reversals in the swinging balls case, predicts no reversals with planar ball trajectories, as shown in Figure 2. To further investigate this discrepancy we attempted to replicate Montagne et al.'s findings.

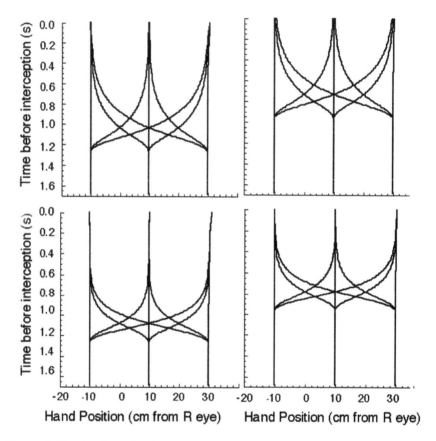

Figure 2. Hand trajectories based on Michaels et al.'s (2004) model, using the optical ratio time-series as the input. The sample predictions vary *delay,* the average time taken to initiate movement (distinguishing the left and right pairs), and the slope of the VITE go-function (distinguishing the upper and lower pairs).

Method

Five undergraduates from the University of Connecticut used their right hands to intercept glowing balls approaching across a tabletop in a dark room. Rolling down an unseen ramp, the ball reached a velocity of 2.5 m/s, and traveled a distance of 4 m before being caught at the table's edge. Prior to trial-onset, participants placed their hand on the instructed initial position. Head position was fixed using a cushioned forehead rest set 10 cm above the table. A 3 x 3 x 3 repeated-measures design was used where approach angle, initial hand position, and final ball position were manipulated. The initial-hand and final-ball positions were -10, +10, and +30 cm relative the fixed eye position. The ball approached at an angle of either -4°, 0°, or 4° relative to a line perpendi-cular to the table's edge. Order of presentation was randomized for all variables and viewing was binocular.

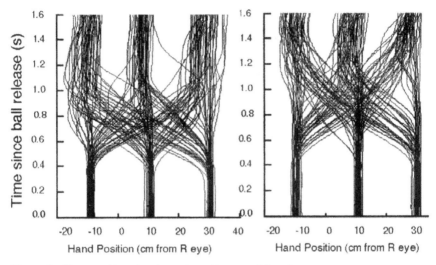

Figure 3. Observed hand trajectories of two participants.

Results and Discussion

Using the reversal criterion of Montagne et al. (1999), we observed no movement reversals on any of the 225 trials in the critical condition. From these results we conclude that planar ball approaches are not generally characterized by movement reversals. Conversely, we found that the observed trajectories, as shown in Figure 3, were similar to those predicted by the optical ratio (Figure 2).

Note also that in the planar case, the optical ratio specifies future passing distance (see also Bootsma & Peper, 1992), which would permit predictive hand movements— where the hand reaches the ball's final position before the ball (see Figures 2). In Figure 3 we observe such predictive movements.

To reiterate, for swinging trajectories, but not planar ones, the optical ratio predicts a unilateral reversals, which were reported. It appears that the time series of the optical ratio, and thus the hand's movement, is strongly affected by the shape of the oncoming ball's trajectory.

It is unclear why Montagne et al. (1999) observed the reversals reported in Figure 1. It admittedly represented the data of one participant, and it is possible that this participant was exploiting a different informational source from that used by the participants in our study. However, they found overall that 41% of critical trials displayed reversals in the predicted direction (though 16% of the reversals were in the wrong direction).

References

Bootsma, R. J., & Peper, C. E. (1992). Predictive information sources for the regulation of action with special emphasis for catching and hitting. In L. Proteau & D. Elliott (Eds.), *Vision and motor control* (pp. 285-314). Amsterdam: North-Holland.

Jacobs, D. M., & Michaels, C. F. (2004). *Lateral interception I: The education of attention and calibration.* Submitted.

Michaels, C. F., Jacobs, D. M., & Bongers, R. M. (2004). *Lateral interception II: Predicting hand movements.* Submitted.

Montagne, G., Laurent, M., Durey, A., & Bootsma, R. J. (1999). Movement reversals in ball catching. *Experimental Brain Research, 129,* 87-92.

Acknowledgement. This research was supported by NSF Grant BCS 0339031.

Studies in Perception and Action VIII
H. Heft & K. L. Marsh (Eds.)
© 2005 Lawrence Erlbaum Associates, Inc.

Effects of Attention on Performance in Baseball Hitting

Brooke Castaneda & Rob Gray

Department of Applied Psychology, Arizona State University East, USA

This study investigated the role of attention on hitting performance as a function of expertise in a high-fidelity baseball batting simulation. Previous research has shown that novices display enhanced performance when directing their attention to the step-by-step actions in a motor task (utilizing their declarative memory knowledge base), whereas experts perform significantly worse when attending to skill execution (e.g., Beilock, Carr, MacMahon, & Starkes, 2002; Gray, 2004).

It has also been found that performance successes and decrements can be dependent on whether performers' attention is directed to the effects of their movements (*external* focus of attention) or to the movements themselves (*internal* focus of attention). Wulf and colleagues' (Wulf & Prinz, 2001) research has mainly focused on novice participants and has found that participants perform better when utilizing an external focus of attention as opposed to an internal focus of attention.

The purpose of the present experiment was three-fold. First, this study was designed to determine the comparability between skill-focused attention conditions and external -focused attention conditions. It is unclear whether conditions for skill-focused attention used by Beilock and colleagues and by Gray can be directly compared to the external conditions by Wulf and colleagues. Second, because various forms of environmental-focused (i.e., external) attention have not been directly compared in previous studies, another objective of this study is to identify how forms of environmental-focused attention affect performance in novices and experts. The third goal was to investigate whether environmental-focused attention is beneficial to experts merely because it prevents experts from attending to their skill execution, or because environmental-focused attention actually assists experts in attaining pertinent information to the task.

Method

Sixteen male baseball players participated in the experiment. The 8 expert participants played for a college baseball team affiliated with the National Junior College Athletic Association (NJCAA). The 8 novice participants varied in baseball experience, but were not currently playing college baseball. Participants were between the ages of 18 and 31.

Novice and expert college baseball players participated in four attention conditions: two conditions that directed attention to skill execution ("skill-bat" and "skill-hands") and two conditions that directed attention to the external environment ("environmental-irrelevant" and "environmental-relevant"). In the skill-bat condition participants judged whether their bat was moving up or down at the instant an auditory tone (displayed randomly during the swing) was presented; while in the skill-bat condition they judged whether their hands were moving up or down at the instant the tone was heard. In the environmental-irrelevant condition, participants judged whether the frequency of the tone was high or low. In the environmental-relevant condition, participants judged whether the simulated ball rotated with over-spin or under-spin as it approached the plate. The spin direction of the ball was correlated with pitch speed (as is the case in real baseball) to make this source of information relevant to the task of hitting. Unlike most previous research in this area, we used the judgment accuracy to perform manipulation checks for the different attention conditions. Temporal swing errors were used to quantify batting performance.

Results

Mean temporal batting errors (MTE) for the four attention conditions are shown in Figure 1. Planned comparisons revealed that the attention conditions had substantially different effects on batting performance for experts and novices. A comparison of the combined mean of the two "skill" conditions versus the combined mean of the two "environment" conditions revealed a significant condition x expertise interaction, $t(14) = 8.0$, $p < 0.001$. For experts, planned comparisons revealed that the MTE for the two "skill" conditions was significantly higher than the MTE for the two "environment" conditions, $t(7) = 26.5$ $p < 0.001$, the MTE in the "skill-hands" condition was significantly higher than the MTE in the "skill-bat" condition, $t(7) = 8.7$, $p < 0.001$, and the MTE in the "environmental-irrelevant" condition was significantly higher than in the "environmental-relevant", $t(7) = 6.9$, $p < 0.001$. None of these comparisons were significant for novices, although it can be seen in Figure 1 that the MTE for novices was highest for "environment-irrelevant" condition and lowest for the "environment-relevant" condition.

Discussion

There are several implications of these findings. Attending to any part of skill execution (either the movement of the body or the bat) degrades performance in experts relative to attending to information in the external environment (consistent with Beilock, Carr, MacMahon, & Starkes, 2002; Gray, 2004). As proposed in these previous studies, this effect was most likely due to the disruption of the experts' proceduralized baseball batting skill. As reported by Wulf and Prinz (2001) for novices, experts in our study performed significantly better when the focus of attention was external to the body (i.e., the bat) as opposed to when attention was directed to the movement of the hands. However, inconsistent with previous research, this difference was not significant for novices in our study. Expert performance in the batting task was significantly better when attention was directed to information in the external

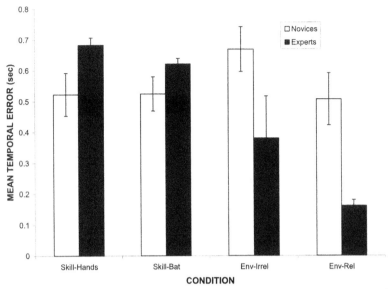

Figure 1. Mean temporal batting errors for novices and experts in the four different attention conditions.

environment that was relevant to the task (i.e., ball rotation) as opposed it when it was not directly relevant to the batting task (i.e., tone frequency). This finding suggests that focusing attention on information in the environment is beneficial to expert performers both because it prevents attention to skill execution, and because it allows the pick-up of informational cues relevant to task performance. This finding also further confirms that picking-up ball rotation direction is an important element of successful baseball batting (Gray, 2002). It also seems that when novices' attention is directed to this relevant cue, hitting performance is improved.

References

Beilock, S. L., Carr, T. H., MacMahon, C., & Starkes, J. L. (2002). When paying attention becomes counterproductive: Impact of divided versus skill-focused attention on novice and experienced performance of sensorimotor skills. *Journal of Experimental Psychology: Applied, 8*, 6-16.

Gray, R. (2002). Behavior of college baseball players in a virtual batting task. *Journal of Experimental Psychology: Human Perception and Perfor-mance., 5*, 1131-1148.

Gray, R. (2004). Attending to the execution of a complex sensorimotor skill: Expertise differences, choking and slumps. *Journal of Experimental Psychology: Applied., 10*, 42-54.

Wulf, G., & Prinz, W. (2001). Directing attention to movement effects enhances learning: A review. *Psychonomic Bulletin & Review, 8*, 648-660.

Acknowledgements. This work was supported by the National Science Foundation Faculty Early Career Development Program (Award # 0239657 to author RG).

Studies in Perception and Action VIII
H. Heft & K. L. Marsh (Eds.)
© *2005 Lawrence Erlbaum Associates, Inc.*

The Influence of Symmetry on Perception of Thrown, Oblong, Symmetrical Projectiles in 3D

Igor Dolgov[1], Michael K. McBeath[1], & Thomas G. Sugar[2]

[1]Department of Psychology, Arizona State University [2]Department of Mechanical & Aerospace Engineering, Arizona State University, USA

In the last few decades a body of literature has been published regarding visual perception and interception of spherical projectiles (Chapman, 1968; McBeath, Shaffer, & Kaiser, 1995; McBeath & Shaffer, 2002), in most cases baseballs. It should be noted, however, that a baseball—nearly a perfect sphere—may be a special case of the above mentioned tasks. The current experiments extend projectile perception and interception research by examining the influence of a symmetry axis on the perception of a thrown, oblong, symmetric projectile, specifically an American football.

Morikawa (1999) has shown that in the 2-dimentional case, perceived direction of motion is influenced by the shape of the animate object. Features such as elongation and symmetry resulted in a perceptual bias of the motion vector toward the axis of symmetry. The following experiments verify the existence of similar perceptual biases in 3-dimensional space, in a real-world, spatial judgment task.

Experiment 1 consisted of a web-survey examining participant's accounts of the in-flight behavior of an American football. In Experiment 2, we empirically examined the physics of the in-flight behavior of a thrown football, with a focus on the relationship of the axis of symmetry to the trajectory. Experiment 3 compared performance in a spatial judgment task that asked participants to predict the final destination of spherical and oblong projectiles, specifically, volleyballs and footballs.

Experiment 1

This experiment was designed to determine whether people have a bias to presume that a football travels along its axis of symmetry. The competing hypotheses were that participants will tend to believe that the axis of a passed football will typically (i) be aligned with its direction of travel, versus (ii) systematically deviate from its direction of travel (i.e. be tilted more upward or downward, leftward or rightward). A secondary hypothesis was that there would be some relationship between the pattern of responses and some biographical factor, such as a measure of athletic experience.

Method

A total of N=124 (51 females and 73 males) participants of various levels of athletic experience were recruited via e-mail and web-forum postings to participate in the experiment. The subjects could use any internet-connected computer to complete a simple web-based survey consisting of a few biographical questions as well as two questions regarding their perception of a thrown football in the horizontal and vertical planes.

Results and Discussion

With regard to overall pattern of responses, in the vertical plane, a majority (59.7%) believed that the axis of the football typically deviates above the trajectory, while only about 10% indicated a downward tilt. In the horizontal plane, a plurality (49.7%) responded that the ball remains aligned with the axis, while only 16.9% reported a deviation to the right. Chi-square tests were performed on survey response counts, but no significant differences were found. The results show a lack of general consensus about the football's behaviour in the horizontal plane.

Experiment 2

In the case of an ideally thrown American football, current physics models (Brancazio, 1985; Soodak, 2002) predict that the drag force acting on the ball should make it behave like a fixed-point gyroscope, with its axis maintaining alignment with its trajectory throughout flight. However, we felt that initial-condition assumptions made by these models were unrealistic and not satisfied in real-world tasks. Experiment 2 was conducted to measure empirically the behavior of a thrown football and to test the hypothesis that the symmetry (also, the rotational) axis of a thrown football maintains an alignment with its trajectory. Two competing hypotheses were compared: (i) The rotational axis of the football will remain generally aligned with trajectory, versus (ii) The rotational axis of the football will systematically deviate from the trajectory.

Method

Three male participants (2 right-handed, 1 left-handed) of varying football throwing expertise (1 professional-level, 2 amateur-level) were recruited to act as passers in the experiment. Football position data were collected using an 8-camera Vicon® motion capture system that records real time position of marked objects at a 120 Hz rate over a volume of approximately 12,000 cubic feet (40' x 30' x 10'). Each passer was asked to throw the football at a comfortable velocity at a target positioned approximately 15 yards away. The trajectory and orientation of the ball were computed for each pass.

Results

Hypothesis ii was supported: the football's axis did not track its trajectory in flight. For both the vertical and horizontal planes, the average absolute deviation of the axis away from trajectory was significantly different from zero for all passers. Specifically, in the horizontal plane, the football systematically deviated away from trajectory in a direction consistent with the handedness of the passer with an average deviation of 17.6° for the amateur-level passers and 7° for the professional-level passer. In the vertical plane, the deviation was not systematically affected by any biological factor, but rather depended on the nature of each specific throw, especially the specific football that was thrown. As in the horizontal plane, the amount of deviation was lowest for the professional-level passer at 4.5°, with the amateur-level passers averaging 9.5°. The results show that the specific behavior of a football, in flight, systematically varies due to biological and physical factors, such as handedness of the passer and ball shape, with the amount of deviation depending on the passer's level of expertise.

Experiment 3

The purpose of this experiment was to investigate whether there was a significant difference in performance on estimating the final destination of a projectile between a spherical object, a volleyball, and a symmetrical, oblong object, an American football. If an American football's axis of symmetry deviates from its trajectory, then perceiving this axis may actually produce a misperception of trajectory and impoverished performance in judgment tasks, and possibly interception tasks. The hypotheses are as follows: (i) Observers will judge the destination of thrown spherical volleyballs more accurately than thrown elongated footballs. (ii) Observers will systematically deviate in their judgments of thrown footballs in the direction that the axes are tilted.

Method

Two groups of five subjects (3 females, 7 males) were positioned adjacent-to and in-front of a 4x3 target array as seen in Figures 1a and 1b, with their backs to the actual targets. Football position data was collected using the Vicon apparatus described in Experiment 2. The subjects were in a position to view the passer, but were directed not to look for overt visual cues, such as eye fixation and arm position. The subjects were asked to judge the final destination of the projectile having been allowed to view only the initial ¾ of the flight-path.

Results and General Conclusions

Hypotheses i and ii were supported. There was a significant difference in performance, $F(1,9) = 17.82$, $p = 0.002$, with the subjects performing better in judging volleyballs. There was also significant correlation, $r^2 = 0.53$, $p < 0.01$, between performance on the judgment task for American footballs, and the number of mistakes made consistent with the orientation of the axis. These results suggest that it is, in fact, the misaligned axis which is causing reduced performance in the case of a thrown, oblong, symmetrical projectile. We must also consider that while above mentioned bias produces a pronounced effect in a stationary judgment task, it may not translate to active tasks such as projectile interception.

The current 3-D perception experiments are consistent with previous work done in perception in a 2-D space. Another interesting finding (Morikawa, 1999) is that symmetric shapes moving along their main axis of symmetry resulted in faster judgments on direction of motion than asymmetric shapes. Morikawa conjectured that these symmetry-based perceptual biases may be adaptive. The ecological motivation, as discussed by McBeath, Schiano, & Tversky (1997), consists of the following observations: (1) Most natural and artificial objects that are capable of locomotion possess at least 1 axis of symmetry, which allows for more economical recognition and/or cognitive processing; (2) Animated objects typically travel along their primary axis of symmetry.

With advancing locomotive technology, the existence of these biases has important implications in perceptual judgments of real-world objects such as naval vessels, airplanes, skidding automobiles and spacecraft. While symmetry played a detrimental role in judgment tasks in Experiment 3, it may actually have the opposite effect when the main symmetry axis is aligned with the trajectory, as is the case with most natural ecologically-consistent motion. Under such circumstances, the axis might actually afford an additional informative visual cue and may aid in many real-world spatial judgment tasks and, possibly, projectile interception and navigation tasks.

References

Brancazio, P. J. (1985). Why does a football keep its axis pointing along its trajectory? *The Physics Teacher,* 23(9), 571-573.

Chapman, S. (1968). Catching a baseball. *American Journal of Physics,* 36, 868-870.

McBeath, M. K., Morikawa, K., & Kaiser, M. K. (1992). Perceptual bias for forward-facing motion. *Psychological Science,* 3, 362-366.

McBeath, M. K., Schiano, D. J, & Tversky, B. (1997). Three-dimensional bilateral symmetry bias in judgments of figural identity and orientation. *Psychological Science,* 8, 217-233.

McBeath, M. K., & Shaffer, D. J. (2002). Baseball outfielders maintain a linear optical trajectory when tracking uncatchable fly balls. *Journal of Experimental Psychology: Human Perception & Performance,* 28, 335-348.

McBeath, M. K., Shaffer, D. J., & Kaiser, M. K. (1995). How baseball fielders determine where to run to catch fly balls. *Science,* 268, 569-573.

Morikawa, K. (1999). Symmetry and elongation of objects influence perceived direction of translational motion. *Perception & Psychophysics,* 61, 134-143.

Soodak, H. (2002). A geometric theory of rapidly spinning tops, tippe tops, and footballs. *Journal of Physics,* 70, 815-828.

Studies in Perception and Action VIII
H. Heft & K. L. Marsh (Eds.)
© *2005 Lawrence Erlbaum Associates, Inc.*

An Information-Based Account of Lateral Interception: Coupling of Hand Movements to Optics in Novel Trajectories

Alen Hajnal, R. W. Isenhower, Steven J. Harrison, & Claire F. Michaels

Department of Psychology & Center for the Ecological Study of Perception and Action, University of Connecticut, Storrs, CT, USA

In recent years two approaches have been proposed to explain the guidance of hand movements in lateral interception tasks. In this task, the participant is to intercept a ball that would pass laterally within arm's reach along some trajectory. A series of studies (Peper, Bootsma, Mestre & Bakker, 1994, Montagne, Laurent, Durey & Bootsma, 1999, Dessing, Bullock, Peper & Beek, 2002, Dessing, Peper & Beek, 2004) have elaborated successive modifications of Bullock and Grossberg's (1988) VITE model and argued that lateral ball position serves as the basis for controlling hand movements. Jacobs and Michaels (2004) and Michaels, Jacobs, and Bongers (2004) using a computationally less demanding version of the VITE model, one that is closer to the original, claimed to have demonstrated that another variable, the ratio of the ball's lateral angular optical velocity to its rate of optical expansion, is used to guide hand movements. This has now been shown with two ball-trajectory types, rolling toward the perceiver on a horizontal plane (Arzamarski, Harrison, & Michaels, 2005) and swinging on a thin line along a circular trajectory toward the perceiver (Jacobs & Michaels, 2004).

In our present contribution we examine the hand-movement trajectories that occur in response to a new ball trajectory. A ball attached to the top of a physical pendulum rotates around a fixed axis toward the catcher. Starting from different initial hand positions, a participant is asked to catch balls approaching different final positions at different incidence angles. The VITE model modification proposed by Michaels et al. (2004) was used to simulate hand movement trajectories, given the trajectory of the ball. The predicted trajectories show one, two or no movement reversals depending on (1) initial hand position, and (2) the variable that is assumed to be informative in guiding hand movements. We compare these predictions to observed hand trajectories.

Method

A single male participant (RWI) caught 50 tennis balls arriving along a horizontal rail at lateral distances from 5cm to 45cm from his right eye. He was seated with his head in a fixed position and was to make no vertical or anterior-posterior hand movements. It took the ball approximately 1 s to travel from its release the horizontal distance of 174 cm and a vertical distance of 57 cm (the ball velocity decelerated to zero as it came to the rail). The experiment was conducted in complete darkness; the participant could see only the ball and his gloved hand (both coated with phosphorescent paint). The trajectories of the ball and hand were recorded with an Optotrak Certus System at a sampling rate of 100Hz.

Results

The ball was caught on every trial.

Hand trajectories and the optical variable $\dot{\theta}/\dot{\phi}$ (ratio between the ball's angular optical velocity and its optical expansion) were computed for each trial to assess the extent to which the participant relied on that optical information.

As one test of the predictive power of the optical variable, we computed the correlation between the specified needed movement (i.e., the difference between the momentary position specified by optics and the initial hand position) and the velocity of the hand 500ms later. A correlation of .736 ($p < .001$) showed a strong reliance on information provided by the optical variable. The agreement between the hand trajectory and the optical variable can be seen when plotted side by side. Three representative trials are presented in Figure 1. The hand position, depicted by the solid lines, moves in the direction of and then follows the optically specified position. Note that the optical variable and the hand movement are synchronized by shifting up the time series of the former by 500 ms. The optical variable appears to be guiding hand movements successfully.

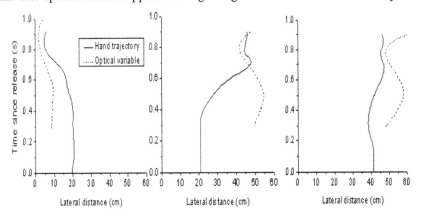

Figure 1. Hand trajectories (solid lines) and the optical variable $\dot{\theta}/\dot{\phi}$ trajectories (dotted lines) for trials 2, 25 and 44.

We used the Michaels et al. (2004) version of the VITE model to predict hand trajectories. Typical results are shown in Figure 2. The VITE model predictions were more accurate in trials with large movements (more than 15cm in trials 2 and 25) than for small hand movements (less than 10cm in trial 44).

The details of movement prediction are easier to see when we compare actual hand movements with optical variable trajectories (Figure 1) due to the fact that the VITE model produces inherently smoother trajectories.

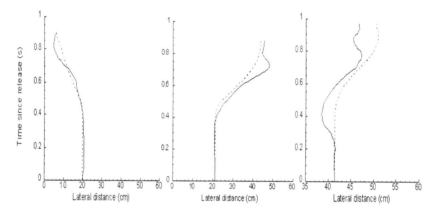

Figure 2. Actual (solid lines) and simulated hand trajectories (dotted lines) predicted by the VITE model for trials 2, 25 and 44.

References

Arzamarski, R., Harrison, S.J. & Michaels, C.F. (2005). Lateral ball interception: Hand movements during planar ball trajectories. Submitted for publication.

Bullock, D., & Grossberg, S. (1988). Neural dynamics of planned arm movements: Emergent invariants and speed-accuracy properties during trajectory formation. *Psychological Review, 95,* 49-90.

Dessing, J. C., Bullock, D., Peper, C. E., & Beek, P. J. (2002). Prospective control of manual interceptive actions: Comparative simulations of extant and new model constructs. *Neural Networks, 15,* 163-179.

Jacobs, D. M., & Michaels, C. F. (2004). Lateral interception I: Attunement and calibration. Submitted for publication.

Michaels, C. F., Jacobs, D. M., & Bongers, R. M. (2004). Lateral interception II: Predicting hand movements. Submitted for publication.

Montagne, G., Laurent, M., Durey, A., & Bootsma, R. J. (1999). Movement reversals in ball catching. *Experimental Brain Research, 129,* 87-92.

Peper, C. E., Bootsma, R. J., Mestre, D. R., & Bakker, F. C. (1994). Catching balls: How to get the hand to the right place at the right time. *Journal of Experimental Psychology:Human Perception & Performance, 20,* 591-612.

Acknowledgements. This research was supported by NSF Grant BCS 0339031.

Studies in Perception and Action VIII
H. Heft & K. L. Marsh (Eds.)
© *2005 Lawrence Erlbaum Associates, Inc.*

The Effects of Task Constraints on the Perceptual Guidance of Interceptive Reaching Toward a Moving Target

Joanne Smith & Gert-Jan Pepping

Perception-in-Action Laboratories, Moray House School of Education, University of Edinburgh, UK

Research on interceptive reaching tends to be divided into one of two distinct categories, viz.: reaching towards a stationary target, and dynamic interception of a moving target. Stationary-reaching research has focused on the key timing characteristics of the transport and grasp-components and how the accelerative and decelerative phases are adapted to meet differing task demands. This research has identified that the acceleration phase of the hand transport remains unaltered despite manipulation of accuracy requirements, whereas the deceleration phase of the movement is typically affected by object properties (Jeannerod, 1984). Zaal (2000) showed that changes to movement time were not dependent on the size of the object—as previously thought—but rather, on the area available for contact. This demonstrates that the constraints placed by the size of the object affect the way we reach. What's more, the subtleties of different actions afforded by a situation can be observed in the refinement of the reaching movement. Here we investigate which elements of the transport phase of an interceptive reach towards a moving target are adjusted to meet the spatial and temporal requirements of a task under varying instructional constraints.

The analysis of interceptive actions of moving targets has focused on the nature of the prospective information used to guide the movement and the strategies employed to regulate it. Lee proposes that guidance of movement is accomplished by τ (Tau) -coupling, that is, by keeping the τs of motion gaps in a constant ratio (Lee, 1998). A second aim was to determine whether the control of interceptive reaching could be explained by the τ–coupling model.

Method

Seven adult participants were asked to remove a small object (65x40x15mm) from a toy train moving at a constant velocity (approx. 226 mms^{-1}) on a stadium shaped track. Three task conditions were used: (1) spatial and temporal requirements were left unspecified; (2) spatial requirements were specified; (3) both spatial and temporal requirements were specified. Hand kinematics were recorded for ten trials in each condition using a 3 camera Qualsys motion analysis system at 240 Hz.

Results and Discussion

Four movement phases were identified for analysis, viz. initiation to peak acceleration, peak acceleration to peak velocity, peak velocity to peak deceleration and peak deceleration to object contact. Figure 1 shows the spatial and temporal contribution of each of these phases in time and in displacement. Analysis revealed an effect of task on movement time, $F(1.19, 42.72) = 79.84$, $p<0.01$, partial $\eta^2 = .69$, with participants displaying significantly shorter movement times in task 3 (see figure 1). There was also an effect of task on movement displacement, $F(2,84) = 389.88$, $p < .05$, partial $\eta^2 = .90$, showing that the object was picked up closer to the body in the anywhere-and-anytime condition (task 1, see also Figure 1). Interestingly, there was no effect of task on the percentage of movement time spent accelerating/decelerating, nor was there an effect of task on the time between peak velocity and peak deceleration.

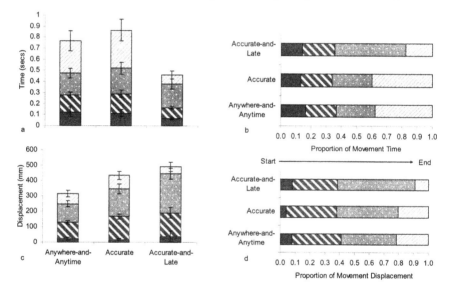

Figure 1. a) Absolute duration of movement phases in time across the three experimental conditions; b) relative movement phase duration as a percentage of total movement time; c) absolute distance of movement phases; d) relative movement phase length as a percentage of total movement displacement.

The analysis highlights that movements were differentiated to accommodate task constraints by altering the composition of the deceleration phase of the hand movement towards the object. The deceleration phase is composed of the initial hand deceleration after peak velocity and the final low-velocity phase beginning with the moment of peak deceleration.

With regards to the second aim, three motion gaps were identified: the gap between the hand and the object (HO), the gap between the hand and the interception location (HI), and the gap between the object and the interception location (OI). Four potentially relevant τ-couplings of motion gaps were considered, viz.: τ_{HO}–τ_{HI}, τ_{HI}–τ_{HO}, τ_{HO}–τ_{OI}, and τ_{HI}–τ_{OI}. Figure 2 shows the continuous ratio K (Kappa), of the τs of the relevant combinations of motion-gaps. Analysis revealed that over the whole duration of the transport phase Ks stayed very stable within a trial (Figure 2), with low variability over trials (Figure 3), supporting the idea that the transport phase of interceptive reaching is guided by means of τ-coupling. The data further lend support for the idea that participants selected the most appropriate motion gaps to τ-couple during different phases of an ongoing movement.

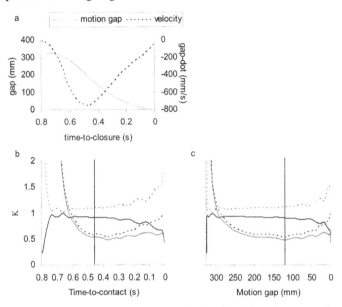

Figure 2. Typical plots of displacement and velocity (a) and K as a function of time-to-contact (b) and K as a function of motion-gap (c). The vertical line in plots b and c indicates the moment of peak velocity, whilst the areas outside the shaded area represent the initial and final low velocity phases. The grey dotted line indicates K for τ_{HO}–τ_{HI}, the black solid line K for τ_{HI}–τ_{HO}, the grey solid line K for τ_{HO}–τ_{OI}, and the black dotted line is K for τ_{HI}–τ_{OI}.

In conclusion, the present study highlights that the control strategy used for guidance of the hand during interceptive reaching to a moving target is dependent upon, and varies according to the specific task requirements. The parameters varied to accommodate differing instructional task constraints are commensurate with previous research on stationary reaching, namely that the final deceleration of the hand towards the object changes according to the varying task constraints. These findings confirm that interceptive reaching toward moving targets follows similar patterns as reaching toward stationary targets and indicates that the reaches made towards a moving target can be analysed in the same way as those made to a stationary target.

A new τ-coupling analysis is introduced by analyzing the continuous ratios of the τs of motion gaps. The data support the theory that τ-coupling occurs during the interceptive reaching movements. Analysis of the selected motion gap couplings provided an explanation of the guidance strategies employed during the transport phase of an interceptive reach of a moving target. What's more, the analysis revealed the subtle differences that result from the different spatial and temporal constraints imposed by the task.

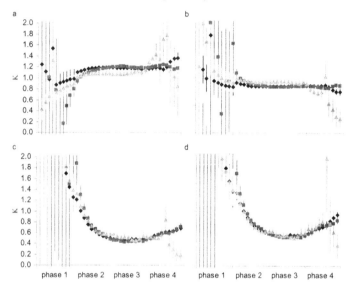

Figure 3. A single participant's Ks of the four τ-couplings analyzed, a) τ_{HO}–τ_{HI}, b) τ_{HI}–τ_{HO}, c) τ_{HO}–τ_{OI}, and d) τ_{HI}–τ_{OI}, across the three experimental conditions. Diamonds represent the anywhere-and-anytime trials, squares represent the accurate trials and triangles represent the accurate-and-late trials. The plots are time normalized for each phase and error bars represent standard deviations.

References

Jeannerod, M. (1984). The timing of natural prehension movements. *Journal of Motor Behavior, 16*, 235-254.

Lee, D. N. (1998). Guiding movement by coupling taus. *Ecological Psychology, 10*, 221-250.

Zaal, F. T. J. M. (2000). *On prehension: Toward a dynamical account of reaching and grasping movements.* Unpublished Doctoral Dissertation, Department of Psychology of the Faculty of Human Movement Sciences, Vrije Universiteit, Amsterdam.

Acknowledgements. This study was supported by grants from the University of Edinburgh and was written whilst the first author was supported by the Economic and Social Research Council (ESRC) award PTA-030-2003-00320.

Audition

Studies in Perception and Action VIII
H. Heft & K. L. Marsh (Eds.)
© *2005 Lawrence Erlbaum Associates, Inc.*

The Influence of Presentation Method on Auditory Length Perception

Brent C. Kirkwood

Technical University of Denmark

Size, shape, and position, spatial properties of many everyday sound-producing sources, have been shown in numerous studies to be perceivable by normal-hearing listeners (Carello, Wagman & Turvey, 2005; Grassi, in press; Heine & Guski, 1993). Live presentation of stimuli, as has been done in some of these experiments, has the great advantage of bypassing any limitations of a recording and playback chain and can thereby increase the ecological validity of a listening task. However, this ecological validity comes at a cost in the form of a significant reduction in the choices of test method and in the types of stimuli that can be presented. In an attempt to understand the influence of the stimulus presentation method for a typical everyday listening task, performance in a dropped-rod length-estimation experiment, like that described in Carello et al. (2005), was compared for three cases: 1) live presentation of stimuli, 2) playback of binaural stimuli as recorded from an acoustic head and torso simulator, and 3) diotic presentation of monophonically-recorded stimuli as recorded from a single microphone.

Method

Eight normal-hearing test subjects, all enrolled in an introductory psychoacoustics course, participated as paid listeners. The test subjects were seated facing away from an acoustically transparent but visually opaque screen. Test subjects listened to recordings presented via headphones and to the live presentation of wooden dowels, lengths 15 to 120 cm in 15 cm increments, being dropped on a linoleum floor behind the screen. The dowels were dropped in a similar way on each trial: approximately 3 m behind the subject at an angle of 15° (relative to the floor) with their centers of gravity positioned 59 cm above the floor. The rods were released from the top of a short (1.8 cm) ramp. All dowels were 13 mm in diameter.

The test participants were told they would hear rods dropped on the floor, but were given no other information about the material, size, or shape of the rods. The subjects were asked to produce estimates of the rod lengths by positioning a moveable surface in such a way that it corresponded to a just-reachable distance between it and a stationary surface. A laser-based distance-measuring device was used to automatically measure the length of each estimate. Subjects were given approximately six seconds to respond. No feedback was given.

The recording, playback, and live presentation of the stimuli all occurred in the same acoustically-normal room. Recordings (24 bit, 44.1 kHz) were made in a position typical of where the test subject would be seated, thereby maintaining a similar impression of both the direct and reflected sound as allowed for in particular by the binaural-recording technique. Equalizations of the recorded stimuli were also performed, in order to account for undesirable fluctuations in the frequency responses of the recording and reproduction systems (Møller, 1992). Playback sound levels were calibrated to closely match those of the live case. Participants were told that they would "wear headphones" for some of the experiments, but it was intentionally left unstated that they would be listening to recordings. Open headphones were used for playback in order to make the presence of the headphones as transparent as possible to the wearer.

The test was broken into four sessions, one for each presentation method plus a repetition of the first session, conducted in order to enable checks of training effects. The sequence of the first three sessions was systematically randomized. Within each session, subjects listened to the eight different dowel lengths being dropped onto the floor five times each. In the case of the recordings, five different recordings of each rod being dropped were used for the five replicates, with the binaural and monophonic stimuli recorded simultaneously. Test subjects produced unique length estimates for each drop. Eight drops, one for each rod length, were considered as a block, and all rods in a block were dropped prior to a new block beginning. To help minimize the influence of order effects, the sequence of rod drops within each block was systematically randomized.

Results and Discussion

An average of all subject data for each presentation method indicates very accurate estimations of rod lengths. In Figure 1 it can be seen that the mean length estimates in the live case are generally closer to perfect performance (the dotted line), however the means were not found to be statistically different at a 95% confidence level.

Inspection of the errors in the responses for each method, however, reveals some differences between presentation methods. Figure 2 compares the mean percent error magnitudes for each of the presentation techniques. Comparisons using multiple-comparison 95% confidence intervals reveal that subjects made larger errors on average when performing the task from monophonic recordings than from live presentation. Subject performance with the binaural-recording presentation method was not statistically different than the live or monophonic presentation methods.

In the case of the binaurally-recorded stimuli, subjects were often unaware that they were listening to recordings during the listening test. Many subjects apparently believed they were wearing headphones for some other purpose, in-

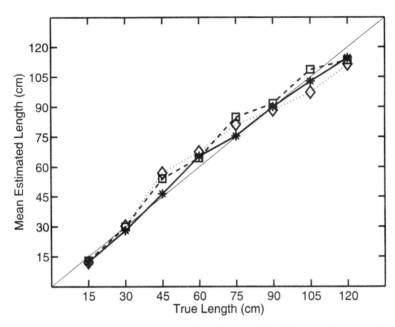

Figure 1. Mean length estimates for live (asterisks), binaural (squares), and monophonic (diamonds) presentation methods.

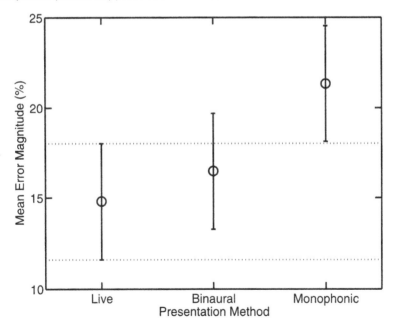

Figure 2. Mean length estimation %-error magnitudes (circles) for each presentation method, with multiple-comparison 95% confidence intervals.

indicated by questions like, "Is it okay that the headphones aren't working?" This was not the case for the monaurally recorded stimuli, for which it was generally obvious to the subjects that they were listening to reproductions. It is apparent from the subjective comments that there are properties of the sound, likely the spatial ones, present in the binaural-recording and presentation technique that are important for maintaining realism.

Comments from test subjects indicated that some believed they were able to recognize rods being redropped in the test, though their stated guesses at how many rods were being used were always lower than the true number. Subjects mentioned that, as the test progressed, they may have been simply responding with length estimates that matched what they remembered previously reporting for a rod that they recognized. This provided reason to suspect possible training effects. Simple comparisons of the data, however, indicated no statistically significant differences, at a 95% confidence level, between the first and last sessions.

The results from this experiment indicate that, for normal-hearing subjects, using a monophonic recording and playback method to produce auditory stimuli for a length estimation experiment produces greater variability in the results than live presentation produces for similar stimuli. It appears that equalized binaural recordings made with an acoustic mannequin may offer the best solution when recordings are chosen, if for no other reason than the subjective realism experienced when using such recordings. Monophonically-recorded stimuli should be used with caution.

References

Carello, C., Wagman, J. B., & Turvey, M. T. (2005). Acoustic specification of object properties. In J. D. Anderson & B. F. Anderson (Eds.), *Moving image theory: Ecological considerations.* Carbondale, IL: Southern Illinois University Press.

Grassi, M. (in press). Do we hear size or sounds: balls dropped on plates. *Perception and Psychophysics.*

Heine, W. D. & Guski, R. (1993). Can listeners catch approaching sound sources? In S. S. Valenti & J. B. Pittenger (Eds.), *Studies in perception and action II: Posters presented at the VIIth International Conference on Event Perception and Action* (pp. 238-241). Hillsdale, NJ: Lawrence Erlbaum Associates.

Møller, H. (1992). Fundamentals of binaural technology. *Applied Acoustics, 36,* 171-218.

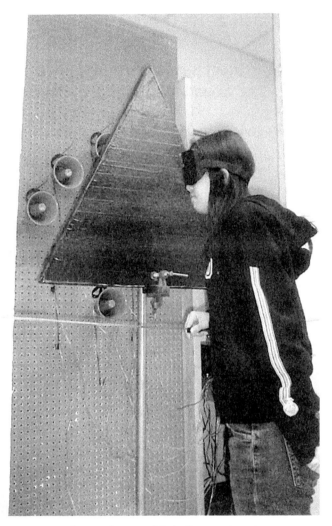

Figure 1. The apparatus and procedure used in both experiments.

Three shapes—square, circle, triangle—each with a surface area of 7575 cm^2 (Kunkler-Peck & Turvey, 2000) were cut from 3.81 cm thick sound insulating foam board. Each shape was covered with black electrical tape to ensure that the foam board would not fray with use. The shapes rested on a stand positioned 30.48 cm in front of the loudspeaker array. The vertical position of the shapes was different for each subject so that the bottom of the shapes was 31.75 cm below the subject's ear-height (and in the center of the loudspeaker configuration). To help the subjects move comfortably and safely during trials, a 162.56 cm long guide wire was positioned 104.14 cm from the ground and 36.83 cm in front of the shape stand.

Studies in Perception and Action VIII
H. Heft & K. L. Marsh (Eds.)
© *2005 Lawrence Erlbaum Associates, Inc.*

Hearing Silent Shapes: Identifying the Shape of a Sound-Obstructing Surface

Ryan L. Robart & Lawrence D. Rosenblum

University of California, Riverside, USA

While most psychoacoustics is concerned with perception of sound sources, there is evidence that surfaces that reflect or obstruct sound can also be detected and can guide behavior (e.g., Rice, 1967; Rosenblum & Gordon, 2004). It has long been known that both blind and sighted listeners can echolocate a sound-reflecting surface well enough to judge its position, size, shape, and even material (e.g., Rice, 1967). With regard to sound-obstruction, Gordon and Rosenblum (2004) showed that blindfolded listeners could judge whether they could fit through an aperture created between sound-obstructing walls. For these purposes, two moving walls partially obstructed an array of sound-emitting loudspeakers. On each trial, the walls were positioned so that their inside edges created various aperture widths. Untrained listeners judged whether they could fit through the aperture based on how the sound field was obstructed. Results showed that listeners were accurate at this task and were sensitive to the acoustic aperture in body-scaled dimensions.

The research described below uses a related methodology to examine whether listeners can determine the shape of sound obstructing surfaces. While there is evidence that listeners can hear the shape of sound-emitting and sound-reflecting surfaces (e.g., Kunkler-Peck & Turvey, 2000; Rice, 1967), it is not known whether the shape of sound-obstructing surfaces can be heard. In two experiments, blindfolded listeners were asked to identify three shapes of equal surface area, which obstructed a set of loudspeakers emitting broad-band noise. The first experiment utilized a single intensity broad-band noise, while the second experiment tested two intensities of noise.

Experiment 1

Methods

Eighteen subjects participated in this experiment for course credit or pay. All subjects reported good hearing.

Broadband noise (82 dB) was generated using a computer and presented through an eight-loudspeaker array. The loudspeakers were 12.7 cm horn speakers and were configured in a diamond-type shape (see Figure 1). Based on pilot experiments, it was decided that the height of the loudspeaker configuration would be adjusted differently for each subject. Specifically, the horizontal center of the diamond configuration was adjusted to match each subject's ear-height.

The experiment took place in a small laboratory room (350.52 x 396.24 cm) with normal reflectances. The walls were constructed of painted drywall, the ceiling consisted of commercial acoustical tile, and the floor was covered with standard linoleum tile.

Subjects had full view of the shapes and apparatus while being given instructions. They were told that they would be blindfolded and for each trial, would be asked to judge which of the three shapes was positioned in front of the loudspeakers. Subjects were instructed to use whatever listening strategies they liked and were told that moving side-to-side in front of the shape (while holding the guide wire) might help with the task. On each trial, the noise was presented for 10 secs after which subjects were asked which shape they thought was positioned in front of the loudspeakers. After responding, subjects were moved back from the guide wire and headphones (emitting white noise) were placed on the subject's ears (Gordon & Rosenblum, 2004). The experimenter then removed the shape and placed another shape on the stand. Subjects were presented with a total of 60 randomized trials (20 per shape). If the same shape was to be presented on consecutive trials, the experimenter still took the shape off of the stand and then placed it back (so that inter-trial interval was roughly constant). No practice trials or feedback were provided to subjects during the experiment.

Results & Discussion

The mean percentage correct identification scores for the square, circle, and triangle were 38.89, 41.11, and 50.83 respectively. T-tests revealed that performance with each of the shapes was better than chance (33.3%), $p < .05$. An ANOVA revealed a significant effect of shape, $F(2, 34) = 5.53$, $p = .008$, and Fisher PLSD tests revealed that the triangle was recognized significantly more often than either the square or circle ($p < .05$).

Overall, listeners were successful at this task, and some listeners showed near perfect performance. Based on post-experiment interviews, subjects reported similar strategies for shape determination. Most reported that head movement aided in their determinations, and that they could hear the edges of the shapes. Furthermore, many subjects referred to differences in the sound loudness of the occluded noise based on the shapes: e.g., "the circle seems more muffled than the square". Based on these comments, and results from our previous acoustic aperture experiment (Rosenblum & Gordon, 2004), a follow-up experiment was conducted to examine the salience of overall acoustic intensity in judging sound-obstructing shapes. In Experiment 2, two levels of broad-band noise were used in the experiment. It was thought that if overall intensity is an important informational dimension for judging shape, then hearing multiple loudspeaker intensities randomly presented, would degrade perfor-mance relative to that of the first experiment.

Experiment 2

Method

Nineteen subjects participated in this experiment for course credit or pay. All subjects reported good hearing. The materials and apparatus for Experiment 2 were exactly the same with the exception that two intensity levels were emitted from the loudspeakers: 82 dB and 73 db.

In this experiment, there were 90 randomized trials (3 shapes x 2 sound intensities x 15 trials). The same procedure as Experiment 1 was used with additional instructions alerting listeners that two intensities of broadband noise would be heard through the loudspeakers.

Results & Discussion

The mean percentage correct identification scores for the square, circle, and triangle were 52.95., 48.63, and 52.95 for the lower intensity, and 41.84, 48.63, and 61.37 for the higher intensity, respectively. All shapes were recognized at better than chance levels (p < .05) at both intensities with the exception of the square at the higher intensity which was judged better than chance at the $p = .051$ level. A 3 (shape) x 2 (intensity) ANOVA revealed no significant effects for either shape or intensity, or their interaction at the $p < .05$ level. To examine whether performance was inhibited by the inclusion of two loudspeaker intensities, an analysis was conducted testing performance in this experiment and Experiment 1. For these purposes, a test was conducted comparing the means of subjects in Experiment 1 with the means of performance in Experiment 2 with the higher intensity trials (the same intensity used in Experiment 1). In fact, an ANOVA revealed that despite hearing multiple loudspeaker intensities, subjects performed more accurately in Experiment 2 than in Experiment 1 for all shapes, $F(1, 35) = 6.39$, $p = .016$. The fact that judgments improved when subjects could not rely on a single loudspeaker intensity could suggest that subjects were generally using information other than overall intensity for their shape judgments, and that this information remained invariant (and was made more salient) over multiple intensities. Future research will be directed at determining the salient acoustic information for determining the shape of sound-obstructing objects.

References

Gordon, M.S. & Rosenblum L.D. (2004). Perception of sound-obstructing surfaces using body-scaled judgments. *Ecological Psychology 16,* 87-113.

Kunkler-Peck, A. & Turvey, M. T. (2000). Hearing shape. *Journal of Experimental Psychology: Human Perception and Performance, 1,* 279-294.

Rice, C. E. (1967). Human echo perception. *Science, 155,* 656–664.

Acknowledgments. This research was supported by a University of California Intramural grant awarded to the second author.

Studies in Perception and Action VIII
H. Heft & K. L. Marsh (Eds.)
© 2005 Lawrence Erlbaum Associates, Inc.

Hearing Space: Identifying Rooms by Reflected Sound

Ryan L. Robart & Lawrence D. Rosenblum

University of California, Riverside, USA

When we enter a room, we have an immediate impression of the room's size as well as the layout and composition of its major surfaces. Certainly, much of this impression comes from sight. However, the immediacy of the impression suggests that we apprehend these properties before fully exploring the space visually. It could very well be that some of our early sense of a space comes from the sounds that are emitted and reflected in the space. Consider the differences heard when entering a small walk-in closet vs. a large public restroom. Not only would the emitted sounds differ, but the differences in reflected sound between the rooms (one dampened by soft material; one amplified by hard tile and linoleum) would likely be noticeable to even the acoustically naïve observer. In fact, the entertainment industry makes exactly this assumption in dedicating vast resources to enhance and simulate acoustic spaces. Much of this craft is accomplished by manipulation of sound reflections and reverberations. Moreover, the empirical acoustic engineering literature has shown that listeners are sensitive to the sound reflecting properties of spaces so as to judge the acoustic quality and general dimensions of the space (e.g., Bradley, Reich, & Norcross, 2000). There is also speculation on the perceptual skills listeners use to apprehend properties of spaces (e.g., Clifton, Freyman, & Meo, 2002). Still, there is no research testing whether listeners can simply recognize different types of rooms based on reflected structure. The experiment reported below examined this question by asking listeners to identify four different rooms based on hearing how the rooms structured (reflected; reverberated) emitted sounds.

Method

Fifteen subjects participated in this experiment for course credit. All subjects reported normal hearing.

Five different sound sources were binaurally recorded in four different acoustic spaces. The sources ranged from human speech to white noise bursts. The human speech stimulus was a recording of a male speaker uttering the 'Rainbow Passage'—a short paragraph often used in psychological experiments because of its diverse phonetic content. A struck cowbell was used as a live sound source in each space. The remaining three sound sources were synthesized broadband noise bursts: (a) 4 repetitions of a 3 ms burst with a 300 ISI; (b) 6 repetitions of a 5 ms burst with a 200 ms ISI; and (c) 5 repetitions of a

Figure 1. A picture of the gym and loudspeaker used for recording some of the stimuli. A similar picture, along with pictures of the other rooms, was shown to subjects as they listened to the stimuli.

50 ms burst with a 200 ms ISI. All of the sounds (with the exception of the cowbell) were emitted through a portable studio loudspeaker connected to a laptop computer. The sounds were emitted at an amplitude of 82 db +- 6 db. The loudspeaker rested on a tripod with the center of the cone at 61" high and 67" from the back wall of each room (see Figure 1).

The rooms included a large indoor gymnasium, a moderately-sized classroom, a public restroom, and a small laboratory room. The rooms were chosen on the basis of their differences in sizes as well as reflective surfaces. The gymnasium (95'5" width x 115'10" length x 80' height) contained a hardwood floor and had fold-up bleachers along the walls, which were brick and concrete. The ceiling was composed of concrete reinforced with large steel beams (see Figure 1). The classroom (19'5" x 23'7" x 10') was cluttered with numerous desks, and the walls (drywall) contained chalkboards and whiteboards. The classroom ceiling was composed of acoustical tile and the floor was made of standard linoleum tile. In the restroom (9'8" x 17'5" x 8'), the walls were composed of ceramic tile and drywall, the floor consisted of linoleum tile, and the ceiling was made of standard acoustical tile. The restroom was also cluttered with various reflective surfaces such as sinks, stall walls, mirrors, etc. Finally, the small laboratory room (5'6" x 7'6" x 9'5") had a carpeted floor with painted drywall for walls and an acoustical tile ceiling. A small table and (silent) computer with monitor occupied the room.

The recordings were made using two small binaural microphones (SoundPro SP-MICRO-1) placed in the ears of a 5'3" female listener. The listener stood against the back wall of the rooms with her head facing the loudspeaker (or cowbell). The binaural microphones were connected to a Digital Audio Tape (DAT) recorder (SONY TCD-D8). The recordings were then digitally downloaded to a computer where they were edited into individual stimuli.

Untrained listeners heard each sound (presented from computer) over headphones as they looked at photographs of the four rooms presented on a computer screen (e.g., see Figure 1—but for the photographs shown to subjects, the speaker and stand were not visible). Subjects were asked to choose the room in which they thought each sound was recorded. Stimuli were organized in blocks based on sound source. Each of the five blocks contained 20 trials of a single type of sound (e.g., voice) randomly presented in each of the four rooms (5 times each). Subjects judged 100 trials total: 5 sounds (blocked) x 4 rooms x 5 trials each, and the presentation ordering of blocks was randomized across subjects. On each trial, the stimulus recording was played three times after which listeners made their room choice by typing the number (1-4) assigned to the room in which they thought the recording was made. Participants received no feedback during the experiment, which lasted about 45 minutes.

Results and Discussion

The mean percent correct values for each room and each sound are displayed in Figure 2. A series of t-tests revealed that every room was recognized at significantly better than chance levels (25%) for every sound tested ($p < .05$). An ANOVA revealed significant main effects for both room, $F(3,42) = 6.12$, $p = .002$, and sound $F(4, 56) = 4.66$, $p = .01$, but no significant interaction of these factors ($p > .05$). Pairwise comparison tests for rooms indicated that the gym was recognized significantly more often than any other room ($p < .05$). Pairwise comparison tests for the sounds showed that the cowbell as well as the 3ms-300ms ISI noise burst led to judgments significantly less accurate than with the 5ms-200ms ISI and 50ms-200ms ISI sounds ($p < .05$). No other pairwise tests were significant at the $p < .05$ level.

Overall, listeners were outstanding at the task, displaying mean room identification accuracy of 78% and means ranging from 50-93% correct across the different sounds. In post experiment interviews, subjects reported using the "echoes" and "reflections" they heard in the rooms. Most subjects also reported that they found the task relatively easy depending on the type of sound source they were hearing.

These results suggest that listeners can recognize rooms by based on how the rooms structure emitted sounds. The findings add to echolocation demonstrations (e.g., Rice, 1967) showing that listeners can use acoustic structure that is reflected from silent surfaces to identify perceptual properties. Along these lines, the results add to a growing literature showing that human listeners are sensitive to a wider range of acoustical properties than is usually considered in

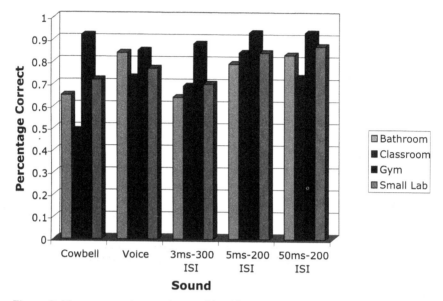

Figure 2. Mean percent correct room identifications as a function of sound source and room (see text for details).

the psychoacoustics literature (Gordon & Rosenblum, 2004). Many questions arise from the current findings including the acoustical support for recognizing rooms; whether more subtle differences between rooms (e.g., differences in room height only) can be detected; and whether listeners can hear from what position in a room the recordings were made. These and other questions are currently being explored in our laboratory.

References

Bradley, J.S., Reich, & Norcross, S.G. (2000). On the combined effects of early- and late-arriving sound on spatial impression in concert halls. *Journal of the Acoustical Society of America 108 (2),* 651-662.

Clifton, R.K., Freyman, & J. Meo (2002), What the precedence effect tells us about room acoustics. *Perception & Psychophysics, 64,* 180-188 .

Gordon, M.S., & Rosenblum L.D. (2004), Perception of sound-obstructing surfaces using body-scaled judgments. *Ecological Psychology, 16,* 87-113.

Rice, C. E. (1967). Human echo perception. *Science, 155,* 656–664.

Acknowledgments. This research was supported by a University of California Intramural grant awarded to the second author.

Studies in Perception and Action VIII
H. Heft & K. L. Marsh (Eds.)
© *2005 Lawrence Erlbaum Associates, Inc.*

The Role of Instrument Properties in Music Performance: Variations in Sound and Movements Induced by Baroque-Violin Playing

R. Goasdoué & B. Bril

Groupe de Recherche Apprentissage et Contexte,
École des Hautes Etudes en Sciences Sociales, Paris, France

Since the end of the 1960's both musicologists and musicians have made a significant contribution towards the revival of ancient instruments and repertoire, as well as towards the reconstruction of interpretative style. The interesting point here is that one single repertoire is played in different ways, on different instruments. This peculiarity in the history of interpretation provides an unique opportunity to study the effects of various constraints on musical performance. According to K. Newell's (1986) definition of action as emerging from the interaction between organism, environment and task, music performance may be viewed as resulting from the interplay between performer, interpretative tradition, instrument and musical work. This unique situation is also a way to assess the lag between musical plans (projects) and their performance (achievement).

Method

Three groups of violinists of roughly equal expertise participated in the study (high level students of Paris Conservatories). The first group consisted of musicians specializing in ancient instruments (i.e. baroque violin) and is considered as the control group. The second group involved musicians specializing in both baroque and modern instruments. Lastly, the third group was composed of modern violinists who have never tried to play an ancient instrument.

All participants had to play the first two musical phrases from the "Gavotte en Rondeau" BWV1006 by J.S. Bach along two different interpretative styles (baroque vs. modern) and on two different violins (baroque vs. modern). This imitation task has the advantage to impel the musical intention of the musician, hence to exert control on the sound production. Besides the musicians of the first group who played only baroque violin (control group), all performers played the musical phrases along the two "styles" (baroque and modern) on both violins (baroque and modern). Consequently we are able to compare the arm movement and the sound production of each violinist while performing baroque and modern interpretation on both instruments.

Each performance was recorded by means of a minidisc recorder synchronized with two video cameras (sampling rate 50 hz).

Results

For each performance we conducted an analysis of the sound signal, and a kinematic analysis of the right arm movements (bow arm). These analyses should allow us to characterize: (1) the variation in sound production due to instrument's properties, (2) the adaptation of the bow movements and the arm coordination to the instrument's properties, and (3) the effect of musicians' competencies (familiarity with baroque instruments) on arm coordination.

Sound analysis: A "baroque" musical scale

A specific method of sound analysis based on acoustical correlates of interpretative styles was developed to assess the imitation task of interpretative styles. The first step of this method was to establish sounds parameters that allow for characterizing each note along its temporal and dynamic traits (note duration, parameters of sound envelope, attack, sustain, release, symmetry). In order to determinate acoustical correlates able to differentiate interpretative styles we performed multivariate statistics on 28 commercial recordings classified as modern or baroque versions. This research of acoustical correlates was also driven by the principles of interpretation described in various treatises from the Baroque period. A set of 18 criteria was established: 9 criteria describe timing variations and 9 characterize dynamics. To evaluate in a synthetic way the imitation task, we ended up establishing an interpretative style scale on the basis of the previous analysis and in agreement with the methodological principles developed in psychometry. Application of this method to the 28 commercial recordings revealed a significant difference between modern and baroque recordings ($p < 0.01$ Mann-Whitney, see Figure 1). We consider this result to be a kind of validation of the scale.

This global analysis confirms that all violinists are able to imitate the two interpretative styles. There is a significant difference between versions that do not depend on the violin type except for musicians of third group (modern violinists) who had difficulties imitating a modern style on the baroque violin. Their modern versions on baroque instruments were surprisingly a bit more baroque than their baroque version on modern violin! This result suggests that experience is most probably needed to use an instrument in an unexpected way.

Movement analysis

The kinematic analysis was based on a 3D reconstruction of the movement from the video recordings. We focused on two main aspects of bowing movements: the bow trajectory and the coordination of the right arm (bow arm). The main goal of this analysis was to describe the immediate variations induced by the different constraints (type of violin and interpretative style). See Figure 2.

The variations in bow use contrasted with the reorganization of the arm coordination across the three groups. All the violinists tended to use a smaller portion of the bow when playing with a baroque bow; furthermore, playing a

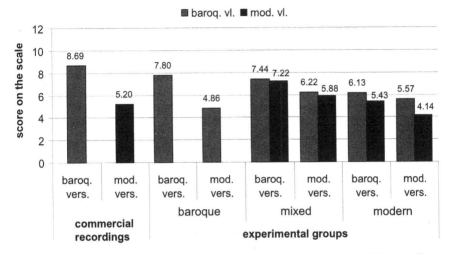

Figure 1. Baroque scale applied to baroque and modern commercial recordings of the "Gavotte en Rondeau" BWV1006 by J.S. Bach (left) and experimental performances from the three groups of violinists when playing in baroque and modern interpretative styles; baroque violinists play on baroque violin (gray bars) whereas mixed & modern violinists play on modern ones (black) as well.

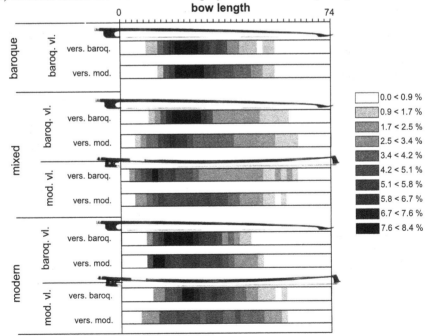

Figure 2. Bow use depending on musician (baroque, mixed or modern experts), violin (baroque or modern) and interpretation mode (baroque or modern): frequency of use of the bow (in 2cm segments) over whole musical performance.

baroque version enhanced this outcome (Figure 2). Concerning the arm coordination measured through the contribution of the elbow joint to the total elbow-shoulder angular variation (Figure 3), modern violinists showed differences neither attributable to the instrument nor to the interpretation. Baroque and mixed violinists exhibited a significant difference depending on the interpretation (smaller contribution of elbow for baroque version on baroque violin), while mixed violinists show no difference between interpretative version when playing a modern violin.

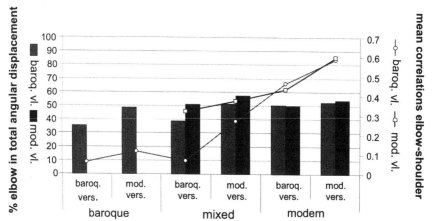

Figure 3. Right arm coordination, contribution of elbow to the elbow-shoulder angular displacement for baroque, mixed, and modern violinists when they play on baroque (grey bars) or modern (black bars) violins; correlation (dots) are between angle variations of the elbow and the shoulder.

Discussion

As shown in more simple tasks (Vereijken 1991; Goldfield 1993), this experiment stresses the importance of mastering the instrument's properties to develop specific and adapted movements. While all violinists adapted to the bow properties, this was not the case for their right arm coordination. "Mixed violinists" only exhibited different patterns of coordination depending on the violin. This could explain why, contrary to mixed violinists, modern violinists have a sound production significantly different when playing a modern version on a baroque or modern violin. These results highlight the fact that the arm movements and the working point trajectory (bow movements) do not refer to the same reality. However these preliminary results allow us to reconsider the direct links often regarded by musicians between movements and sound production.

References

Newell, K. M. (1986). Constraints on the development of coordination. In M. G. Wade & H. T. A. Whiting (Eds.), *Motor skills acquisition* (pp. 386). Dordrecht: Martinus Nijhoff.

Vereijken, B. (1991). *The dynamics of skill acquisition.* Amsterdam: Amsterdam : Free University Press.

Goldfield, E. C., Kay, B. A., & Warren, W. H., Jr. (1993). Infant bouncing: The assembly and tuning of action systems. *Child Development, 64,* 1128-1142.

Acknowledgements. The violin players, Eva David and the members of the Groupe de Recherche Apprentissage et Contexte are warmly acknowledged. This work was supported in part by the French Ministry of Research, ACI 3T 02 20440 and by the ACI CNRS Complexité.

Studies in Perception and Action VIII
H. Heft & K. L. Marsh (Eds.)
© *2005 Lawrence Erlbaum Associates, Inc.*

Does Length Sound Like What Length Feels Like?

Jeffrey B. Wagman, Kimberly M. Hopkins, & Jennifer L. Minarik

Department of Psychology, Illinois State University, USA

In the ecological view, environmental properties structure energy arrays so as to provide information about those properties to a perceiver. For example, an object's physical characteristics (e.g. its size, shape, and material) characteristically affect how the object vibrates when mechanically disturbed, and such vibration patterns provide information about the sound-producing object or event (see Carello, Wagman, & Turvey, 2005). Such structure in the acoustic array is rich enough for listeners to perceive with metrical accuracy. For example, listeners can perceive the sizes of struck plates (Kunkler-Peck & Turvey, 2000) and the lengths of rods dropped to the floor (Carello et al., 1998).

In fact, the acoustic array is rich enough for perceivers to show comparable performance in perceiving properties by audition as perceiving them by vision or by touch (see Carello et al., 2005 for a review). This fact suggests that the information for perception may be independent of a particular energy array (i.e., it may be modality-neutral, see Stoffregen & Bardy, 2001). For example, haptic perception of a wielded rod and auditory perception of a rod dropped to the floor are each constrained by the mass distribution of the object (quantified by I_{ij}). In both cases, perception of length scales positively to the maximum principal moment of inertia (I_1) and negatively to the minimum principal moment of inertia (I_3) (see Carello et al., 1998).

The rods used in Carello et al. (1998) were plain wooden rods. Therefore, I_{ij} always co-varied with the length of the rod, and the effects of I_{ij} and actual length on perceived length could not be independently evaluated. The current experiment attempts to evaluate the effect of I_{ij} on auditory perception of length on a set of objects in which inertial properties are decoupled from geometric properties.

Method

The 15 objects used in this experiment were constructed from PVC pipe. The rods were internally weighted to decouple I_{ij} from length. A given object consisted of two layers of PVC pipe—an outer shell and an inner shell. In the most generic object design, the inner shell was filled with lead shot, sealed at both ends, wrapped in foam padding and inserted into the outer shell which was also sealed at both ends (see Figure 1).

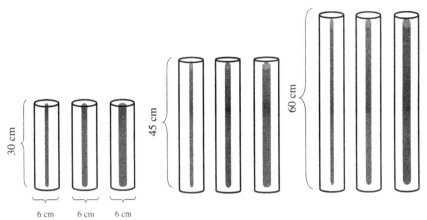

Figure 1. Examples of the experimental stimuli. Nine of the fifteen objects are pictured.

Outer shells and inner shells were cut to three different lengths (30cm, 45cm, and 60cm). For each set of lengths, the radius of the inner shell determined the amount of lead shot. Four different radii of inner shells were used at each length (2cm, 1.25cm, 1cm, and 0.75cm) (see Figure 1). The fifth object at each length contained no inner shell and no lead shot. The rods were rolled to the floor one at time from a support surface approximately 30 cm from the ground. Rods and dropping apparatus were occluded from the participant by a curtain. The participant reported perceived length by magnitude production. They adjusted the distance of a moveable flag to correspond to the perceived length of the rod (see Figure 2). Rods were dropped three times each, and order of presentation of the rods was randomized.

Results and Discussion

Internally weighting the rods served to decouple geometric properties (i.e., length) and inertial properties (i.e., I_{ij}). This makes it possible to independently evaluate the contributions of actual length and I_{ij} to perceived length. If perceived length is a function of actual length, we would expect length to account for a large portion of variance in perceived length despite this manipulation (cf. Carello et al. 1998). If perceived length is a function of I_{ij}, perceived length should scale positively to I_1 and negatively to I_3. For the sake of simplicity, analyses from the current experiment focus solely on the contribution of I_1 to perceived length.

In the current experiment, actual length failed to account for any variance in perceived length ($r^2 = 0.001$, *ns*). I_1, on the other hand, accounted for 33% of the variance in perceived length ($r^2 = .33$, $p < .05$). As predicted, perceived length scales positively to I_1 (see Figure 3, left). The fact that I_1 accounts for only 33% of the variance in perceived length precludes a conclusion that I_1 is the information for auditory perception of length. However, the results suggest that when actual length and I_{ij} are decoupled, perceived length of a rod dropped to the floor is constrained by I_{ij} and not actual length.

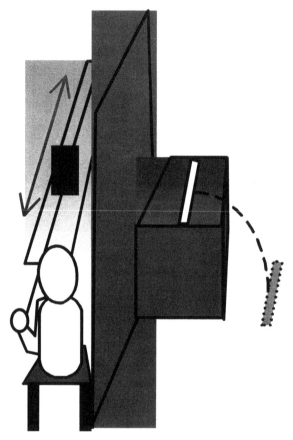

Figure 2: Experimental paradigm. Rods were rolled off of a support surface. Rods were occluded from the participant by a curtain. Participants reported perceived length by means of magnitude production. Here the participant is pictured from behind. (I thank Claudia Carello for drawing the figure).

Interestingly, when the rods of different lengths are analyzed separately, I_1 accounts for 82% of the variance in perceived length of the small (30cm) rods ($r^2 = 0.82$, $p < 0.05$), 98% of the variance in perceived length of the medium (45cm) rods ($r^2 = 0.98$, $p < 0.05$), and 73% of the variance in perceived length of the long (60cm) rods ($r^2 = 0.73$, $p = 0.06$), (see Figure 3, right). The fact that the influence of I_1 on perceived length seems to depend on whether rods of different lengths are grouped together is somewhat difficult to interpret. It may be that the range of inertial variables used in the current experiment is too narrow to exhibit the expected lawfulness across object of different sizes. Alternatively, it may be that a "higher" higher-order stimulation variable is specific to auditory perception of length (see Carello et al., 2005).

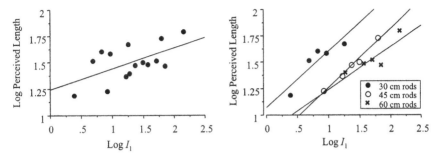

Figure 3. When all three rod lengths are considered together, log l_1 accounts for only 33% of the variance in perceived length (left). When small, medium, and long rods are considered separately, log l_1 accounts for between 73% and 98% of the variance in perceived length (right).

References

Carello, C., Anderson, K. L., & Peck, A. (1998). Perception of object length by sound. *Psychological Science, 9*, 211-214.

Carello, C., Wagman, J. B., & Tuvey, M. T. (2005). Acoustic specification of obejct properities. In J. Anderson & B. Anderson (Eds.). *Moving Image Theory: Ecological Considerations*. Carbondale, IL: Southern Illinois University Press.

Gaver, W. W. (1993a). What in the world do we hear? An ecological approach to auditory event perception. *Ecological Psychology, 5*, 1-29.

Kunkler-Peck, A., & Turvey, M. T. (2000). Hearing shape. *Journal of Experimental Psychology: Human Perception and Performance, 1*, 279-294

Stoffregen, T. A., & Bardy, B. (2001). On specification and the senses. *Behavioral and Brain Sciences, 24*, 195-261.

Intermodal and Bimodal Perception-Action

Studies in Perception and Action VIII
H. Heft & K. L. Marsh (Eds.)
© *2005 Lawrence Erlbaum Associates, Inc.*

Coupling of Movement to Acoustic Flow in Sighted Adults

ChungGon Kim[1], Thomas A. Stoffregen[1], Kiyohide Ito[2], & Benoît G. Bardy[3]

[1]University of Minnesota, Minneapolis, USA; [2]Future University, Japan
[3]Université de Paris XI, France

Typically, we think that sound is for listening, not for controlling movement. However, there is reason to question this traditional assumption. A theoretical framework for these efforts originates from vision and its contribution to the control of action (Gibson, 1966). Body sway creates changes in the optic array that are known as *optic flow*, and these changes are known to influence the control of standing posture (e.g., Lee & Lishman, 1975; Stoffregen, 1985). Body sway also creates changes in the acoustic array that can be understood as *acoustic flow*. Just as optic flow provides information about relative motion between the observer and the illuminated environment, acoustic flow provides information about relative motion between the observer and the audible environment. This similarity between optic and acoustic flow motivates the hypothesis that people might use acoustic flow for the perception and control of stance. This hypothesis has been confirmed in blind people (Ito, Stoffregen, Donahue, & Nelson, 2001). Here, we evaluate it in the context of blindfolded sighted people.

Method

Acoustic flow was created using a moving room. The room was a 2.4 meter cube mounted on wheels that rolled along rails (Figure 1). The room was moved by an electric motor under computer control. The room moved with the amplitude of 22 cm at 0.2 Hz. At each interior corner of the room was attached a speaker (Cambridge SoundWorks satellite), 1.7 m above the floor, facing inward. In Experiment 1 the speakers were rigidly attached to the wall. In Experiment 2 the speakers were attached to poles that were fixed to the floor. During acoustic flow conditions computer generated pink noise was presented through the speakers at 79.5 dB. Head and body motions were recorded using the Fastrak (Polhemus, Inc.) magnetic tracking system. One motion sensor was attached to the room and another to the posterior surface of a bicycle helmet that participants wore.

Experiment 1. We aimed first to determine whether the blindfolded sighted people could use acoustic flow to guide body sway. Twelve subjects participated. They were instructed to listen to room motion, and to move their head forward and backward so as to maintain a constant distance from the front wall (an acoustic version of the tracking task used by Bardy, Marin, Stoffregen, & Bootsma, 1999). They performed four trials in this condition. The duration of each trial was 60 seconds. They wore a blindfold during the task. Because the speakers were attached to the room and faced inward, subjects received motion information in reflected sound (reflected from the moving walls) but also from direct sound (arriving direct from the moving speakers).

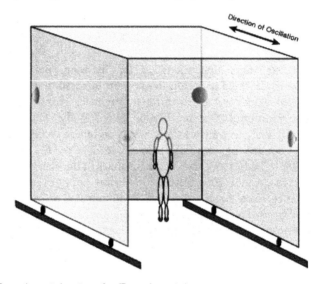

Figure 1. Experimental set-up for Experiment 1.

Experiment 2. We sought to determine whether acoustic flow patterns were sufficient for performance of the tracking task. When the speakers were mounted on stationary stands within the room, information about room motion was available solely in reflected sound (i.e., acoustic flow). Because the speakers faced the center of the room acoustic flow in reflected sound was masked by (louder) direct sound from the stationary speakers. Subjects again performed the tracking task over four trials. Two electro-goniometers (Biopac Systems, Inc.) were used to record angular displacements of the right ankle and right hip.

Results

Experiment 1. Sample data for one trial are shown in Figure 2. We computed the cross-correlation, phase, and gain of head motion relative to room motion. For analysis, cross-correlation coefficients between room-head position as a function of time were computed. As predicted, head positions were significantly related to acoustic stimulation; the mean cross-correlation (0.78) differed from 0, $t(11) = 7.34$, $p < 0.05$. Head motion was in-phase with the acoustic motion (mean relative phase = 8.2°) and the mean gain was 1.3.

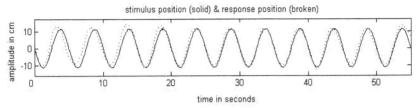

Figure 2.   A sample trial from Experiment 1 showing motion of the room (solid line) and the head (dashed line) during the tracking task.

Experiment 2. Head motion was again strongly coupled to room motion (mean cross correlation = 0.95; $t(11) = 169.49$, $p < 0.05$). The mean relative phase was 19.0° and the mean gain was 1.36. The mean peak-to-peak angular displacement of the hip joint was 2.9° (SD = 3.75°) and that of the ankle joint was 1.1° (SD = 1.45°). As predicted, the mean relative phase between hip and ankle angles was close to anti-phase (151.9°, SD = 46.14°). The goniometer data confirm that the tracking task involved movements of the torso and legs, as well as of the head.

Discussion

In two experiments we found that blindfolded sighted persons could use acoustic information to precisely guide whole body movement, and we found that the auditory guidance of movement was robust when motion information was limited to acoustic flow. Our results extend the earlier finding that blind people can use acoustic information for the control of stance (Ito et al., 2001). In particular the current results indicate that acoustic guidance of whole body motion is robust even among people (in this case, sighted people) who, presumably, do not have a strong prior motivation to pursue this type of perception-action coupling.

References

Bardy, B. G., Marin, L., Stoffregen, T. A., & Bootsma, R. J. (1999). Postural coordination modes considered as emergent phenomena. *Journal of Experimental Psychology: Human Perception & Performance, 25,* 1284-1301.

Gibson, J. J. (1966). *The senses considered as perceptual systems.* Boston: Houghton-Mifflin.

Ito, K., Stoffregen, T. A., Donahue, S., & Nelson G. (2001). Blind adults exhibit postural responses to a moving room. In G. A. Burton and R. C. Schmidt (Eds.), *Studies in perception and action VI* (pp. 1-4). Mahwah, NJ: Lawrence Erlbaum Associates, Inc.

Lee, D. N. & Lishman, J. R. (1975). Visual proprioceptive control of stance. *Journal of Human Movement Studies, 1,* 87-95.

Stoffregen, T. A. (1985). Flow structure versus retinal location in the optical control of stance. *Journal of Experimental Psychology: Human Perception and Performance, 11,* 554-565.

Acknowledgements. Supported by *Enactive Interfaces*, a network of excellence (IST contract #002114) of the Commission of the European Community, and by the National Science Foundation (BCS-0236627).

Studies in Perception and Action VIII
H. Heft & K. L. Marsh (Eds.)
© *2005 Lawrence Erlbaum Associates, Inc.*

Intermodal Specification of Egocentric Distance in a Target Reaching Task

Bruno Mantel[1], Benoît G. Bardy[1,2], & Thomas A. Stoffregen[3]

[1]Research Center in Sport Sciences, University of Paris Sud XI, Orsay
[2]Institut Universitaire de France
[3]School of Kinesiology, University of Minnesota, Minneapolis, USA

The ecological notion of specification is traditionally understood within a single perceptual modality, with the structure of a given ambient (say optic) energy uniquely related to physical reality. This presumed *1:1* mapping between reality and energy structure can, however, turn into a *1:many* relation, because (i) a given physical reality will, in many cases, give rise to multiple structures within the same energy (e.g., optical invariants for layout perception), and (ii) one physical property usually constrains the structure of several ambient energies, producing redundancies in the information available to perceptual systems. The 'single-energy' specification hypothesis is therefore questionable when multiple forms of ambient energy are concerned.

Stoffregen and Bardy (2001) have proposed that specification can exist only in the multi-dimensional energy flow emerging out of the observer-environment interaction. The *global array* contains information that is not present in individual energy arrays and that can be useful for perception. Information is present in the co-variation of energies, just as in a triangle, where triangularity exists only in the relation between the three segments. Testing the global array involves two distinct steps. The first is to identify analytically global array parameters that specify particular aspects of the animal-environment interaction. The second is to test empirically whether the global array is perceived and used by humans.

In the experiment reported below, we evaluated the existence of the global array in the context of layout perception, which is often assumed to rely on vision. We formalized an intermodal invariant (i.e., a parameter of the global array) specifying the egocentric distance between a moving observer and a static object (Equation 1):

$$D = \frac{Vx \cos \alpha \pm \sqrt{Vx^2 \cos^2\alpha + 4\dot{\alpha}\, Vy\, Sx}}{2\dot{\alpha}} \qquad \text{(Equation 1)}$$

where Sx is the linear position of the head along the frontal axis, Vx and Vy are its linear speed (with Vy along the antero-posterior axis). These are inertial terms. In optics, α and $\dot{\alpha}$ are respectively the angular position and velocity of the target. A similar equation describes the movement in the antero-posterior plane (with Vz instead of Vy). Equation 1 can be easily simplified, for example at some key moments of the movement (central point, extremities) or when the observer's motion is unidirectional. Equation 1 can also be reformulated, for example in approximating the body-target system as a mass-spring system and using τ as the optical variable to characterize optical flow (Bingham & Stassen, 1994). Equation 2 and 3 illustrate two of these simplifications for, respectively, side-to-side and antero-posterior unidirectional movements (with c constant). However, using this relation to behave does not necessarily imply to have independent access to each terms of the equation.

$$D = \frac{Vx \cos \alpha}{\dot{\alpha}} \qquad \text{or} \qquad D = \pm \sqrt{\frac{Vy\,c}{\dot{\alpha}}} \qquad \text{(Equations 2 and 3)}$$

Method

Participants ($N=12$) were asked to judge (yes/no) whether, with just a movement of their preferred arm, they could reach a simulated object (a target on a screen) located at different distances. They were seated in a dark room and their viewing was monocular. Head position and orientation were captured with an electromagnetic sensor (Ascension Technology's Flock of Bird). Displays of the target were driven in real time by the motion of the observer's head, allowing the target to be virtually located at any distance between the subject and the screen (or even behind the screen), as illustrated in Figure 1. Three main conditions were tested: Vision-Movement (VM - all terms of Equation 1 were present), Vision only (VO - only optical terms), Movement only (MO - only inertial terms). Egocentric distance was specified only in the VM condition, and we expected participants to detect it only in that condition. In addition, we settled another intermodal condition (VMg), in which we introduced a gain in the equation (G=1.05), to test its influence on perceived distance. Finally, in the VOpb condition, target movements were produced passively by recorded movements of the same participant from earlier trials. This playback condition was used to verify that optical flow was not sufficient on its own to perform the task. Finally, two control conditions (VMr and VOr) with real vision (i.e., in which virtual and actual target were confounded on the screen) were used to validate our virtual set up.

In each condition five target distances were used (90%, 95%, 100%, 105% and 110% of actual reaching distance) and each target was presented 4 times. Dependent variables were yes/no responses, response time, and head movements (described by SD and amplitude, along x, y and z axes). Responses were approximated with a logistic function and thus were analysed through their precision (slope at Y=50%), their accuracy (abscissa of Y=50%) and the accuracy of data approximation for each curve (associated R^2).

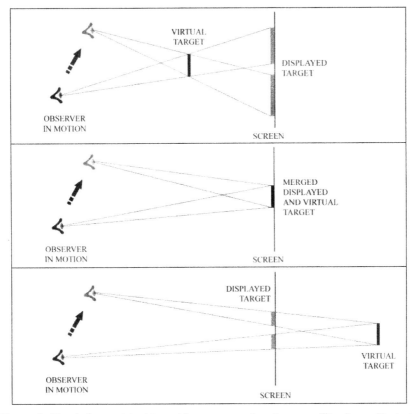

Figure 1. Simulating a virtual target for a monocular observer. The figure illustrate three examples of where the virtual target can be simulated, when the displayed target is moved as a function of the observer movements.

Results and Discussion

Figure 2 represents actual vs. perceived maximal reaching distance for the three intermodal conditions. Reachability judgments were precise only when the relation between energy flows was preserved (VM condition). Judgement accuracy in that condition corresponded to the actual reaching distance, but was slightly overestimated (5%). Judgements in the VO and MO conditions were close to random. Introducing a gain in the intermodal relation (VMg condition) did not change the precision of judgements, but modified the perceived distance, as expected. Performances in the condition combining real vision and movements (VMr) was almost exactly the same as the two other intermodal conditions (VM and VMg), which used virtual display. Finally, responses in the playback condition (VOpb) were inaccurate and significantly different from the responses in intermodal conditions (Wilcoxon tests $T(11)=1$, $Z(11)=2.84$, $p<.05$, $T(12)=9$, $Z(11)=2.35$, $p<.05$ and $T(12)=8$, $Z(12)=2.43$, $p<.05$, for comparisons with VM, VMg and VMr, respectively). This result confirms that optical flow alone provides no information about egocentric distance in this task. Response

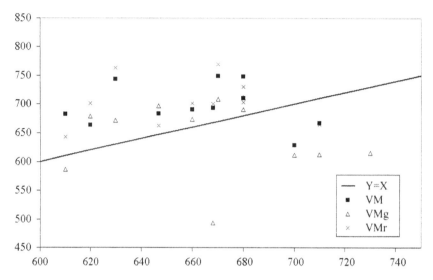

Figure 2: Perceived maximal reachable distance as a function of actual maximal reachable distance (both in millimeters), for the three intermodal conditions: Vision-Movement, Vision-Movement with gain and Vision-Movement with real target (not virtual).

time and head movements did not change with the estimated distance. Participants, although they were free to move (in some conditions) did not show any collective preference between moving forward and moving laterally.

In conclusion, the reachability of an object is specified across optical and inertial energy structure (Equation 1), that is, in the global array. Human participants are sensitive to Equation 1 and, on this basis, detect accurately the egocentric distance.

References

Bingham, G. P. & Stassen, M. G. (1994) Monocular egocentric distance information generated by head movement. *Ecological Psychology*, 6, 219-238.

Stoffregen, T.A. & Bardy, B.G. (2001). On specification and the senses. *Behavioral and Brain Sciences*, 24(2), 195-261.

Acknowledgements. Research supported by Enactive Interfaces (European IST contract #002114), and by NSF (BCS-0236627).

Studies in Perception and Action VIII
H. Heft & K. L. Marsh (Eds.)
© *2005 Lawrence Erlbaum Associates, Inc.*

Exploiting New Perception-Action Solutions in Ball Bouncing

A. Morice[1], I. A. Siegler[1], & B. G. Bardy[1,2]

[1]Research Center in Sport Sciences, University of Paris, France
[2]French University Institute, Paris, France

A physical model of ball bouncing (Schaal, Atkeson, & Sternad, 1996), simulated a task that consists of the repeated bouncing of a ball on a planar surface, demonstrating the existence of a stable attractor when the racket impacts the ball with negative acceleration. This indicates that small perturbations do not have to be corrected to maintain stable bounces. Ball trajectories relax back to their limit-cycle attractors within a few cycles. Sternad, Duarte, Katsumata, & Schaal, (2001) have evidenced in human experiments that regular bouncing is guided by these stability properties, and Dijkstra, Katsumata, de Rugy and Sternad (2004) have shown, in turn, that over 40 practice trials, racket acceleration values are optimized and decrease toward negative values that provide optimal stability. Perceptual information seems to play a crucial role in this optimization process.

In both the Sternad et al. and the Dijkstra et al. cases, the same event—bouncing—produces temporally synchronized optic, acoustic, and haptic patterns, i.e., the moment of contact between the racket and the ball is optically, acoustically, and haptically specified. In the present experiment, we test the human ability to perform adaptive actions in bouncing under circumstances where perceptual synchrony has been artificially changed. Temporal relations between vision and proprioception were manipulated in order to investigate the consequences on performance stability and learning. The introduction of a new synchrony between the kinesthetic information and the visual consequences of bouncing had another consequence: the sensory-motor attractors discovered by Schaal et al. (1996) were shifted. New attractors for ball bouncing were thus created, and we investigated the routes taken by human subjects to discover the new solutions.

Method

Subjects ($N = 26$) stood in front of a large screen and held a (real) table tennis racket whose position was recorded by an electromagnetic tracker. We used a virtual reality set-up (in which real and virtual rackets were desynchronized) in order to create new attractors. The real racket controlled a virtual racket that bounced a virtual ball on the screen. Participants (4 groups) were tested in three sessions (50, 50 and 25 trials 40 sec. long, respectively). In session 1 and session 3, the phase lag between real and virtual rackets was zero. In session 2, the lag between the two rackets was 45°, 90°, 135°, or 180°, depending on the group, thus changing the location of stable attractors. Virtual Racket Period (VRP), Signed Bounce Error (SBE), Virtual Racket Acceleration at Contact (VRAC), Virtual (VRCP) and Real (RRCP) Racket Contact Phase were used as main variables to capture learning and performance. ANOVAs (10 blocks of 5 trials x 4 independent groups) were conducted to investigate the learning effect in each session (Block factor) for each phase lag group (Group factor).

Results

In session 1, ANOVAs showed a significant effect of Block on mean values of VRP ($F(9, 225) = 4.08, p < .05$), SBE ($F(9, 225) = 6.39, p < .05$), and VRAC ($F(9, 225) = 4.16, p < .05$). This suggests that participants adjusted their behaviors over the 10 blocks of trials. Exponential convergence analyses were performed on VRAC to evaluate the learning time constant (τ) as well as initial mean values and final asymptotic values (see Figure 1). τ was equal to 12.5 trials, initial value to 5.2m/s², and final value to 3.2m/s².

Contrary to earlier work (Sternad et al., 2001), the acceleration at impact produced to reach a good performance was slightly positive. Performances and ball-racket contact behaviors were shown to be stabilized within the 10 blocks.

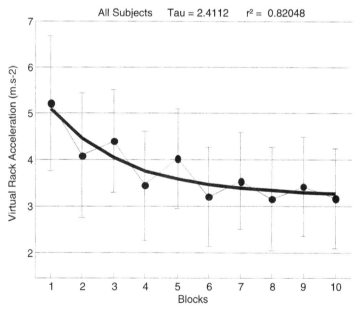

Figure 1. Mean VRAC (± mean standard error) as a function of trial block for all participants (N=26) during the first 50 trials (session 1). The bold line represents the exponential fit, together with τ and R² values.

In session 2, ANOVAs showed significant interactions between Group and Block for mean values of SBE, $F(27, 198) = 2.09$, $p < .05$, and VRP, $F(27, 198) = 2.35$, $p < .05$. Significant interactions between Group and Block factors were found also for mean and standard deviation values of RRCP, $F(27, 198) = 4.583$, $p < .05$, and VRCP, $F(27, 198) = 2.91$, $p < .05$. At the end of session 2, the four groups reached similar task performances, however, learning was different between groups, with a 45° phase lag being more rapidly learned than 90°, 135° and 180° (see Figure 2). Irrespective of the new sensori-motor relation, final performances were similar in session 2 and session 1 (no lag), indicating that learning occurred in all groups by making appropriate adjustments of real racket motion. Participants could easily and quickly perform the task with an end-to-end latency as small as 83.75 ms, but for larger lags, a longer time scale was needed to reach optimal performances.

In session 3, ANOVAs showed a primary effect of Block but no Group effect and no Group x Block interaction for any of the variables. This led us to conclude that there was no lag-dependent destabilization of coordination.

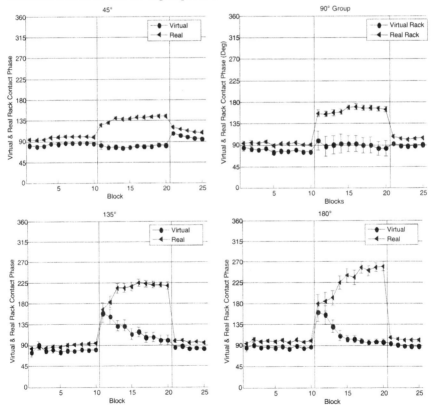

Figure 2. Mean VRCP and RRCP (± mean standard error) plotted as a function of trial block for the four groups during the first, second and third session. Initial and final differences between the two curves in each condition are due to the small but incompressible 30 ms delay present in the racket-racket loop.

Discussion

First, these results suggest that new perception-action solutions for ball bouncing can be learned. A good performance was achieved for all groups within each session. Second, the stable attractors discovered by Schaal et al. (1996) and exploited by humans in ball bouncing (Sternad et al., 2001) were not exploited by our participants in our virtual ball bouncing task; thus, their exploitation remains an open question. Third, the new solutions were learned differentially depending on the phase lag between the real and virtual racket: 90°, 135° and 180° phase lags were more difficult to learn than 45°. Because the increase in phase lag co-varied with an increase in absolute delay in this task, it remains an open question whether the dynamics of discovering new perception-action solutions depend on the stability of initial attractors or on the time delay between the (visually and proprioceptively) specified contacts.

References

Dijkstra, T. M. H., Katsumata H., de Rugy, A., & Sternad D. (2004). The dialogue between data and model: Passive stability and relaxation behavior in a ball bouncing task. *Journal of Nonlinear Science.*

Schaal, S., Atkeson, C. G., & Sternad, D. (1996). One-Handed Juggling: A Dynamical Approach to a Rhythmic Movement Task. *Journal of Motor Behavior, 28,* 165-183.

Sternad, D., Duarte, M., Katsumata, H., & Schaal, S. (2001). Bouncing a ball: tuning into dynamic stability. *Journal of Experimental Psychology: Human Perception and Performance, 27,* 1163-1184.

Acknowledgments. Supported by *Enactive Interfaces,* a network of excellence (IST contract #002114) of the Commission of the European Community.

Studies in Perception and Action VIII
H. Heft & K. L. Marsh (Eds.)
© *2005 Lawrence Erlbaum Associates, Inc.*

The Effects of Bimodal and Unimodal Familiarization on Infants' Memory for Unimodal Events

Joe Schmutz, Dan Hyde, Seth Gunderson, Katie Gordon & Ross Flom

Department of Psychology, Brigham Young University, Provo, UT, USA

We live in a world of objects and events that are multimodal and dynamic. Historically, however, much of the research in the area of sensory development has focused on the development of a single sense modality such as infants' ability to visually discriminate various faces/patterns or their ability to auditorally recognize a particular voice, despite the fact that these abilities develop in a multimodal context. While researchers have begun to examine infants' capacity for intersensory perception, as well as generate hypotheses regarding the nature of its development and its relationship to learning in early development (Lewkowicz & Lickliter, 1994; Lickliter & Bahrick 2000), little research has examined the relationship between intersensory perception and early memory development in human infants. Much of the research that has examined the development of memory in human infants has also largely focused on infants' memory for modality specific properties such as form, pattern, orientation, and color (e.g., Cohen & Gelber, 1975; Slater, 1985). More recently, however, research has begun to examine infants' memory for dynamic events (Bahrick & Pickens, 1995; Bahrick, Hernandez-Reif, & Pickens, 1997; Courage & Howe, 1998) as well as infants' long-term event memory using the mobile conjugate reinforcement paradigm (Davis & Rovee-Collier, 1983; Hayne, Rovee-Collier, & Perris 1987; Rovee-Collier & Fagan, 1981). Still, little is known regarding the effects of intersensory perception and early memory development, and it is important to do so given the multimodal nature of infants' environment and the fact that infants use multisensory information in learning about and organizing their world in a largely veridical manner. Given that the presence or absence of multimodal stimulation affects infants' perceptual attention; it is also possible that the presence or absence of multimodal information affects what infants remember about a particular event. The purpose of the current study was to examine the effects of redundant (audio-visual) and non-redundant (visual) familiarization on infants' memory for the unimodal property of visual orientation.

Method

Forty-eight three-month-olds, seventy-two five- and seventy-two nine-month-olds were familiarized (120s) to films of a brightly colored plastic hammer moving up and down striking a light colored wooden surface in a distinctive pattern. Infants were randomly assigned to one of two familiarization conditions (bimodal auditory-visual or unimodal visual) and one of three retention intervals (5-minutes, 2-weeks, or 1-month). Following the familiarization phase, infants received two 60s test trials. The visual preference memory test for orientation consisted of two silent, side-by-side, 60s trials of the hammer moving at familiar orientation, and the adjacent monitor presented the same hammer moving at the novel orientation (i.e., rotated 180°).

Results

Following either unimodal or bimodal familiarization at the 5-minute as well as the 2-week retention intervals, three-month-olds did not demonstrate any preference for either the event used during familiarization or the novel event. No three-month-olds were tested at the one-month delay. At the 5-minute retention interval five month-olds, however, preferred the novel orientation following unimodal familiarization (Figure 1), $M = 61\%$; t (11) = 2.87, p = .02, but not bimodal familiarization (Figure 2), $M = 53\%$; t (11) = 1.53, p = .2. At the two-week retention interval 5-month-olds demonstrated no preference for either the familiar or unfamiliar event following bimodal or unimodal familiarization. Following the 1-month retention interval however, 5-month-olds in the unimodal familiarization condition showed a significant preference for the familiar event, $M = 44\%$; t (11) = 3.03, p = .011. Five-month-olds in the bimodal condition did not exhibit a visual preference for either the familiar or unfamiliar event following a 1-month delay. The 9-month-olds, however, showed a preference for the novel orientation given either bimodal, $M = 59\%$; t (11) = 3.87, p = .003, or unimodal stimulation, $M = 63\%$; t (11) = 7.4, p = .001, following a 5-minute delay. At the 2-week delay, 9-month-olds demonstrated a null preference for the novel orientation when provided bimodal or unimodal familiarization (all p's >.1).Finally following a 1-month delay, 9-month-olds in the bimodal, $M = 42\%$; t (11) = 3.01, p = .012, and unimodal, $M = 38\%$; t (11) = 3.9, p = .002, conditions demonstrated a familiarity preference.

Discussion

Three-month-olds failed to show reliable memory for the orientation of an event when the event was presented silently (i.e., unimodaly), or when the event could be seen and heard (i.e., bimodally). Five-month-olds, however, demonstrated a novelty preference at the 5-minute delay when the event was presented unimodally, but not bimodally. No preference for either the familiar or novel event was demonstrated at the 2-week retention interval. Finally, only those 5-month-olds in the unimodal condition showed memory for the event (in this case a familiarity preference) at the 1-month retention interval. These results are consistent with previous research assessing infants' memory for dynamic events. That is, others have demonstrated that infants' early memories are exhibited by a novelty preference, after an intermediate delay infants often show a null preference and following longer delay infants frequently exhibit a familiarity preference.

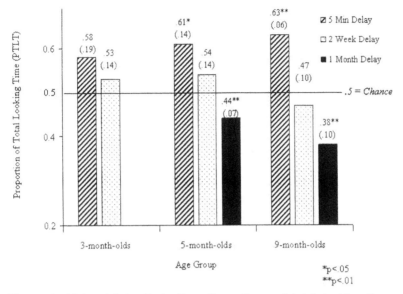

Figure 1. Unimodal familiarization: Proportions of total looking time and standard deviations to the novel visual orientation across retention intervals of 5-minute, 2-week, and 1-month delay as a function of age.

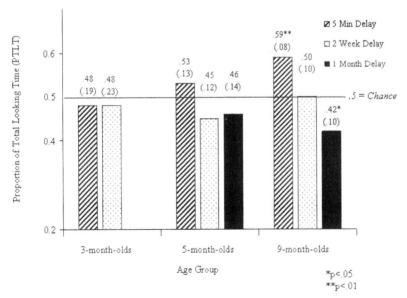

Figure 2. Bimodal familiarization: Proportions of total looking time and standard deviations to the novel visual orientation across retention intervals of 5-minute, 2-week, and 1-month delay as a function of age.

These results confirm and extend Bahrick et al.'s (2004) intersensory redundancy hypothesis which states that in early development or when first perceiving an event, those properties specific to the visual modality (i.e., color, orientation) are most easily perceived when presented unimodally (i.e. silently) but not when presented bimodally (i.e. seen and heard). A second prediction, based on the intersensory redundancy hypothesis, is that with development/experience older infants, however, should be able to perceive and subsequently remember a unimodal property when presented under either unimodal or bimodal conditions. The results of the 9-month-olds confirm this prediction. Nine-month-olds in both the unimodal and bimodal conditions showed memory (i.e., a novelty preference) following the 5-minute delay. Nine-month-olds in the bimodal and unimodal conditions exhibited a familiarity preference following a 1-month delay. Together these results replicate the shifting pattern of infant memory (novel, null and familiarity) for dynamic events as a function of short, intermediate, and longer retention intervals, respectively, and these results demonstrate that predictions based on the intersensory redundancy hypothesis extend to infants' memory for dynamic events.

References

Bahrick, L. E., Hernandez-Reif, M., & Pickens, J. N. (1997). The effect of retrieval cues on visual preferences and memory. *Journal of Experimental Child Psychology, 67*, 1-20.

Bahrick, L. E., Lickliter, R, & Flom, R. (2004). Intersensory redundancy guides infants' selective attention, perceptual and cognitive development. *Current Directions in Psychological Science, 13*, 99-102

Bahrick, L. E. & Pickens, J. N. (1995). Infant memory for object motion across a period of three-months: Implications for a four-phase attention function. *Journal of Experimental Child Psych, 59*, 343-371.

Cohen, L. & Gelber, E.R. (1975). Infant visual memory. In L. Choen & P. Salapatek (Eds.), *Infant perception: From sensation to cognition*, Vol. 1 (pp. 347-403). NY: Academic.

Courage, M. L. & Howe, M. L. (1998). The ebb and flow of infant attentional preferences: Evidence for long-term recognition memory in 3-mo-olds. *Journal of Experimental Child Psychology, 70*, 6-53.

Davis, J. M., & Rovee-Collier, C. K. (1983). Alleviated forgetting of a learned contingency in 8-week-old infants. *Developmental Psychology, 19*, 353-365.

Hayne, H., Rovee-Collier, C. K., & Perris, E. E. (1987). Categorization and memory retrieval by three-month-olds. *Child Development, 58*, 750-767.

Lewkowicz, D. J., & Lickliter, R. (1994). (Eds.), *The development of intersensory perception: Comparative perspectives*. Hillsdale, NJ: Erlbaum.

Lickliter, R. & Bahrick, L.E. (2000). The development of infant intersensory perception: Advantages of a comparative convergent-operations approach. *Psychological Bulletin, 126*, 260-280.

Rovee-Collier, C.K. & Fagan, J. W. (1981). The retrieval of early memory in infancy. In L. P. Lipsitt (Ed.), *Advances in infancy research* (Vol. 1. pp. 225-254). Norwood: Ablex

Slater, A. (1995).Visual perception and memory at birth. In C Rovee-Collier & L.P. Lipsitt (Eds.), *Advances in infancy research* (Vol. 9. pp. 107-125). Norwood: Ablex.

Studies in Perception and Action VIII
H. Heft & K. L. Marsh (Eds.)
© 2005 Lawrence Erlbaum Associates, Inc.

Optical Gain and the Perception of Heaviness

Matt Streit & Kevin Shockley

University of Cincinnati, USA

Haptic perception of wielded objects (including perception of one's own limb orientation) has been shown to be reliably constrained by an object's rotational inertia (see Turvey, 1996 for a review). That is, perception of a wielded object is directly related to the response of an object to the muscular forces applied during wielding. Several studies have also shown that perception of wielded objects is also influenced by vision. Riley and Turvey (2001), using prism goggles and arm splints with differential weight-distributions, found that visual and inertial information about limb orientation appear to influence perception of limb orientation in an independent and additive fashion. Masin and Crestoni (1988) and Ellis and Lederman (1993) showed that objects of the same mass, when lifted via a string, feel lighter with increasing volume with only visual access to object volume. Amazeen (1997) demonstrated that the mapping between rotational inertia and perceived heaviness is scaled by visual access to volume. Other studies have shown that kinematic information alone is sufficient to perceive weights of objects lifted by others (Runeson & Frykholm, 1981) and the relative mass of colliding balls (Flynn, 1994).

The purpose of this study was to determine if perception of the heaviness of a wielded object is influenced by the optical response to applied muscular forces. That is to say, if the visual and haptic information about object movement differs, how will that affect a person's perception of an object's heaviness? We hypothesized that for a given value of rotational inertia, perception of heaviness will be influenced by optical gain—the ratio of the degree of optically presented rotation to the actual rotation of the object. We predicted that if the optical response to the applied muscular forces is amplified (high gain) the object will feel lighter than normal. In contrast, if the optical response to the applied muscular forces is attenuated (low gain) the object will feel heavier.

Method

Four men and seven women at the University of Cincinnati participated in partial fulfilment of a course requirement. Participants were seated in a wooden chair with armrests. On their right side was an occlusion screen that they reached through in order to hold the object handle. They were asked to grasp a wooden handle into which one of three removable wooden dowels was snugly inserted. Attached to each of the three dowels was a 100g mass positioned at either the near end of the rod (low inertia), the middle of the rod (medium inertia), or near the tip of the rod (high inertia). Attached to the bottom of the handle was a magnetic motion capture sensor (Polhemus, Inc., Colchester, VT). The motion data of the wielded object was linked to the motion of a graphical representation of the wielded object projected onto a screen viewed by the participant.

Prior to wielding any object, the experimenter assigned the computer gain setting out of view of the participants. Before beginning the experiment proper, participants were allowed a few test swings of the object to get used to the wielding motion and to the visual display. During this time the system was assigned a canonical optical gain (1 × actual rotation). Participants were instructed to wield the occluded object in a full range of motion in the sagittal plane and to watch the movements of the virtual object on the screen (see Figure 1). During the experiment proper, each participant completed ten total trials for an object of a given value of inertia (low, medium, or high). Two optical gain settings were used—low gain (0.8 × actual rotation) and high gain (1.2 × actual rotation). A single trial consisted of wielding the object at one optical gain setting to achieve a good feel for the heaviness of the object and then wielding the same object at a different optical gain setting. Within a given trial, one optical gain setting was randomly assigned to the first wielding of the object and the other optical gain setting was assigned to the second wielding of the object.

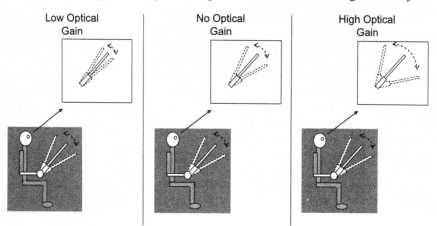

Figure 1. A participant wielding an object about the wrist, through an occlusion screen. The participant is looking at a projection of the object moving. Left panel: Low optical gain. Middle panel: No optical gain. Right panel: High optical gain.

The wooden dowel was removed and replaced between the two wielding motions within a given trial so that it was not obvious that the participants were wielding the same two objects within a trial. When the participant was not actively wielding the object to gain an impression of heaviness, the participant was asked to orient the object upright, following which the experimenter firmly grasped the top of the handle. This was done to prevent the participant from gaining any haptic information about the objects through wielding and to prevent the optical projection from moving during gain setting changes. After the pair of trials for a given trial, participants were asked to report which object felt heavier, the first or the second—a two-alternative, forced-choice paradigm.

Results and Discussion

For a given participant the dependent measure was the proportion of trials of a given rotational inertia for which the low optical gain setting was reported as heavier than the same rotational inertia with a high optical gain setting. For each of the three levels of inertia, the proportions reported as heavier for low optical gain were compared to chance (0.5) using t-tests (low moment of inertia $M = 0.64$, SD = 0.11; medium moment of inertia $M = 0.77$, $SD = 0.15$; high moment of inertia $M = 0.65$, $SD = 0.076$). Participants performed as expected. For each inertial value, objects with a low optical gain were perceived as heavier than objects with a high optical gain (low moment of inertia $t(6) = 3.33$, $p = .0079$; medium moment of inertia $t(6) = 4.80$, $p = .0015$; high moment of inertia $t(6)=5.24$, $p = .00097$). This suggests that people use visual, as well as haptic, information about an object's response to applied muscular forces in order to perceive the heaviness of an object. Future investigations will be required to determine the nature of the integration of the visual and haptic information about an object's heaviness (i.e., if they are independent and additive). This will be important to our theoretical understanding of how different modalities are integrated. This will also be useful for applied settings in which there is a mis-match between applied muscular forces and the consequences of those applied forces. For example, for the successful and efficient operation of an industrial robotic arm, or for the manipulation of implements in minimally invasive, robotic, or tele- surgery environments, it is important to know how visual and haptic information are perceptually cross-calibrated to effectively control one's actions in such environments.

References

Amazeen, E. (1997). The effects of volume on perceived heaviness by dynamic touch: With and without vision. *Ecological Psychology, 9*, 245-263.

Ellis, R. R. & Lederman, S. J. (1993). The role of haptic versus visual volume cues in the size-weight illusion. *Perception & Psychophysics, 53*, 315-324.

Flynn, S.B. (1994). The perception of relative mass in physical collisions. *Ecological Psychology*, 6, 185-204.

Masin, S. C. & Crestoni, L. (1988). Experimental demonstration of the sensory basis of the size-weight illusion. *Perception & Psychophysics, 44*, 309-312.

Riley. M.A. & Turvey, M.T. (2001). Inertial constraints on limb proprioception are independent of visual calibration. *Journal of Experimental Psychology: Human Perception and Performance, 27*, 438-455.

Runeson, S. & Frykholm, G. (1981). Visual perception of lifted weight. *Journal of Experimental Psychology: Human Perception and Performance, 7,* 733-740.

Turvey, M.T. (1996). Dynamic Touch. *American Psychologist, 51*, 1134-1152.

Action & Coordination Dynamics

Studies in Perception and Action VIII
H. Heft & K. L. Marsh (Eds.)
© *2005 Lawrence Erlbaum Associates, Inc.*

Stability and Variability of Rhythmic Coordination with Compromised Haptic Perceptual Systems

Claudia Carello[1], Geraldine L. Pellecchia[1,2], Polemnia G. Amazeen[3], & M. T. Turvey[1]

[1]Center for the Ecological Study of Perception and Action, University of Connecticut; [2]Department of Physical Therapy, University of Connecticut, Storrs, CT, USA; [3]Department of Psychology, Arizona State University, Tempe, AZ, USA

The synchronizing of rhythmically moving limbs and limb segments is one of the most fundamental achievements of the human movement system. It attracts considerable scientific attention because it is a primary expression of how movements are organized in space and time, how they resolve issues of efficiency, and how they meet the competing challenges of stability and flexibility. More broadly, 1:1 frequency locking can be viewed as one of human movement's original models for a collective form of organization in which many component parts, distributed across the body, act coherently to produce a global action.

A complex system's collective dynamics are relatively independent of the specific details of the internal and external interactions of its component subsystems. Accordingly, the collective dynamics—for example, of synchronized rhythmic hand movements—can be usefully modeled in relative ignorance of the constituent dynamics. As developed by Kelso (1995) and colleagues, the elementary rhythmic 1:1 synergy can be modeled by a motion equation in the collective variable of relative phase ϕ—the difference in the phase angles ($\theta_{left} - \theta_{right}$) of the left and right limbs. Thus,

$$\dot{\phi} =\ ^2 \omega - a \sin(\phi) - 2b \sin(2\phi) + \sqrt{Q}\zeta_t \qquad (1)$$

The overdot signifies the first time derivative, $\Delta\omega$ is a detuning term that can be equated with the difference ($\omega_{left} - \omega_{right}$) between the uncoupled frequencies of the limbs, and a and b are coefficients that determine the relative strengths of attractors for the coordination at or in the vicinity of the values $\phi = 0$ and $\phi = \pi$. The faster interactions among the internal subsystems are identified with ζ_t, a Gaussian white noise process of strength $Q > 0$. The predictive successes of the state dynamics expressed through Equation 1 (summarized in Amazeen, Amazeen, & Turvey, 1998) indicate the intimate connection between motor timing and stability and the significance of symmetry breaking ($\Delta\omega \neq 0$).

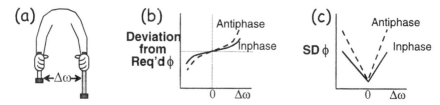

Figure 1. (a) A method for studying rhythmic synergies. Differences in pendulums control the asymmetry or detuning $\Delta\omega$. Typical data, showing changes in (b) phase deviation and (c) the standard deviation of phase as a function of $\Delta\omega$ and required phase (in vs. anti).

Figure 1a shows a method for investigating the predictions of Equation 1. Pendulums held in the two hands can be of varied lengths and masses, thereby manipulating their preferred frequencies. In this example, movement speed is freely chosen. If the pendulums are the same, $\Delta\omega = 0$. Among the basic facts of bimanual rhythmic coordination are: (a) increased deviation from required relative phase when $\Delta\omega \neq 0$; (b) greater change in stable relative phase per change in $\Delta\omega$ for intended antiphase than intended inphase coordination (Figure 1b); and (c) increased variability in relative phase (SDϕ) when $\Delta\omega \neq 0$ (Figure 1c).

Rhythmic coordination in older adults

Establishing spatio-temporal relations among body segments is made possible by information about the states of muscles, limb segments, and limb attachments. This information is realized in the patterned activity of mechanoreceptors in response to distortions of the body's tissues due to movement and environmental contacts. Mechanoreceptors decline with age and certain illnesses, however, leaving individuals with reduced awareness of their bodies and of the surfaces and objects they are in contact with. This neuropathy results in the loss or partial loss of sensitivity in touch and the muscle sense, with unknown consequences for everyday functionality (manipulating objects, using tools, walking). For example, it may have consequences for the on-line tuning of muscular synergies that enables coordinated manual behaviors.

How similar are the collective dynamics of interlimb coordination across age levels? We have compared 4 younger (mean 25 years) and 4 older (mean 68 years) adults in the task shown in Figure 1a. In an experiment with inphase and antiphase coordination and three values of $\Delta\omega$ (0, ±2 rad/s), ANOVA found no age effects on relative phase or its fluctuations in either coordination mode and no interactions of age with $\Delta\omega$ (Figure 2). Within the limits of the experiment, it would seem that both groups abide by Equation 1. Variability of performance measures are reported to be greater in the elderly (e.g., Darling, Cooke, & Brown, 1989). The results shown in Figure 2 suggest that the opposite may be true when one is considering the moment-to-moment variability of a rhythmic coordination. Despite age-related decrements in sensory structures, older adults showed no apparent deterioration in rhythmic coordination of homologous limbs at a self-selected pace. It remains to be seen whether interlimb behavior of individuals with reduced proprioceptive information may be affected when the coupling between limbs is weakened—in tasks that require, for example, movement at faster speeds or coordination of nonhomologous limbs.

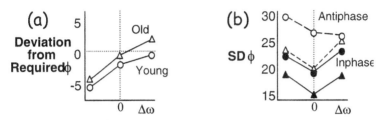

Figure 2. Deviation in degrees from intended relative phase (a) and variability in degrees of relative phase (b) as a function of $\Delta\omega$. Anti-phase (dashed lines) produces greater fluctuations than in-phase (solid lines) both for young and old participants.

Rhythmic coordination and peripheral neuropathy

A more dramatic loss of sensitivity accompanies the clinical condition *peripheral neuropathy*, a functional deafferentation that accompanies certain diseases or injury. Individuals with neuropathy cannot feel anything touching the affected limb, nor can they feel the limb itself (its location, orientation, or extent). Given that proprioceptive information may be particularly important for maintaining the co-ordination of the limbs during bimanual movements, peripheral neuropathy presents an interesting test of Equation 1.

The patient CA was diagnosed with peripheral neuropathy in the left arm, extending from the hand through the elbow with some involvement of the shoulder. The condition was due to a growth on the sensory tract at the top of the spine that appeared at 40 years of age. The lack of sensation in the left arm was confirmed by an identification task in which a succession of plastic numbers (approximately 2 cm × 2 cm × 1 cm deep) were placed in her hand. Without being able to see the numbers, she correctly identified all using the unaffected (right) hand. With her left hand, however, she could identify none of the numbers correctly (and, indeed, dropped them because she could not feel that they were in her hand).

The pendulum task was used again: Inphase and antiphase coordination performed without vision, freely chosen movement speed, and five values of $\Delta\omega$ (0, ±1 rad/s, ±2 rad/s). Figure 3 shows the pattern of results as a function of intended phase and $\Delta\omega$. But note how large the phase deviation is compared to the elderly participants (Figure 2a vs. Figure 3a). SDϕ, in contrast, is not unusual (Figure 2b vs. Figure 3b). A phase deviation of 30° typically is seen only under especially challenging conditions (e.g., speeded coordination with concomitant cognitive activity; Pellecchia & Turvey, 2001). The observed phase deviation may reflect an attentional asymmetry. Attention directed to the left limb leads to a coordination dynamic that is more left leading (Amazeen et al., 1997). Given the loss of proprioceptive information about the left arm, CA may well have directed attention to that side (e.g., so as not to drop the pen-dulum). Of note, SDϕ was lowest for zero detuning, suggesting this was still the most stable condition, despite a phase shift greater than that demonstrated for the negative detuning conditions.

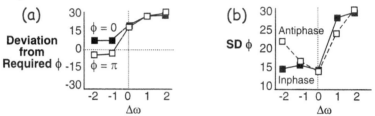

Figure 3. (a) Phase deviation follows the standard topology but is shifted for individual with peripheral neuropathy in one arm. (b) SDϕ replicates the standard result.

Conclusions

The human ability to synchronize the movements of two limbs is fundamental. It has been argued that the coupling between limbs is informational (rather than neural). Just as the contribution of cognitive activity plays out in the fundamental coordination equation so, too, does the damping of information that accompanies neuropathy. Nonetheless, the field-like structure of the mechanoreceptor support for haptic perception allows the basic features of bimanual coordination to be preserved.

References

Amazeen, E. L., Amazeen, P. G., Treffner, P. J., & Turvey, M. T. (1997). Attention and handedness in bimanual coordination dynamics. *Journal of Experimental Psychology: Human Perception and Performance, 23*, 1552-1560.

Amazeen, P. G., Amazeen, E., & Turvey, M. T. (1998). Breaking the reflectional symmetry of interlimb coordination dynamics. *Journal of Motor Behavior, 30*, 199-216.

Acknowledgments. This research was supported by NSF Grant SBR 023036 and a grant from the Provost's Office at the University of Connecticut.

Studies in Perception and Action VIII
H. Heft & K. L. Marsh (Eds.)
© *2005 Lawrence Erlbaum Associates, Inc.*

(De)Stabilization of Required vs. Spontaneous Postural Dynamics with Learning

Elise Faugloire[1], Benoît G. Bardy[1,2], & Thomas A. Stoffregen[3]

[1] Research Center in Sport Sciences, University of Paris Sud 11, Orsay, France, [2] Institut Universitaire de France, [3] School of Kinesiology, University of Minnesota, Minneapolis, USA

The dynamical perspective of motor learning emphasizes reciprocal influence between the pre-existing coordination modes (those naturally preferred) and the learning process (e.g., Zanone & Kelso, 1992). The theory predicts that learning a new coordination mode will destabilize pre-existing modes. However, studies of bi-manual coordination (e.g., Zanone & Kelso, 1992; Lee, Swinnen, & Verschueren, 1995) have yielded conflicting results. We examined the consequences of learning a new coordination mode on coordination dynamics in stance. In previous studies (e.g., Bardy et al., 1999), two pre-existing ankle-hip coordination modes have been revealed: an in-phase mode for low frequencies or amplitudes (ankle-hip relative phase around 30°), and an anti-phase mode for higher frequencies or amplitudes (ankle-hip relative phase around 180°). We evaluated ankle-hip coordination dynamics in two complementary tasks, before and after participants learned a relative phase of 90°. In Task 1, the goal for standing participants was to track a moving target with their head: the ankle-hip coordination emerged *spontaneously*, without instruction about the relative phase to produce. In Task 2, participants were asked to produce specific values of ankle-hip relative phase; hence, the ankle-hip mode was *required*. We investigated how learning 90° influenced the coordination dynamics in Task 1 (spontaneous) and Task 2 (required).

Method

Twelve participants performed the four sessions of the experiment over 5 days: the pre-test (day 1), the learning sessions (days 2, 3 and 4), the post-test (end of day 4) and the retention test (day 5, one week after day 4). Days 1, 2, 3 and 4 were consecutive. In each session, participants stood upright in front of a large screen (3 m H × 2 m V). Electro-goniometers (Biometrics, Inc.) fixed on the left hip and ankle measured the angular joint motion. Postural coordination was characterized by the ankle-hip relative phase (ϕ_{rel}) and its standard deviation ($SD\phi_{rel}$).

Test sessions (pre-test, post-test and retention test) consisted of the two tasks mentioned above. *Task 1 (spontaneous coordination):* The screen displayed a square target oscillating at 0.2 Hz along the antero-posterior axis. Participants tried to maintain a constant distance between their head and the target. According to previous results (e.g., Bardy et al., 1999), two target amplitudes were tested in order to evaluate both pre-existing postural patterns: a small target amplitude (8 cm) favouring the emergence of the in-phase pattern, and a large target amplitude (25 cm), favouring the anti-phase pattern. Three trials of 8 oscillations were performed for each amplitude. *Task 2 (required coordination):* Participants were asked to perform twelve ankle-hip relative phases in a randomized order: 0°, 30°, 60°, 90°, 120°, 150°, 180°, 210°, 240°, 270°, 300°, 330°. Three trials of 8 oscillations were performed for each required pattern, with an imposed frequency of 0.2 Hz. Participants received real-time visual feedback about their performance through a Lissajous figure (ankle angle vs. hip angle) showing the required relative phase (elliptic shape to follow) and the actual movements performed (a trace drawn in real time in the figure).

During the learning sessions, participants practiced a non-spontaneous relative phase of 90° using the real-time visual feedback. Sixty trials of 8 oscillations were performed, with 25 trials on Day 2, 25 trials on Day 3 and 10 trials on Day 4. Here we present no data relating to performance in the learning sessions.

Results

Spontaneous coordination. At pre-test, 7 participants produced the expected in-phase pattern for the small target amplitude (the 5 others produced an anti-phase mode), and 9 performed the expected anti-phase pattern for the large target amplitude (the 3 others produced an in-phase mode). Only the results for the participants who produced the expected coordination mode are presented here. At post-test, a modification of the initial spontaneous pattern was observed in the direction of the learned pattern (90°) for the majority of participants: 5 out of the 7 in-phase participants for the small target amplitude (Figure 1A), and 6 out of the 9 anti-phase participants for the large target amplitude (Figure 1B), Watson-Williams, $Fs(1, 40) > 5.15$, $p < .05$. This modification in the direction of the learned pattern persisted one week after the post-test (i.e., at the retention test) for all participants in the small target amplitude, and for 4 participants (out of 6) in the large target amplitude (Watson-Williams between post-test and retention test, $Fs(1, 40) < 1.06$, *ns*).

Required coordination. Absolute error AE (absolute difference between required and performed relative phases), and $SD\phi_{rel}$ are presented in Figure 2. At pre-test, accuracy (AE) and stability ($SD\phi_{rel}$) were greater for the required patterns around anti-phase, and decreased as the required patterns moved away from 180°. The curves for post-test and retention test revealed that learning 90° improved and homogenized accuracy and stability for all required patterns. This

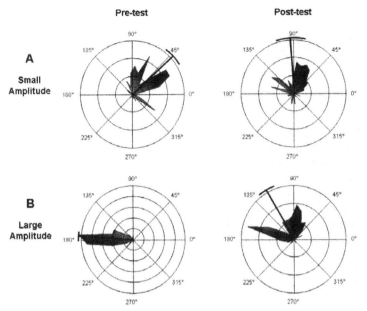

Figure 1. Frequency distributions for spontaneous relative phase (Task 1) at pre-test and post-test. A: *N* = 5. B: *N* = 6 (cf. text). Each concentric circle corresponds to 5% of the total distribution of observed relative phase values. The dark radial line and the arc of circle represent the circular mean direction and its 95% confidence interval, respectively.

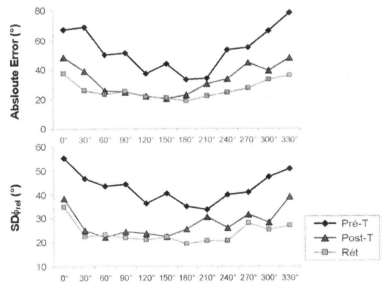

Figure 2. Performance (absolute error and standard deviation of relative phase) for the 12 imposed patterns (Task 2) at pre-test, post-test and retention test.

improvement was confirmed by Pattern (12) × Test (3) repeated measures ANOVAs conducted on AE and $SD\phi_{rel}$, showing a significant effect of Pattern, $Fs(11, 121) > 11.99$, $p < .05$, of Test, $Fs(2, 22) > 52.26$, $p < 0.05$, and of the Pattern × Test interaction, $Fs(22, 242) > 1.75$, $p < .05$.

Discussion

Our results for the *spontaneous* postural modes are in accordance with the theoretical predictions: as a new coordination mode was learned, its emergence competed with pre-existing in-phase and anti-phase patterns. However, for the *required* postural modes, the general improvement of all tested patterns was unexpected, given the theoretical principles and previous results on bi-manual coordination. Despite the fact that our Task 2 and our experimental design were very close to classical bi-manual studies, the increase in performance for every required coordination mode contrasted with the destabilization effect (e.g., Zanone & Kelso, 1992) or the absence of modification (e.g., Lee et al., 1995) observed for the bi-manual system. It seems that learning an ankle-hip relative phase of 90° led to improvement of this pattern of coordination itself, but also to better control of ankle and hip movements in general. The practice of any ankle-hip pattern could have led to the progress and homogenization of performance for any phase relation. The different results observed in postural and bi-manual systems suggest that the consequences of learning are not equivalent for different effector systems.

References

Bardy, B. G., Marin, L., Stoffregen, T. A., & Bootsma, R. J. (1999). Postural coordination modes considered as emergent phenomena. *Journal of Experimental Psychology: Human Perception and Performance, 25,* 1284-1301.

Lee, T. D., Swinnen, S. P., & Verschueren, S. (1995). Relative phase alterations during bimanual skill acquisition. *Journal of Motor Behavior, 27,* 263-274.

Zanone, P. G., & Kelso, J. A. S. (1992). Evolution of behavioral attractors with learning: Nonequilibrium phase transitions. *Journal of Experimental Psychology: Human Perception and Performance, 18,* 403-421.

Acknowledgements. Research supported by Enactive Interfaces (European IST contract #002114), and by NSF (BCS-0236627). We thank Bruno Mantel for the design of the real-time visual feedback display.

Studies in Perception and Action VIII
H. Heft & K. L. Marsh (Eds.)
© *2005 Lawrence Erlbaum Associates, Inc.*

Effects of Task and Individual Characteristics on Microslips of Action

Naoya Hirose

School of Human Sciences, Sugiyama Jogakuen University, Japan

In daily life, we sometimes perform erroneous actions against our intentions. These errors are called action slips, and the frequencies of their occurrence have been reported at about three times per week in a diary study (Reason, 1984). In this regard, slips rarely take place, and most of our actions are carried out correctly and smoothly. If we turn our eyes to the environment, we are surrounded by many objects. Living in such a cluttered environment, can we smoothly perform appropriate actions relative to specific objects in most cases? From close observation of everyday task performance, Reed and Schoenherr (1992) found that people made slip-like small corrections frequently. These are called *microslips* (Reed & Schoenherr, 1992) or *micro-explorations* (Sasaki, Mishima, Suzuki, & Ohkura, 1995). Reed and Schoenherr categorized microslips into four types: (a) *hesitations*, such as reaching towards an object, stopping momentarily, then continuing to reach and grasp it; (b) *trajectory changes*, such as reaching an object, and then shifting to another object; (c) *hand shape changes*, any rapid changes in hand shape; (d) *touches and take/gives*, such as touching an irrelevant object before reaching the target. Basically, microslips are microscopic corrections of the hand that are commonly observed in everyday activities. Previous studies of microslips have been devoted to examining the occurrence of microslips using the same task; thus they have given little attention to different task demands. The main purpose of this study was to investigate how different task constraints influence the occurrence of microslips. In addition to this main purpose, it is known that there are considerable individual differences in microslip incidence, so it would be interesting to see if the individual characteristics maintain over different tasks. Thus, the present study examined the occurrence of microslips in two different tasks using a within-subject design.

Method

Fourteen female undergraduates participated in the experiment, receiving partial course credit. The participants were asked to engage in a coffee making task and a block building task. In the first session, participants were instructed to make two cups of instant coffee: one with cream and sugar, and one with cream only. Materials such as coffee powder and sugar were contained in plastic cups on the table. Unnecessary items such as forks, a pot of cold water and others were also placed on the table. In the second session, participants were asked to use Lego® blocks to create anything they would like on a building plate. The intervals of two sessions were about six months. All actions that the participant performed were videotaped by a camera placed in front of her.

Coding of video clips was done independently by two coders other than the author. The inter-rater agreement of the occurrence of slips was 0.85, and any coding differences were settled by the author. In addition to microslips, erroneous actions such as action slips and mistakes were also coded. Thus, slips of action were classified into six categories: the erroneous action, the four types of microslips in the previous studies, and others. A microslip was also coded in terms of its action transition (alter, cancel, resume), pause (or not) and touch (or not) at the time of occurrence, based on a newly developed coding scheme (Hirose, 2004).

Results and Discussion

Participants made more slips in the block than in the coffee task (41.93 vs. 13.00, $t(13) = 3.37$, $p < .005$). The rates per minute for slips were also different between the block and coffee tasks (10.44 vs. 6.75, $t(13) = 2.97$, $p < .05$), whereas participants took more time in the block than in the coffee task (235.9s vs. 117.0s, $t(13) = 3.71$, $p < .005$). The difference in rate per unit of time between the two tasks suggests that the larger number of slips in the block task was not due to the longer time to complete the task. Thus, the block task should have some essential features that cause more slips.

All slips were classified into six types (Figure 1). A two-way repeated measures ANOVA revealed significant main effects of task, $F(1, 13) = 8.85$, $p < .05$, and of slip type, $F(5, 65) = 38.86$, $p < .001$, and a significant interaction between them, $F(5, 65) = 9.21$, $p < .05$. Closer inspection of the results revealed that there were more trajectory changes and touches in the block than in the coffee task ($t(13) = 2.48$, $p < .05$, $t(13) = 6.21$, $p < .001$, respectively). As is the case with the previous studies (Reed & Schoenherr, 1992; Sasaki et al. 1995), in the coffee task, hesitations and trajectory changes accounted for the majority of microslips, and touches and hand shape changes were rarely observed. In the block task, however, touches were also frequently observed.

Microslips were further analyzed in terms of transitions, pauses and touches. Because of the differences in frequencies between tasks, the following analyses of microslips were based on percentages, and statistics were carried out on the transformed variables. Action transitions at the occurrence of microslips are shown in Figure 2. A two-way repeated measures ANOVA revealed a significant main effect of transition, $F(2, 26) = 39.70$, $p < .001$, and a significant interaction, $F(2, 26) = 6.96$, $p < .01$. Closer inspection of the results revealed that there were more alter and less resume transitions in the block than in the coffee task ($t(13) = 2.50$, $p < .05$, $t(13) = 3.29$, $p < .01$, respectively). The result suggests that because the block task involves more freedom in choice of action, participants more frequently altered the target (block to reach or place to put), and less frequently resumed the same action.

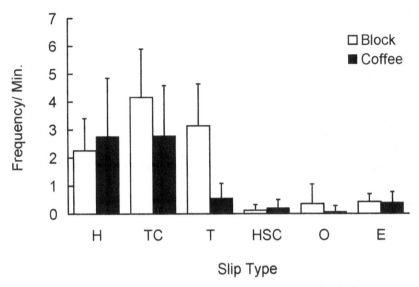

Figure 1. Mean rates of frequency per minute for types of slips in both tasks. H: hesitations, TC: trajectory changes, T: touches and take/gives, HSC: hand shape changes, O: other microslips, E: erroneous actions (action slips and mistakes).

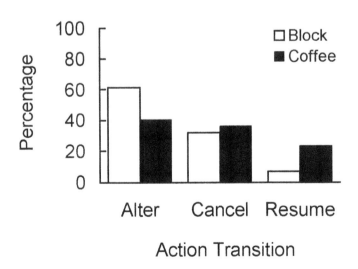

Figure 2. Percentages of action transition of microslips in both tasks.

Percentages of pauses at the occurrence of microslips were 45.84% in the block task and 51.46% in the coffee task, and they did not differ, $t(13) = 0.293$, *ns.* On the other hand, percentages of touch were 35.93% in the block task and 10.53% in the coffee task, and they differed significantly, $t(13) = 5.55, p < .001$. This result is consistent with the above slip-type analysis. One possible reason for the larger number of touches in the block task is that touches are influenced by the hand-object relations.

Correlations between tasks were calculated on the number of frequency, duration and slip types, and the percentages of action transition, pause and touch. None of the correlation coefficients were very high ($rs < .35$) nor statistically significant. Participants made different slips in the different tasks, and individuals' characteristic slips across tasks were not found. Consequently, the present study suggests that the incidence of microslips depends more on the task constraints than on the individual characteristics. Because the number of participants was not large enough to reliably detect medium-sized relationships, future research should confirm this conclusion.

References

Hirose, N. (2004). How to describe non-smooth action sequences: Categorization of microslips. *Journal of Ecological Psychology*, *1*, 19-24. (In Japanese)

Reason, J. (1984). Lapses of attention in everyday life. In R. Parasuraman & D. R. Davies (Eds.), *Varieties of attention* (pp. 99-102). New York: Academic Press.

Reed, E. S., & Schoenherr, D. (1992). *The neuropathology of everyday life: On the nature and significance of micro-slips in everyday activities.* Unpublished manuscript.

Sasaki, M., Mishima, H., Suzuki, K., & Ohkura, M. (1995). Observations on micro-exploration in everyday activities. In B. G. Bardy, R. J. Bootsma & Y. Guiard (Eds.), *Studies in perception and action III* (pp. 99-102). Hillsdale, NJ: Lawrence Erlbaum Associates.

Acknowledgment. This research was supported by NSF Grant SBR 00-04097.

Studies in Perception and Action VIII
H. Heft & K. L. Marsh (Eds.)
© *2005 Lawrence Erlbaum Associates, Inc.*

Complexity and Stability in Isometric Force Production

S. Lee Hong, Jacob J. Sosnoff, & Karl M. Newell

Department of Kinesiology, The Pennsylvania State University, USA

Slifkin and Newell (1999, 2000) have found that increasing the required constant level of isometric force results in an inverted-U pattern of output complexity, indexed by ApEn (approximate entropy). Pincus (1994) proposed that the decrease in the complexity of a system's output is due to the increased isolation of its components, while Von Holst (1939/1973) suggested that greater coupling strength between two oscillating limbs leads to greater stability in their global dynamics. Whether or not these ideas are congruent is dependent on whether stability at the global level leads to greater variability at the local level and vice-versa. This study is aimed at examining the relation between the non-linear coupling of components and the complexity of the normal force output from the perspective of global and local complexity.

Method

Adults (mean age 26.3 years) participated in this study. All subjects were right hand dominant, with normal or corrected-to-normal vision, and no history of any neuromuscular disorders. All the subjects signed informed consent forms prior to participation, with approval for the experimental protocol from the Pennsylvania State University Institutional Review Board. A 3-dimensional load cell (ATI Industrial Automation, Garner, North Carolina) was placed in the center of a table top 75 cm above the ground, with the surface of the load cell 2 cm above that of the table (Figure 1). Each participant completed an isometric constant force production task with their index finger at 5%, 15%, 25%, and 35% of their maximal voluntary contraction (MVC), completing 3 trials at each percentage of MVC. The 3 force dimensions were defined as the subcomponents, or local variables, while the relative phase between the resultant force vectors and the transducer surface served as the global variable. ApEn values were calculated for the vertical force (Fz) vector and absolute continuous relative phase values of these angles were then divided into $10°$ bins ranging from 0 to $360°$ (Figure 2). The percentage of the total time series in the bin with the highest frequency counts was then calculated as an index of the stability of the global parameter.

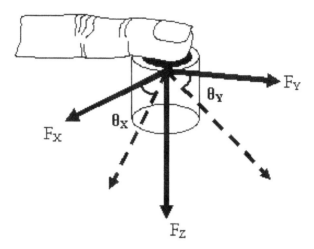

Figure 1. Schematic illustration of the force vectors and resultant force angles.

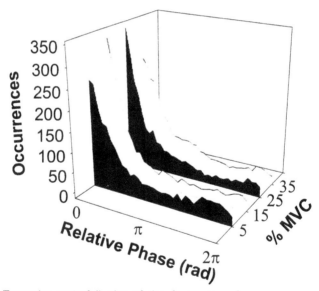

Figure 2. Exemplar waterfall plot of the frequency of occurrences at various phase values at each % MVC condition for a single participant.

Results and Discussion

Similar to Slifkin and Newell (1999, 2000), mean force increased linearly with percentage of MVC while the changes in the standard deviation (SD) of the force output were curvilinear with an increasing rate. ApEn values showed an inverted-U shaped change as the percentage of MVC increased. This curvilinear change was fitted with a second-order polynomial, with an r^2 value of 0.90 (Figure 3). An inverted-U change was also found in the stability of the preferred relative phase mode and the function for the percentage of the time series captured by the peak relative phase value bin was similar to that of ApEn. This curve was also fitted with a second-order polynomial with an obtained r^2 value of 0.92.

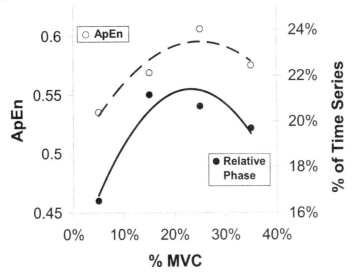

Figure 3. Fitted 2nd order polynomial curves for both ApEn values and peak relative phase percentages of the total time series.

The findings of the force variability in this study have replicated those of Slifkin and Newell (1999, 2000), but have extended them by finding similar patterns of changes of all the force vectors, in both mean force and its standard deviation within a trial. The similarity between the patterns of change in ApEn values and the stability of the preferred relative phase pattern supports both Von Holst and Pincus' hypotheses, as increases in the irregularity of the normal force output, the local behaviours, were reflected in increases in non-linear coupling strength, the stability of the global behaviour, despite the fact that only visual feedback of the normal force had been provided. Overall, these findings also suggest the possibility that the control of motor actions occurs primarily through the constraining of the global dynamics. The flexibility of biological systems lies in its ability to change its local output complexity so as to adapt to changes in the task goal or environment, adapting to the confluence of constraints placed upon it by increasing or decreasing the coupling strength between its subcomponents.

References

Pincus, S. M. (1994). Greater signal regularity may indicate increased system isolation. *Mathematical Bioscience, 122,* 161-81.

Slifkin, A. B., & Newell, K. M. (1999). Noise, information transmission and force variability. *Journal of Experimental Psychology: Human Perception and Performance, 25,* 837-851.

Slifkin, A. B. & Newell, K. M. (2000). Variability and noise in continuous force production. *Journal of Motor Behavior, 32,* 141-50.

Von Holst, E. (1973). *The collected papers of Erich Von Holst: Vol 1. The behavioral physiology of animal and man* (R. Martin, Ed. & Trans.). Coral Gables: University of Miami Press (Work in original language published in 1939).

Studies in Perception and Action VIII
H. Heft & K. L. Marsh (Eds.)
© *2005 Lawrence Erlbaum Associates, Inc.*

A New Method for Studying Non-Stationary Signals in Human Movement: The Cross-Wavelet Transform

Johann Issartel[1], Ludovic Marin[1], Thomas Bardainne[2], Philippe Gaillot[2-3], & Marielle Cadopi[1]

[1]Motor Efficiency and Motor Deficiency Laboratory, University of Montpellier 1, France; [2]Geophysic Imagery Laboratory, University of "Pau et des pays de l'Adour", Pau, France; [3]Center for Deep Earth Exploration, Japan Agency for Marine-Earth Science and Technology, Yokohama Kanagawa, Japan

The goal of this study was to present a new method for analyzing non-stationary signals in human motor behavior: the wavelet transform (WT). We particularly focused on the cross-wavelet transform (an extension of the WT) that gives information about interactions between two signals. Although this method finds its application in several fields like physiology (Jobert et al., 1994) and neuroscience (Karrasch et al., 2004), almost no studies exist in experimental psychology and particularly in motor control.

The cross-wavelet transform (CWT) has two major advantages over other more classical methods. Firstly, the CWT permits us to characterize the nature of the interactions (e.g. motor coordination) between two signals regardless of the nature of data (stationary and non-stationary). Secondly, this method permits us to analyze the temporal evolution of the frequency, amplitude and phase properties of a (non-stationary) signal. The originality of the CWT (and the WT) is to transform the signal into a time-frequency representation that contains the same amount of information as the original time-series.

Explanation of the Method

The cross-wavelet transform's method is based on the time-frequency plane. The interest in performing the analysis in the time-frequency plane is justified by the fact that typically, for non-stationary signals, interpretation of temporal analysis results without a frequency component is difficult, as interpretation of frequency analysis results is difficult without any temporal information. The time-frequency plane (Figure 1a) is defined by the time interval that spans the signal and the frequency ranging from zero to the Nyquist frequency. The idea is to 'tile' a plane with rectangles, usually called Heisenberg cells, and assign to each cell a magnitude representing the power of the signal in the time-frequency interval spanned by the cell. Each cell can be compared to a window. Moreover, the wavelet transform provides a flexible time-scale window that narrows when focusing on small-scale features and widens on large-scale features (Figure 1a). The highest frequencies can be well localized in time, and the lowest frequency components can be accurately quantified. Such tiling is obtained since this method outstrips the window Fourier transform (WFT) by introducing the notion of dilatation/contraction of the time-scale window. The tiling of the plane depends on the choice of the analyzing function called the mother function. The choice of the mother function (the wavelet) is neither unique nor arbitrary. The mother function is a function with unit energy chosen so that it has (1) compact support, or sufficiently fast decay to obtain localization in time, and (2) zero mean. The requirement of zero mean is called the admissibility condition of the wavelet. These two conditions open up the possibility to create different functions as wavelets (Torrence et al., 1998). The determination of the mother function depends on the nature of the signal and the kind of information that has to be pointed out (see Daubechies, 1992). Consequently, several mother functions exist. The most popular wavelet is Morlet wavelet (Figure 1b), a complex mother function (Torrence et al., 1998) that allows any analysis of the interaction between two signals. The results obtained with such a wavelet are represented in two spectrograms. A spectrogram is the name of the time-frequency representation of the wavelet transform (Flandrin, 1988). The first spectrogram illustrates the CWT spectrum (or its square root, i.e. modulus). On this spectrogram, we can analyze the evolution of intensity of the interaction between the two signals for each frequency as function of the time. In the second spectrogram, we have complementary information that is the temporal evolution of the difference of phase between the two signals for each frequency. Statistically, to consider if a

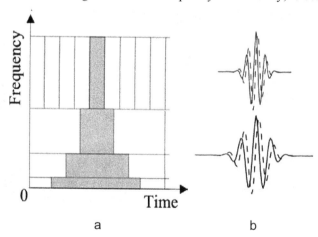

a   b

Figure 1. Tiling of the time-frequency plane (Figure 1a). The highest frequencies can be well localized in time, and the lowest frequency components accurately quantified. This time-frequency plane representation is obtained by a translation and a dilatation/contraction of the complex mother function: Morlet (Figure 1b). The Morlet mother function is a complex-valued function (real part = solid line, imaginary part = dashed line) allowing a difference of phase measure.

frequency is significantly present in the signal, we define a level in the CWT spectrum. Above it the frequencies are statistically significant (details of this test are explained by Torrence et al., 1998).

Illustration

As an illustration of the CWT method, let's consider the displacement of the center of gravity of two players during a fencing match. The CWT method is the most relevant method to analyze the temporal evolution of the interaction of the frequencies of their displacements. In Figure 2a (CWT spectrum), we can observe that the two players systematically move at a common frequency. We can notice that, in the middle of Figure 2a, both players change from a low frequency to a high frequency. In Figure 2b (difference of phase), we can observe

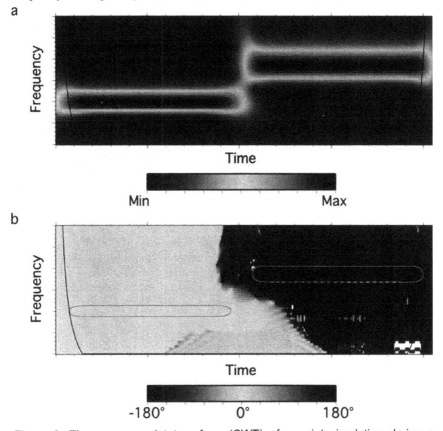

Figure 2. The cross-wavelet transform (CWT) of a point simulation during a fencing match. In both spectrograms, the curved black lines represent edge-effects and the statistically significant frequencies are inside areas delimited by the black (or white) lines. Figure 2a represents the CWT spectrum. The two players perform the same frequency in the first half of the point then they

simultaneously change frequency. Figure 2b, represents the difference of phase between the two players - they shift from in phase to out of phase of 180°.
that this modulation of frequency produces a phase shift of 180° between the two players. Before the frequency change they were in phase (for the low frequency), after the frequency change they converge to an anti-phase pattern (for the high frequency). These two spectrograms (Figures 2a and b) give us a good estimation of the nature of the relationship (phase and frequency evolution in time) between two persons during a fencing match. These properties could be interesting for the coaches of these players as they can observe individual strategies and the relationship of domination between the players.

Conclusion

In conclusion, the method of the CWT is available to study non-stationary movements in human motor behavior. This method can reveal small changes (amplitude and frequency modulation) in the interaction of two signals while also revealing multi-scale properties of the signal (frequency combinations, difference of phase) by conserving the temporal evolution of the signals. Hopefully motor control researchers will be able to use the CWT to open new perspectives in human movement analysis.

References

Daubechies, I. (1992). *Ten lectures on wavelets*. Philadelphia, PA: SIAM.
Flandrin, P. (1988). Separability, positivity and minimum uncertainty in time-frequency energy distributions. *Journal of Mathematical Physics, 39*, 4016-4040.
Jobert, M., Tismer, C., Poiseau, E., & Schulz, H. (1994). Wavelets - a new tool in sleep biosignal analysis. *Journal of Sleep Research, 3*, 223–232.
Karrasch, M., Laine, M., Rapinoja, P., & Krause, C.M. (2004). Effects of normal aging on event-related desynchronization/synchronization during a memory task in humans. *Neuroscience Letters, 366*, 18-23.
Torrence, C., & Compo, G.P. (1998). A practical guide to wavelet analysis. *Bulletin of the American Meteorological Society, 79*, 61-78.

Studies in Perception and Action VIII
H. Heft & K. L. Marsh (Eds.)
© *2005 Lawrence Erlbaum Associates, Inc.*

Stability of Coordination Between Upper and Lower Body Rhythms During Treadmill Walking: Response to Changes in Walking Speed

B.A. Kay, T. G. Rhodes, A. Hajnal, & R. W. Isenhower

Department of Psychology & Center for the Ecological Study of
Perception and Action, University of Connecticut, Storrs, CT, USA

In previous work (Kay, Harrison, & Rhodes, in preparation), we investigated the coordination that occurs when participants rhythmically swung hand-held pendulums while also walking on a treadmill, under steady-state conditions. We found (1) low-integer frequency locking (e.g., 1:1, 2:1) between the upper body and locomotory rhythms in about 1/3 of the trials, (2) intermittent frequency locking, or (3) no apparent locking at all between the two rhythmic tasks. In this experiment, we address the stability of these modes of coordination between the upper and lower body tasks by changing the treadmill speed while participants perform the task, resulting in discrete shifts in stride frequency. If the coupling between the two tasks is significant, mode of coordination· and coupling strength should be stable to this parametric perturbation. In addition, we hypothesize that, although the two rhythms are apparently independent when no locking is present, some dependence will be evident in changes in frequency of the upper body task as the lower body frequency changes.

Method

11 participants swung hand-held pendulums of three lengths (short, medium, and long) about the wrist joint while walking on a powered treadmill at 2 mph (3.22 kph). After 30s, the treadmill was either sped up or slowed down 0.5 mph (0.8 kph), and remained in the altered speed for the remainder of each 80s trial. Control trials with no speed change were also collected. Portable electrogoniometers were used to record wrist and knee angles. Synchrograms were used to detect the presence of frequency locking (Figure 1). T-tests were used to evaluate whether rhythmic frequencies had changed after the speed change. Coherence and cross-average mutual information measures were used to assess the magnitude of coupling among the four joints.

Results and Discussion

As previously observed, frequency locking, intermittent, and non-locking modes of coordination were found, both before and after the speed change, depending on the combination of pendulum length and treadmill speed. Exclud-

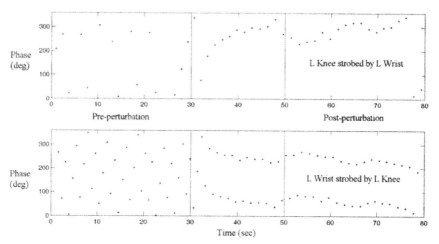

Figure 1. Example synchrogram, showing non-mode locked behavior before the speed change and 1:2 frequency locking (knees:wrists) after the change.

ing intermittent behavior, for most trials the same mode was maintained across the speed change (Table 1). Intermittent behavior was much less stable, and transitioned most often to no apparent locking. No transitions from one frequency lock to another were observed. Treadmill speed changes always induced frequency shifts in the locomotory rhythm, and in most trials induced changes in the upper body frequency as well, even when the two rhythms were not mode locked (62% of such trials; Figure 2). Intra- and inter-girdle coherence and cross average mutual information measures were statistically invariant across the speed change (Figure 3).

		Mode, Post-Perturbation			
		Intermittent	Not Locked	1:1	1:2
Mode, Pre-perturbation	Intermittent	27.3	45.5	21.2	6.1
	Not Locked	22.2	63.0	9.3	5.6
	1:1	12.8	20.5	66.7	0
	1:2	0	16.7	0	83.3

Table 1. Mode transition matrix, i.e., percentage of modes observed pre- and post-perturbation.

The results indicate, overall, that although the two rhythms are nominally independent of each other, there appears to be a graded level of obligatory coupling between the two. Both qualitatively and quantitatively that coupling was stable in the face of the parametric change in stride frequency in most cases. Influences between the two rhythms were almost always seen, even when obvious inter-rhythm coordination was not present.

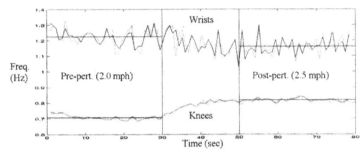

Figure 2. Example of frequency shifts in both rhythms, even though no mode locking was detected before or after the speed change for this trial.

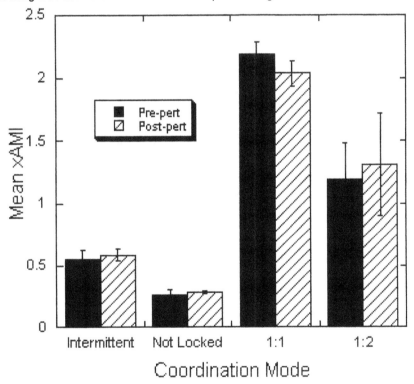

Figure 3. Mean cross average mutual information between girdles for trials in which the same coordination mode was observed before and after the speed change, by coordination mode found. Error bars represent 1 standard error.

References

Kay, B. A., Harrison, S. J., & Rhodes, T. G. (in preparation). *Coordination between upper and lower body rhythms during treadmill walking.*

Acknowledgements. Supported by UConn UCRF Grant FRS 444889 .

Studies in Perception and Action VIII
H. Heft & K. L. Marsh (Eds.)
© *2005 Lawrence Erlbaum Associates, Inc.*

Effects of Coordination Stability on Simple Reaction Time in Dual Task Performance

Annie J. Olmstead[1,2], Ryan Arzamarski[1], Miguel Moreno[1,2], & Geraldine L. Pellecchia[1,3]

[1]Center for the Ecological Study of Perception and Action, University of Connecticut, Storrs, Connecticut, USA; [2]Haskins Laboratories, New Haven, Connecticut, USA; [3]Department of Physical Therapy, University of Connecticut, Storrs, Connecticut, USA

Humans routinely engage simultaneously in motor and cognitive tasks. For instance, it is not out of the ordinary to carry on a conversation while walking with a friend. Psychologists have long been interested in humans' ability to perform such task combinations. Recently, considerable research has investigated the influence of cognitive activity on the dynamics of interlimb coordination. Pellecchia and Turvey (2001) examined effects of performing arithmetic tasks on rhythmic coordination using a wrist pendulum paradigm in which participants swung hand-held pendulums back and forth. A series of experiments showed that performing cognitive tasks shifted the attractors, i.e. the stable states, of the coordination. Such research demonstrates that seemingly unrelated cognitive activity impacts coordination dynamics, and raises the reciprocal question of whether coordination influences cognition. Results of earlier studies addressing this question are equivocal. Temprado, Zanone, Monno, and Laurent (1999) examined whether cognitive task performance changed as a function of coordination stability. Participants performed simultaneous bimanual coordination and reaction time (RT) tasks. The coordination task involved holding a joystick in each hand and performing forearm pronation and supination in both more stable, in-phase, and less stable, anti-phase, patterns. The RT task required participants to respond as quickly as possible to an auditory signal by pressing joystick triggers. Results showed that mean RT was significantly faster (15 ms) for in-phase than for anti-phase movements. In a subsequent study using a similar experimental set-up, (except that RT responses were made via foot pedals), Temprado and colleagues (2001) reported RT was statistically equivalent for in-phase and anti-phase patterns.

Employing additional methods to vary coordination stability may clarify the impact of rhythmic movement on cognitive task performance. The wrist pendulum paradigm is well suited for this purpose. In addition to manipulations of required phase relation, the paradigm allows for the introduction of other factors known to compromise coordination stability, namely, movement frequency and detuning, i.e. the difference in preferred frequency of two limbs engaged in coordinated movement. In the present study, we used the wrist pendulum paradigm to examine whether RT in a cognitive task is a function of coordination stability.

Method

Participants (n=10) performed a bimanual coordination task and a simple RT task. In the coordination task, participants oscillated hand-held pendulums in the sagittal plane through radial and ulnar deviation of the wrists. Wooden dowels were used to create two pairs of pendulums, a symmetric pair and an asymmetric pair, with detuning values of 0 rad/s and 2 rad/s, respectively. The natural frequency of both pendulum pairs was 1 Hz. Participants oscillated the symmetric pendulum pair at 1 Hz. The asymmetric pendulum pair was oscillated faster than natural frequency, at 1.2 Hz, to decrease coordination stability. Both detuning/frequency conditions were performed in-phase (required phase relation = 0°) and anti-phase (required phase relation = 180°) to yield four levels of coordination stability. At the start of each trial, participants synchronized their movements with an auditory metronome for 20s, after which time the metronome was shut off and participants continued to swing at the required pace for an additional 50s.

For the RT task, participants responded to an asterisk presented on a computer screen by saying the syllable 'pa'. By requiring a voiced response in the RT task, we hoped to minimize the effects of motor interference. Each trial contained 20 stimulus presentations, with inter-stimulus intervals randomized between 800 and 1800 ms. There were a total of 9 experimental conditions—five single task conditions consisting of the RT task and the four coordination stability tasks performed separately, and four dual task conditions in which the RT task was combined with each of the four stability tasks. There were 3 trials in each condition for a total of 27 trials. Movement trajectories of the two pendulums were captured using 6D Motion Capture and Analysis System (Skill Technologies, Inc., Phoenix, AZ). Voiced responses were captured using a serial response box.

Analyses were performed on response times in the RT task, and standard deviation (SD) of relative phase and phase shift in the coordination task. Phase shift was computed as the difference between actual and required phase relations between limbs. For each participant, means of the three trials in each condition were calculated for all three dependent measures. RT data were subjected to a one-way analysis of variance (ANOVA) for task condition (single task condition - RT only, 4 dual task conditions), and a 2 (detuning/frequency) × 2 (required phase) repeated measures ANOVA within the dual task conditions. Separate 2 (task – single vs. dual) × 2 (detuning/frequency) × 2 (required phase) repeated measures ANOVAs were performed on phase shift and SD of relative phase.

Results

Response times were longer under dual task conditions than when the RT task was performed singly ($p < .001$). Response times did not differ, however, within the dual task situation for different levels of detuning/frequency and required phase (see Figure 1). For phase shift, ANOVA showed main effects of required phase ($p < .05$), and detuning/frequency ($p < .001$), with larger deviations for in-phase and the less stable detuning/frequency condition. In addition, there was an interaction of task condition and required phase. Pairwise comparisons revealed greater phase shift for required in-phase than for anti-phase under dual task conditions ($p < .05$), as shown in Figure 2. Analysis of SD of relative phase revealed main effects of required phase ($p < .001$) and detuning/frequency ($p < .001$). Variability was greater for anti-phase and for the less stable detuning/frequency condition.

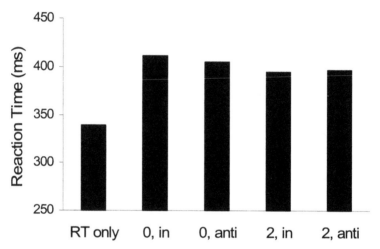

Figure 1. Reaction time (RT) as a function of task condition. RT only = single task condition, i.e. no concurrent coordination task. Dual task conditions combined RT and interlimb coordination tasks: 0, in = 0 rad/s detuning, in-phase coordination; 0, anti = 0 rad/s detuning, anti-phase coordination; 2, in = 2 rad/s detuning, in-phase coordination; 2, anti = 2 rad/s detuning, anti-phase coordination. Reaction times were significantly shorter in the single task condition than in the dual task conditions. There were no differences among the dual task conditions.

Discussion

Verbal response times in an RT task were slowed by concurrent perfor- mance of bimanual coordination. Less stable movement patterns did not have greater impact on RT than more stable movements. Within the limitations of the present study, it seems that performance in an RT task is not a function of coordination stability. Results did provide, however, further evidence of cognition's impact on coordination. Previous research on rhythmic movements performed in the absence of unrelated cognitive tasks demonstrated that, for detuned coordination, phase shift was greater for anti-phase than for in-phase patterns. On the contrary, we found larger deviations from required phase for in-

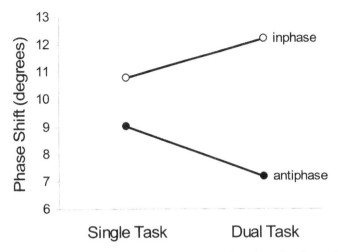

Figure 2. Phase shift in bimanual coordination as a function of task condition and required phase. Single Task = coordination task only; Dual Task = reaction time and coordination tasks combined. For the dual task condition, phase shift was greater for in-phase than for anti-phase movements.

phase coordination. In an investigation of effects of an arithmetic task on in-phase bimanual coordination, Pellecchia, Shockley, and Turvey (in press) reported phase shifts due to detuning and movement frequency were amplified by the unrelated cognitive task. Results of cross recurrence analysis suggested that cognitive activity acted as a source of noise for interlimb coordination. One explanation for phase shifts observed in the present experiment is that the noise injected into the movement system by the RT task affected in-phase patterns more so than anti-phase patterns.

References

Pellecchia, G. L., Shockley, K., & Turvey, M. T. (in press). Concurrent cognitive task modulates coordination dynamics. *Cognitive Science.*

Pellecchia, G.L., & Turvey, M. T. (2001) Cognitive activity shifts the attractors of bimanual rhythmic coordination. *Journal of Motor Behavior, 33,* 9-15.

Temprado, J.J., Zanone, P.G., Monno, A., & Laurent, M. (1999). Attentional load associated with performing and stabilizing preferred bimanual patterns. *Journal of Experimental Psychology: Human Perception and Performance, 25,* 1579-1594.

Temprado, J.J., Zanone, P.G., Monno, A., & Laurent, M. (2001). A dynamical framework for understanding performance trade-offs and interference in dual tasks. *Journal of Experimental Psychology: Human Perception and Performance, 27,* 1303-1313.

Acknowledgement. This research was supported by National Science Foundation award BCS 0423036.

Postural Stabilization

Studies in Perception and Action VIII
H. Heft & K. L. Marsh (Eds.)
© *2005 Lawrence Erlbaum Associates, Inc.*

Postural Stabilization of Looking: Eye Movement Data

Cedrick T. Bonnet[1], Thomas A. Stoffregen[1], Benoît G. Bardy[2]

[1]University of Minnesota, Minneapolis, USA
[2]University of Paris XI, Orsay, France

Postural movements can be controlled so as to facilitate visual performance (Riccio & Stoffregen, 1988; Stoffregen, Smart, Bardy, & Pagulayan, 1999, Stoffregen, Pagulayan, Bardy, & Hettinger, 2000). In the present study, we asked whether eye movements might influence body sway. Oblak, Gregoric, & Gyergyek (1985) found that body sway was reduced during visual tracking, relative to sway during fixation. This suggests that body sway may be modulated to facilitate changes in the direction of gaze. We replicated and extended the work of Oblak et al., but our study differed from theirs in several ways. First, we analyzed body sway separately for the AP and ML axes. Second, we varied the frequency of eye movements. In two experiments, we examined differences in postural behavior when maintaining gaze moving and stationary with eyes open or closed. We predicted that sway amplitude (1) would be reduced only during visually guided eye movements; (2) would correlate negatively with the frequency of eye movements.

Method

In two experiments (respectively fourteen and twelve subjects), subjects stood barefoot with their feet together. They had their hands together and were 100 cm far from a computer screen adapted to their height. The visual target was a red circle presented on the computer monitor, subtending 1.15° of visual angle. Postural sway was recorded using a 6-df (Experiment 1) and 3-df (Experiment 2) magnetic tracking system (Flock of Birds; Ascension Technology, Inc.), sampled at 47 Hz. One receiver was attached to a bicycle helmet, while a second was attached between the shoulder blades using cloth medical tape. Eye position and movement were measured using a standard EOG system (Biopac Systems, Inc., Goleta, CA) sampled at 62.5 Hz.

Experiment 1 had four experimental conditions: Eyes open stationary target (ST); eyes open moving target (MT); eyes closed stationary (CS); eyes closed, moving (CM). In the stationary target condition, the target remained in the center of the display for the duration of the trial. In the moving target condition, the target alternated (at 0.5 Hz) between two positions that were separated by 11° of visual angle in the horizontal plane, and subjects were asked to keep their gaze on the dot. During the eyes closed moving condition, subjects were asked to move their eyes horizontally in time with a metronome (0.5 Hz). In Experiment 2, there were four conditions: stationary target, and target moving horizontally at 0.5, 0.8 or 1.1 Hz (the eyes were always open). There were three trials in each condition, each of which lasted for 65 seconds.

Results

Eye movements. When subjects were instructed to move their eyes, we determined the mean and standard deviation of the amplitude of eye movements. For the stationary conditions, we report only the standard deviation of eye position. In the MT condition and the 0.5, 0.8, and 1.1 Hz conditions, the mean amplitudes of eye movements did not differ from 11°, while the mean amplitude was 73.59° in the CM condition. All standard deviations were below 5° for the eyes open conditions and below 9° for the eyes closed conditions. A representative EOG record for the moving target condition is illustrated in Figure 1.

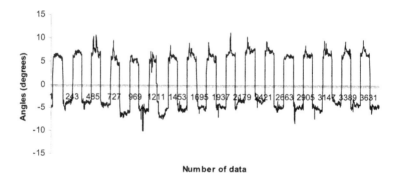

Figure 1. Simulating a virtual target for a monocular observer. The figure illustrates three examples of where the virtual target can be simulated, when the displayed target is moved as a function of the observer movements.

Postural motion. The dependent variables were the positional variability of the head and torso in the AP and ML axes.

In Experiment 1, the main effect of condition was significant for the four dependent variables (torso ML: $F_{(3,39)} = 4.273$, $p < .05$; torso AP: $F_{(3,39)} = 4.419$, $p < .05$; head ML: $F_{(3,39)} = 3.576$, $p < .05$; head AP: $F_{(3,39)} = 3.962$, $p < .05$). Figure 2 illustrates results for Head AP, but the pattern of results was the same for all four dependent variables. The main effect of trials was never significant, nor was the condition X trials interaction. Planned comparisons were conducted using a criterion alpha of .0125. The only significant result was for the difference between the ST and MT conditions in each of the four dependent variables (torso ML: $t_{(13)} = 3.489$; torso AP: $t_{(13)} = 3.526$; head ML: $t_{(13)} = 3.552$; head AP: $t_{(13)} = 3.548$).

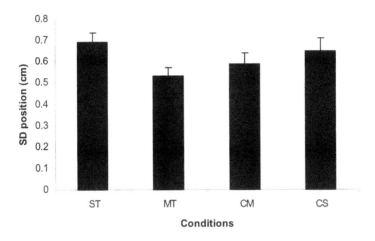

Figure 2. Experiment 1. Standard deviation of head position in the AP axis, in four conditions: ST = Stationary Target; MT = Moving Target; CM = Close Moving; CS = Close Stationary. The error bars are standard error.

In Experiment 2, the main effect of condition was significant in the AP axis for both head and torso (head AP: $F(3,33)$ =10.503, $p < .05$; torso AP: $F(3,33)$ = 12.125, $p < .05$), but not in the ML axis for either head or torso. The main effect of trials was significant in the AP axis (head AP: $F(2,22)$ = 4.185, $p < .05$; torso AP: $F(2,22)$ = 3.195, $p < .05$). The condition X trials interaction was not significant. Planned comparisons were conducted using a criterion alpha of .0083. All comparisons between stationary target and moving target (0.5, 0.8 and 1.1 Hz) gave significant results for the torso AP and the head AP.

Discussion

We examined relations between postural control and performance of suprapostural visual tasks that required eye movements. Our hypothesis was that changes in the gaze (i.e., visually guided eye movements) would constrain body sway more tightly than fixation of stationary targets or eye movements that were not visually guided.

The measured amplitude of eye movements was equal to the movement amplitude of the visual target (11°), indicating that subjects complied with our instructions. When the eyes were closed, eye movements were larger (73.59°) but despite this had no effect on postural motion.

The results in Experiment 1 are consistent with our hypotheses. Body sway was reduced in the two axes for both head and torso when subjects used eye movements to track moving targets (relative to fixation of a stationary target) but only when eye movements were visually guided. Thus, reductions in postural movement can be attributed to the control of gaze, rather than to movement of the eyes as such.

Usually, sway amplitude is greater when the eyes are closed than open but we did not find that result (Figure 2). Stoffregen et al. (1999) found that body sway was significantly reduced when subjects stood in a confined space (a small booth); in Experiment 1, of the present study, a similar effect may have occurred since subjects had very little room around them.

In Experiment 2, postural sway did not vary with the frequency of target motions. The lack of differences in sway with changes in target frequency did not support our hypothesis that sway amplitude would scale negatively to the frequency of target motion. However, at each frequency of target motion, postural sway with moving targets was reduced compared to sway with the stationary target. This result is consistent with our earlier finding of functional reduction of head and torso motion during visually guided eye movements.

References

Oblak, B., Gregoric, M., & Gyergyek, L. (1985). Effects of voluntary eye saccades on body sway. In M. Igarashi & F. O. Black (Eds.), *Vestibular and visual control on posture and locomotor equilibrium* (pp. 122-126). New York, NY: Karger.

Riccio, G. E., & Stoffregen, T. A. (1988). Affordances as constraints on the control of stance. *Human Movement Science, 7*, 265-300.

Stoffregen, T. A., Pagulayan, R. J., Bardy, B. G. & Hettinger, L. J. (2000) Modulating postural control to facilitate visual performance. *Human Movement Science, 2*, 203-220.

Stoffregen, T. A., Smart, L. J., Bardy, B. G. & Pagulayan, R. J. (1999) Postural stabilization of looking. *Journal of Experimental Psychology: Human Perception and Performance, 25*, 1641-1658.

Acknowledgements. Supported by *Enactive Interfaces*, a network of excellence (IST contract #002114) of the Commission of the European Community, and by the National Science Foundation (BCS-0236627).

Studies in Perception and Action VIII
H. Heft & K. L. Marsh (Eds.)
© *2005 Lawrence Erlbaum Associates, Inc.*

Intention to Sway Stabilizes Postural Coordination

Olivier Oullier [1], Benoît G. Bardy [2,3], Reinoud J. Bootsma [1], & Thomas A. Stoffregen [4]

[1]Movement & Perception Lab, CNRS-Université de la Méditerranée, Marseille, France ; [2]Research Center in Sport Sciences, Université de Paris XI, Orsay, France ; [3]Institut Universitaire de France; [4]Human Factors Research Lab, University of Minnesota, Minneapolis, USA

In several experiments, participants have been asked to move their head intentionally so as to track the motion of a visual target (e.g., Bardy, Oullier, Bootsma, & Stoffregen, 2002). They were not given any instructions about postural control *per se*; rather, postural coordination emerged as a means to achieve the required supra-postural tracking task. The motion of different body segments underlying the movement of the head has been analyzed by focusing on the relative phase ϕ between rotations around the ankles and hips. When tracking a target that oscillates at low frequencies, participants were found to spontaneously adopt an in-phase pattern ($\phi \approx 20°$), while tracking at higher frequencies of target motion led to the adoption of an antiphase pattern ($\phi \approx 180°$). Interestingly, transitions from one postural mode to the other—evoked by a gradual change in target frequency—exhibited typical signatures of self-organized systems: differential stability, critical fluctuations, phase transitions, critical slowing and hysteresis (Bardy et al., 2002).

In addition to these findings, manipulation of various parameters revealed that postural coordination dynamics emerge from the interaction of constraints falling into different classes; mainly those arising from properties of the environment, from the body, and from the goal of the task (see Oullier, Bardy, Stoffregen, & Bootsma, 2004 for a review). Previous research has shown that, separately, environmental and bodily constraints can provoke qualitative changes in the dynamics of the postural system. For instance, the mechanical constraints imposed by standing on a narrow beam (therefore reducing the surface of support) favour the antiphase pattern (Marin, Bardy, Baumberger, Flückiger, & Stoffregen., 1999). However, little is known regarding how intention to sway (or not) affects postural coordination dynamics. For instance, whether the preferred in-phase and antiphase postural modes of coordination emerge when participants do not intentionally sway remains uncertain.

In the present study, we address this question by simultaneously varying intentional and mechanical constraints to examine the possible effects of their (competitive/cooperative) interactions on postural coordination dynamics.

Method

Participants stood barefooted in a moving room, arms folded on their chest facing a target attached to the front wall at eye level. Motion around the neck and the knee axes were restricted with adhesive tape. The room was oscillating back and forth in the anterior-posterior axis with a constant peak-to-peak amplitude (4 cm). Its frequency was varied within a trial increasing or decreasing between 0.15 and 0.75 Hz in 0.05 Hz steps. Each frequency plateau lasted 10 cycles. Data from these increasing and decreasing trials were collapsed *a posteriori* to control for possible hysteresis effects. Participants (N = 42) were randomly divided into four groups (N = 13). To avoid fatigue effects (one trial lasting approximately for 8 minutes) each group performed one of four experimental conditions resulting from fully crossing two *intention* conditions with two *support surface* conditions.

Intention was manipulated by asking participants to simply look at the target while the room was oscillating (looking conditions) or to intentionally maintain a constant target-head gain (ideally 1) and phase (ideally 0°; tracking conditions). Surface support was manipulated by asking participants to either perform the looking and tracking tasks while standing on the concrete floor of the laboratory (floor conditions) or standing on a 10-cm narrow beam (beam conditions), i.e. shorter than the length of their feet. Because of format restrictions only the results concerning the (point-estimate) ankle-hip relative phase ϕ and its circular deviation will be presented here.

Results

Floor. When performing the tasks on the floor a clearly bimodal distribution of relative phase values was observed (Figures 1A & B). For the looking and the tracking tasks, the in-phase (close to 20°) and the antiphase (close to 180°) postural coordination modes were adopted for low and high frequencies of the moving room, respectively, as consistently found in our previous work (e.g. Bardy et al., 2002). This finding suggests that, when standing on the concrete floor, postural coordination patterns adopted to perform an intentional or a non-intentional supra-postural task are similar. Interestingly, the values of circular deviation found for both coordination patterns in the tracking tasks were significantly smaller compared to those of the same two patterns adopted in the looking condition. This result clearly indicates that when standing on the floor, the intention to sway had a stabilizing effect on postural coordination (Oullier, Bardy, Stoffregen, & Bootsma, 2002).

Beam. Our results replicate those of Marin et al. (1999), since when standing on the beam the antiphase pattern was the only one adopted regardless of the intention to move. However, the analysis of the circular deviation of ϕ revealed that the antiphase pattern, adopted in the execution of both tasks, was more variable when looking than when tracking (see Figures 1C and D). This result suggests that similarly to the 'floor' results, coordination was more stable when tracking the target in spite of the compelling effect imposed by standing on a narrow beam (Oullier et al., 2004). This stabilizing effect found when tracking was confirmed by the difference between the number of falls from the beam in each task (10 in the looking group against 3 in the tracking group).

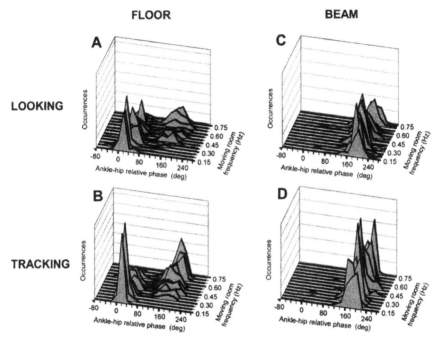

Figure 1. Frequency distribution of ankle-hip relative phase φ values as a function of the room frequency (all individual φ values were sorted in 20° bins). A) Looking task performed on the floor, B) Tracking task performed on the floor (adapted from Oullier et al., 2002). C) Looking task performed on the beam, D) Tracking task performed on the beam (adapted from Oullier et al., 2004).

Discussion

Bardy et al. (2002) documented the emergence of two preferred modes of postural coordination when participants used voluntary movements of the head to track motion of a target in the antero-posterior axis. The present results suggest that similar modes emerge whether participants standing on the floor track the target, or merely look at it. Thus, coordination dynamics underlying the maintenance of upright stance appears similar regardless of the intention to sway, therefore challenging the distinction between quiet stance and sway (Creath, Kiemel, Horak, Peterka, & Jeka, 2005). The beam exercised a powerful influence on coordination but, despite this mechanically-based effect, coupling of head motion with room motion was strongly modulated by the manipulation in supra-postural task instructions, i.e. intention. The persistence of supra-postural task effects despite the constraining influence of the beam is the most important result of this study. As to the role played by each constraint (frequency, surface of support and intention) on the postural system, it seems that in spite of a strong mechanical effect of standing on a beam, the effect of intention does not disappear. Therefore, the present results indicate a coexistence between the environmental (beam) and intentional (looking versus tracking) constraints, rather than one constraint being overwhelmed by the other. The strong mechanical constraint exercised by the beam did not annihilate the stabilizing effect of intention (Oullier et al., 2004). These results further attest that (postural) coordination dynamics emerge from a coalition of constraints of different natures.

References

Bardy B. G., Oullier O., Bootsma R. J., & Stoffregen T. A. (2002). Dynamics of human postural transitions. *Journal of Experimental Psychology: Human Perception and Performance, 28*, 499-514.

Creath, R., Kiemel, T., Horak, F., Peterka, R., & Jeka, J. (2005). A unified view of quiet and perturbed stance: Simultaneous co-existing excitable modes. *Neuroscience Letters, 377*, 75-80.

Marin, L., Bardy, B. G., Baumberger, B., Flückiger, M., & Stoffregen, T. A. (1999). Interaction between task demands and surface properties in the control of goal-oriented stance. *Human Movement Science, 18*, 31-47.

Oullier O., Bardy B. G., Stoffregen T. A., & Bootsma R. J. (2002). Postural coordination in looking and tracking tasks. *Human Movement Science, 21*, 147-167.

Oullier O., Bardy B. G., Stoffregen T. A., & Bootsma R. J. (2004). Task-specific stabilization of postural coordination during stance on a beam. *Motor Control, 8*, 174-187.

Acknowledgements. The research reported in this article was supported by the *National Science Foundation* (INT-9603315 and BCS-0236627), and by the French *Ministère de l'Education Nationale, de la Recherche et de la Technologie* (CNRS/NSF-3899).

Studies in Perception and Action VIII
H. Heft & K. L. Marsh (Eds.)
© *2005 Lawrence Erlbaum Associates, Inc.*

Effects of a Concurrent Memory Task on the Maintenance of Upright Stance

V. C. Ramenzoni & M. A. Riley

Perceptual-Motor Dynamics Laboratory, Department of Psychology, University of Cincinnati, USA

In everyday life we often engage in activities that require the coordinated performance of different tasks. For instance, while maintaining a balanced, upright posture we often perform cognitively demanding activities, such as engaging in abstract thinking. A growing literature has questioned the assumption of relative independence of the systems involved in postural control and cognition. Recent evidence shows that postural control can be affected by the performance of concurrent cognitive tasks, and vice-versa (see Woollacott & Shumway-Cook &, 2002). The literature is inconsistent, however, in two regards: (1) whether cognition degrades or facilitates postural control, and (2) whether postural control is differentially affected by distinct types of cognitive activity. When confounding factors associated with cognitive-task reports are eliminated, results suggest a reduction in postural sway variability—an apparent facilitation of postural control—during cognitive activity (Andersson, Hagman, Talianzadeh, Svedberg, & Larsen, 2002; Riley, Baker, Schmit, & Weaver, in press). A further concern regards the validity of the cognitive tasks employed in previous studies (e.g., verbal vs. visual/spatial) and whether they provide distinct measures of the intended memory processes (Dault, Frank, & Allard., 2001; Maylor, Allison, & Wing, 2001). This study was designed to avoid confounds and questionable procedures that characterize several previous studies and to provide a more comprehensive account of the nature of postural changes in response to different types of memory tasks. We explored how different types of material (verbal or visual) and memory processes (encoding and rehearsal) affected postural sway. Based on Riley et al. (in press), we expected cognitive activity to be associated with reduced sway variability. Given the inconclusiveness of previous studies, no direction of effects was predicted for type of material or memory process.

Method

Prior to the experiment, participants' visual and verbal memory spans were assessed. Memory task difficulty was matched to each participant's span. Participants (n=13) completed a total of 27 trials, each consisting of 50 s of posture data collection. Participants were instructed to stand relaxed on a force platform, breathe normally, and let their arms hang naturally to the side. The position of the feet was measured and marked, and remained constant for the duration of the experiment. Cognitive task material was presented in 88-point font on a PC monitor positioned at eye-height in front of the participant, 50 cm from the front edge of the force platform. The order of presentation of trials was fully randomized. Each trial consisted of a 20 s encoding phase, followed by a 50 s rehearsal phase, and finally a recall task (see Figure 1). During the encoding phase participants were instructed to remember material presented for 20 s. The material consisted of a string of either letters and numbers (verbal task) or Japanese symbols (visual task). For the 30 s rehearsal phase participants were instructed to the actively maintain the string in memory. Posture data collection spanned those two phases. After posture data collection ceased participants recalled the position of a randomly selected item from the string. In a no-task

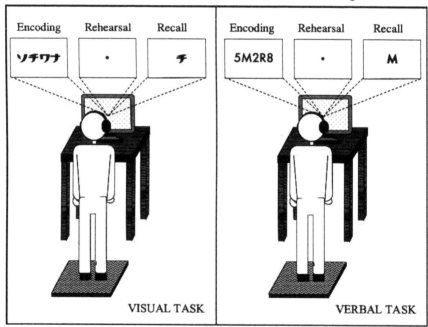

Figure 1. Sequence of events for visual and verbal task trials.

control condition participants were asked to stand relaxed throughout the trial. During all trials (including control), one of three levels of interference (none, visual, or verbal) was introduced during rehearsal. The purpose of interference was to potentially induce overload of specific memory processes—for instance, verbal interference was expected to have a stronger effect during rehearsal of verbal material. Interference effects would suggest that specific cognitive processes are shared by the cognitive task and postural control. In order to ensure dual-task performance for the verbal and visual tasks participants had to perform successfully on at least 2/3 of trials in a given cognitive condition;

failed trials were repeated to obtain at least two trials per condition. Postural sway data were later separated into separate data series for each of the two phases. Postural sway was measured using the standard deviation (SD) and local standard deviation (LSD; the within-trial average of SDs of non-overlapping 1 s data windows) of AP and ML center of pressure (COP) and COP path length (PL).

Results

ANOVAs revealed no effects of the cognitive tasks during encoding. For rehearsal (see Figure 2), ANOVAs and post-hoc tests revealed significantly less lower ML-SD and ML-LSD for either verbal or visual tasks compared to no task, $F(2,24) = 16.52, p < .05$, and $F(2,24) = 7.91, p < .05$, respectively, but for AP-SD, $F(2,24) = 3.41, p < .05$, only the verbal task was associated with less sway variability than the no-task condition. ANOVAs comparing encoding versus rehearsal (see Figure 3) revealed lower LSD values for encoding than rehearsal, $F(1,12) = 15.68, p < .05$, and $F(1,12) = 6.63, p < .05$, respectively, for ML and AP sway, but greater PL for encoding than rehearsal, $F(1,12) = 150.64$, $p < .05$.

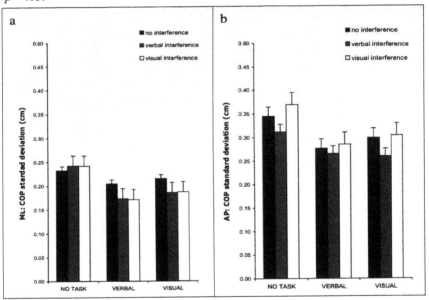

Figure 2. (a) Results for rehearsal phase for ML-SD as a function of type of interference and task condition. (b) Results for rehearsal phase for AP-SD as a function of type of interference and task condition.

ANOVAs revealed no effects of the cognitive tasks during encoding. For rehearsal (see Figure 2), ANOVAs and post-hoc tests revealed significantly less lower ML-SD and ML-LSD for either verbal or visual tasks compared to no task, $F(2,24) = 16.52, p < .05$, and $F(2,24) = 7.91, p < .05$, respectively, but for

AP-SD, $F(2,24) = 3.41$, $p < .05$, only the verbal task was associated with less sway variability than the no-task condition. ANOVAs comparing encoding versus rehearsal (see Figure 3) revealed lower LSD values for encoding than rehearsal, $F(1,12) = 15.68$, $p < .05$, and $F(1,12) = 6.63$, $p < .05$, respectively, for ML and AP sway, but greater PL for encoding than rehearsal, $F(1,12) = 150.64$, $p < .05$.

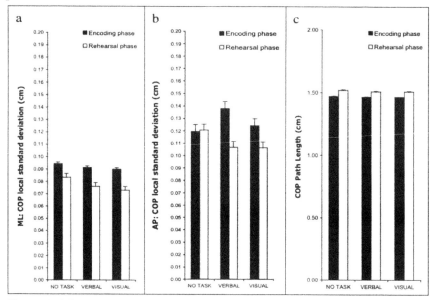

Figure 3. (a) Results for ML-LSD as a function of encoding vs. rehearsal phase and task condition. (b) Results for AP-LSD as a function of encoding vs. rehearsal phase and task condition. (c) Results for Path Length as a function of encoding vs. rehearsal phase and task condition.

Discussion

Overall our findings provide evidence that postural sway variability is diminished during the performance of memory tasks. As predicted, results suggest that the type of memory process and memory material involved differentially affect postural sway, but those differences were not seen for all sway variability measures. The active maintenance of verbal and visual material in working memory reduced AP and ML postural sway variability. Results also indicated that this effect was more pronounced for the rehearsal of verbal material, which suggests that to an extent changes in postural sway may be specific to the memory task used. Furthermore, the comparison of encoding and rehearsal processes for trials with no interference indicates that type of memory process affects the local SD of sway and the total distance traversed by the COP. In summary, this study provides some tentative answers to inconsistencies found in the literature on cognitive activity and postural control. The performance of a concurrent cognitive task not only affects the maintenance of upright balance, but the patterns of the changes observed in postural sway can be partially attributed to the characteristics of the cognitive task and to the dependent measures used.

References

Andersson, G., Hagman, J., Talianzadeh, R., Svedberg, A., & Larsen, H. C. (2002). Effect of cognitive load on postural control. *Brain Research Bulletin, 58*, 135-139.

Dault, M. C, Frank, J. S., & Allard, F. (2001). Influence of a visual-spatial, verbal and central executive working memory task on postural control. *Gait and Posture, 14*, 110-116.

Maylor, E. A., Allison, S., & Wing, A. M. (2001). Effects of spatial and nonspatial cognitive activity on postural stability. *British Journal of Psychology, 92,* 319-338.

Riley, M. A., Baker, A. A., Schmit, J. M., & Weaver, E (in press). Effects of visual and auditory short-term memory tasks on the spatiotemporal dynamics and variability of postural sway. *Journal of Motor Behavior.*

Woollacott, M., & Shumway-Cook, A. (2002). Attention and the control of posture and gait: a review of an emerging area of research. *Gait and Posture, 16,* 1-14.

Studies in Perception and Action VIII
H. Heft & K. L. Marsh (Eds.)
© *2005 Lawrence Erlbaum Associates, Inc.*

Explicitly Minimizing Postural Sway While Performing a Visuo-Spatial Cognitive Task

Nichole E. Saunders & Michael A. Riley

Department of Psychology, University of Cincinnati, OH, USA

Recent experiments on the interplay between mental activity and postural stability have raised questions about dual-task performance and postural control. Some studies found that postural stability is degraded while dual-tasking, while other studies found the opposite, leading to debates regarding the influence of supra-postural cognitive tasks and processing capacity limitations on postural control. Mitra and Frazier (2004) attempted to integrate those disparate findings, along with findings about the facilitation of non-mental supra-postural tasks (e.g., Stoffregen, Smart, Bardy, & Pagulayan, 1999), with their *adaptive resource-sharing model*. One of the predictions of adaptive resource-sharing is that postural control can facilitate supra-postural activity only if postural resources are not exhausted by maintaining postural stability.

Mitra and Frazier (2004) had participants perform easy or difficult visual search tasks while standing in varying postural demand conditions (feet apart vs. together, instructions to stand relaxed or explicitly minimize sway). They found that participants minimized sway when instructed and that, regardless of instructions sway variability increased as search task difficulty increased. The latter effect was magnified when standing with feet together, consistent with adaptive resource-sharing. However, their cognitive task required overt motor responses (pressing a button as quickly as possible after locating a target), which may have introduced artifacts into their postural sway measures. Riley, Baker, and Schmit (2003) reviewed results that suggest when questionable experimental procedures (such as overt motor or vocal responses to cognitive tasks) are eliminated, the bulk of evidence in the literature suggests that postural sway variability is reduced under conditions of higher cognitive load (see also Riley, Baker, Schmit, & Weaver, in press).

The present experiment was inspired by Mitra and Frazier (2004). We had participants perform easy and difficult versions of a visuo-spatial cognitive task while standing with feet together (a less stable stance) or apart (more stable) under instructions to simply stand relaxed or to explicitly minimize postural sway. We used a visuo-spatial delayed-response cognitive task, rather than the visual search task of Mitra and Frazier so that no overt response was necessary during data collection. We predicted reduced postural sway variability during cognitive performance, in contrast to Mitra and Frazier's results but in accordance with the findings of Riley et al. (2003, in press).

Method

Twenty University of Cincinnati undergraduates participated. Participants stood on a Bertec force platform under blocked and counterbalanced instruction conditions of explicitly minimizing postural sway or standing relaxed. In both conditions participants were asked to avoid large movements, keep their arms at their sides, and look straight ahead at a computer monitor that was used for the cognitive task. Participants stood with their feet shoulder width apart or pressed together (randomized within blocks). Three cognitive task conditions (no task, easy task, and difficult task) were presented in random order. A total of 36 trials (3 trials per condition) were performed.

The cognitive tasks consisted of three stages. During the first stage four light gray dots, each with a diameter of 2 cm, were presented on a dark gray background for 10 s (low contrast was used in order to reduce afterimages once the dots were removed from the screen). The second stage consisted of 20 s of postural sway measurement that began after the dots disappeared. During that time four arrows (6 cm long) were presented sequentially on the monitor, each arrow appearing on the screen for 5 s. Participants were instructed to "mentally extend" the arrows in the direction they were pointing and decide which arrows would pierce the previously displayed dots. A random number of arrows pointed toward the previously displayed dots' locations in each trial (all such arrows

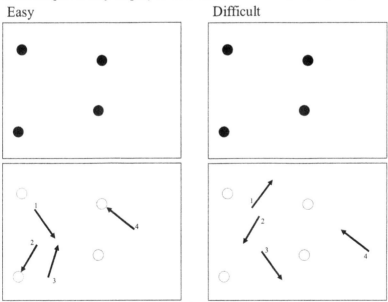

Figure 1. Depiction of the cognitive task for the easy (left) and difficult (right) conditions. The dots were displayed prior to data collection (top) for 10 s and removed from the screen for the 20 s of data collection, during which the arrows appeared on the screen in successive order. During that time the dots were not visible and the arrows were not numbered; those features are depicted here to illustrate what constituted a correct response. In these examples, correct response for both conditions would be "No; Yes; No; Yes".

pointed directly at the center of any dots they would have intersected). In the easy condition any arrow that would be considered a hit had the point of the arrow placed directly next to the dot locations, whereas in the difficult condition the arrows' points were 6 cm (one arrow length away) from the dot locations. An example of this task is shown in Figure 1. The third stage began after data collection ceased. Participants were asked to indicate which arrows would have intersected the dots by expressing four successive yes-no responses. The task thus required visuo-spatial (mentally extending the arrows) and verbal (remembering the yes-no responses) working memory.

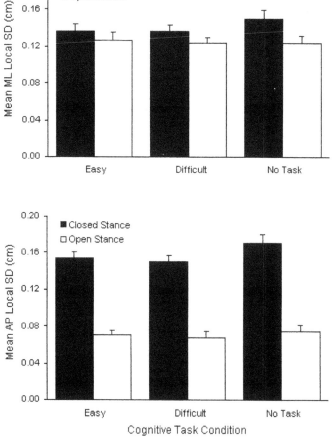

Figure 2. Cognitive task × stance interactions for AP and ML sway. Error bars indicate one standard error of the mean.

Results

Postural sway was operationalized by the *local standard deviation* (within-trial mean of SDs of non-overlapping, 1 s windows; Mitra & Frazier, 2004) of the center of pressure in both the medio-lateral (ML) and anterior-posterior (AP) directions. Participants swayed more with the feet together than with the feet open [ML: $F(1,19) = 17.381$, $p < .05$; AP: $F(1,19) = 101.96$, $p < .05$]. AP variability decreased as task difficulty increased, $F(2, 38) = 9.28$, $p < .05$. Stance × difficulty interactions [$F(2,38) = 6.54$, $p < .05$, and $F(2, 38) = 3.70$, $p < .05$, for ML and AP, respectively] indicated that in the feet-apart condition there was no effect of the cognitive task, but in the feet-together condition sway variability was reduced during cognitive performance (for both easy and difficult tasks) compared to the no-task condition (see Figure 2). For ML sway a stance × instruction interaction, $F(1, 19) = 4.50$, $p < .05$, indicated no effect of the instruction for the feet-together condition, but for feet-apart conditions participants swayed less when instructed to do so.

Discussion

The results of this study do not support Mitra and Frazier's (2004) adaptive resource-sharing model. According to their model, postural sway should have increased under cognitive load, especially in the feet-together condition. Instead, the results provide further support for Riley et. al.'s (2003, in press) proposal that postural sway decreases during cognitive activity because mental tasks divert attention that may interfere with postural control.

Verbal memory tasks were used in previous studies that found reduced sway variability during cognitive performance (Riley et. al., 2003, in press). The present study adds to the body of research by showing that visuo-spatial tasks induce similar effects on postural sway as verbal tasks.

References

Mitra, S., & Fraizer, V. (2004). Effects of explicit sway-minimization on postural-suprapostural dual-task performance. *Human Movement Science*, *23*, 1-20.

Riley, M. A., Baker, A. A., & Schmit, J. M. (2003). Inverse relation between postural variability and difficulty of a concurrent short-term memory task. *Brain Research Bulletin*, *62*, 191-195.

Riley, M. A., Baker, A. A., Schmit, J. M., & Weaver, E. (in press). Effects of visual and auditory short-term memory tasks on the spatiotemporal dynamics and variability of postural sway. *Journal of Motor Behavior*.

Stoffregen, T. A., Smart, L. J., Bardy, B. G., & Pagulayan, R. J. (1999). Postural stabilization of looking. *Journal of Experimental Psychology: Human Perception and Performance*, *25*, 1641–1658.

Acknowledgements. We thank Peter Chiu for his assistance with developing the cognitive task.

Picture Perception and Distance Perception

Studies in Perception and Action VIII
H. Heft & K. L. Marsh (Eds.)
© *2005 Lawrence Erlbaum Associates, Inc.*

Falling Toward a Theory of the Vertical-Horizontal Illusion

Russell E. Jackson

University of Texas at Austin, USA

People recorded distance illusions at least as early as Ancient Egypt and Classical Greece (Winslow, 1933). The vertical-horizontal illusion (VHI) is the perception that a vertical line is longer than a horizontal line of equal length. The VHI was among the first psychological phenomena investigated under modern science (Fick, 1851, as cited in Kuennapas, 1957) and was a focus of the founder of scientific psychology, Wilhelm Wundt (as cited in Winslow, 1933). Despite this history, the ultimate cause of the VHI remains unknown.

Theorized VHI mechanisms include differential eye movements (Wundt, 1874, as cited in Winslow, 1933), discord among retinal, visual, and gravitational orientations (Higashiyama, 1996), and differentially excitatory retinal meridians (Avery & Day, 1969). Proximal mechanisms such as these explain *how* the VHI occurs, but fail to explain *why* the VHI occurs. Why are visual systems designed with what appears to be reliable, systematic error? Why do higher-order brain functions not correct for this source of visual misinformation as they do for many others? Why do we suffer the costs of developing and maintaining this consistently inaccurate perception across age and sex (Walters, 1942; Fraisse & Vautrey, 1956; Chapanis & Mankin, 1967; Brosvic, Dihoff, & Fama, 2002), culture and technology (Rivers, 1905; Segall, Campbell, & Herscovitz, 1966; Bolton, Michelson, Wilde, & Bolton, 1975), and even experience with the VHI paradox (Becker, 1972)? Some mechanism surely produces the VHI, but only a causal theory will answer these long-standing questions.

One causal VHI theory maintains that the VHI is the product of *foreshortening of receding horizontals* (Segall, Campbell, & Herskovitz, 1966). *Foreshortening* applied to the VHI acknowledges that vertical retinal images can represent long horizontal surfaces extending away from the observer. Under this theory, the VHI increases the perceived length of vertical retinal images in order to represent environmental horizontal surfaces accurately.

Alternatively, *Gravity theory* (Howard & Templeton, 1966) explanations of the VHI suggest that perceived distance corresponds with anticipated effort of traversing it. Gravity theory acknowledges that vertical surfaces require more energy to navigate than horizontal surfaces and suggests that this relationship produces over-perception of vertical surfaces.

Theory Under Development: Evolved Fall Avoidance Theory

Evolved Fall Avoidance Theory (EFAT) suggests that some cognitive features reflect natural selection resulting from the risk of falling inherent in vertical surface navigation.

Moving on vertical surfaces presents different, and substantially greater, costs than horizontal surfaces. We can stop, rest, carry items in our hands, or change directions nearly effortlessly while moving horizontally, but vertical movement prevents many actions and increases costs, notably via falling. Common fall outcomes include cuts, dislocations, broken bones, damage to organs such as the lungs or brain, loss of appendages, and death. The smallest of these costs posed critical risk to health and likely influenced reproductive fitness in the environments in which humans evolved. *Evolved Fall Avoidance Theory* suggests that the VHI promotes route choices less likely to result in these costs.

Organisms preferentially pursue nearer navigational goals when benefits and other costs are held constant (Somervill & Somervill, 1977). *Evolved Fall Avoidance Theory* suggests that this preference could be beneficially subverted by making vertical appear longer than horizontal. Such a process would result in a VHI mechanism that weights distance estimation with cost of falling by making vertical surfaces appear longer than horizontal ones.

Comparison of Predictions

In order to test EFAT predictions against other theories, I compared participants' estimates of vertical height from the top and bottom of a large vertical surface. I specify methods below, but will first posit predictions from each theory.

Foreshortening of receding horizontals predicts equal estimates of vertical distance from both the top and bottom of a vertical surface because the actual distances are equal and equally foreshortened.

Gravity theory predicts greater distance estimates from the bottom of a vertical surface than the top because ascending is more energetically expensive than descending.

Evolved Fall Avoidance Theory predicts greater estimated distance while at the top of a vertical surface than the bottom because descending more often results in falls than ascending (Cohen & Lin, 1991).

Method

Sixty-six participants with normal or corrected to normal vision completed a questionnaire containing questions about *EFAT*-relevant variables, including body height, and then proceeded to the outdoor testing site with a researcher.

Participants estimated height from both top and bottom of a 14.39 m vertical surface, as seen in Figure 1. Participants estimated vertical length by adjusting horizontal distance to the researcher with hand signals. Researchers began at a position next to participants and then walked backwards or forwards as participants made as many adjustments as desired, then researchers measured the result. Researchers randomly determined whether participants began at the top or bottom .

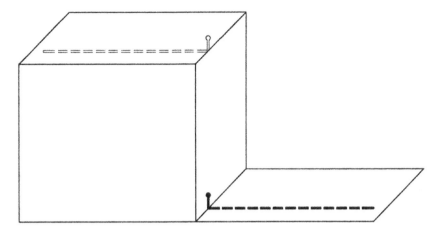

Figure 1. Participant position from top (outline) and bottom (solid) estimates. Dotted icon represents participant. Dashed lines represent the horizontal path in estimating the vertical height. Not drawn to scale.

Testing occurred at a campus parking garage. I selected this site because of its ecological validity to cues likely important in *EFAT* during evolution of the VHI. The vertical distance is large enough to inflict falling costs. Participants, although confined to standing in the same place, were able to turn their head and eyes and lean forward or backward at will. Researchers allowed participants all the time desired to make the estimate. Additionally, both positions were outdoors and the top position was not obstructed impassibly, such as with a window or screen.

I also selected this site for its minimal variance between the top and bottom horizontal surfaces. Texture gradient was minimal and equivalent in both surfaces, due to the same asphalt composition. Linear perspective was very similar and minimized by limited convergence.

Results and Discussion

Mean estimate from the bottom of the vertical was 20.63 m, $SD = 4.70$ m. Mean estimate from the top of the vertical was 26.56 m, $SD = 6.91$ m. A manipulation check suggested the presence of the VHI from both the bottom, $t(65) = 10.879, p < .001$, and top, $t(65) = 14.462, p < .001$.

Results of a paired samples *t*-test suggested significant difference between participants' estimates of length from the top and bottom of the vertical surface, $t(65) = 8.865, p < .001, r = 0.609$. Participants perceived greater vertical distance from the top of the vertical surface than from the bottom. Analysis of variance suggested that order of testing (i.e. beginning at the top or bottom) failed to influence difference scores between top and bottom estimates, $F(1, 65) = 1.038, p = .312$. Analysis of variance suggested that participant height failed to influence difference scores between top and bottom estimates, $F(16, 65) = 1.056, p = .420$.

These data support *EFAT* predictions exclusive from other VHI theories. Support for a causal theory such as *EFAT* helps begin to answer the questions posed at the beginning of this paper. Why do we have reliable 'error' in height estimation? *Evolved Fall Avoidance Theory* suggests that the VHI is not error, but instead functions to weight perception by costs implicit in navigation. Why does our visual system not correct the VHI? Because it serves an adaptive purpose in terrestrial organisms. Why does the VHI persist across all known populations? Because all humans benefit, and descended from organisms that benefited, from distance estimates weighted by the costs of falling. These questions, and the extent to which *EFAT* answers them, are currently being tested in additional studies.

References

Avery, G. C., & Day, R. H. (1969). Basis of the horizontal-vertical illusion. *Journal of Experimental Psychology, 81,* 376-380.

Becker, J. A. (1972). Division and orientation in the vertical-horizontal illusion. *Perceptual & Motor Skills, 34(3),* 899-902.

Bolton, R., Michelson, C., Wilde, J. & Bolton, C. (1975). The heights of illusion: On the relationship between altitude and perception. *Ethos, 3(3),* 403-424.

Brosvic, G. M., Dihoff, R. E., & Fama, J. (2002). Age-related susceptibility to the Mueller-Lyer and the Horizontal-Vertical illusions. *Perceptual & Motor Skills, 94(1),* 229-234.

Chapanis, A., & Mankin, D. A. (1967). The vertical-horizontal illusion in a visually-rich environment. *Perception & Psychophysics, 2(6),* 249-255.

Cohen, H. H. & Lin, L. (1991). A Scenario analysis of ladder fall accidents. *Journal of Safety Research, 22,* 31-39.

Fraisse, P., & Vautrey, P. (1956). The influence of age, sex, and specialized training on the vertical-horizontal illusion. *Quarterly Journal of Experimental Psychology, 8,* 114-120.

Higashiyama, A. (1996). Horizontal and vertical distance perception: The discorded-orientation theory. *Perception & Psychophysics, 58(2),* 259-270.

Howard, I. P, & Templeton, W. B., (1966). *Human Spatial Orientation.* Wiley: New York.

Kuennapas, T. M. (1957). Interocular differences in the vertical-horizontal illusion. *Acta Psychologica, 13,* 253-259.

Rivers, W. H. R. (1905). Observations on the senses of the Todas. *British Journal of Psychology, 1,* 321-396.

Segall, M. H., Campbell, D. T., & Herskovits, M. J. (1966). The influence of culture on visual perception. Oxford: Bobbs-Merrill.

Somervill, J. W., & Somervill, C. Z. (1977). Descent behavior of rats and chicks in a cliff and non-cliff situation. *Perceptual & Motor Skills, 45(2),* 391-397.

Walters, A. (1942). A genetic study of geometrical-optical illusions. *Psychology Monographs, 25,* 101-155.

Winslow, C. N. (1993). Visual illusions in the chick. *Archives of Psychology, 153,* 83.

Studies in Perception and Action VIII
H. Heft & K. L. Marsh (Eds.)
© *2005 Lawrence Erlbaum Associates, Inc.*

Perspective Picture Perception:
A Test of the ART Theory

Igor Juricevic & John M. Kennedy

University of Toronto, Scarborough, Canada

Our experiment concerns perceiving perspective pictures. We propose an ART (Angle and Ratios Together) theory to reconcile robustness (constancy) and its opposite, distortion (Juricevic & Kennedy, 2003). Here we test the ART theory with diamond-shaped tiles, since these are a challenge to theories of constancy.

Figure 1 shows uniform square tiles on a ground using linear perspective. The tiles project many different shapes as a consequence of perspective. Some of the shapes appear to depict square tiles, showing perceptual "constancy". However, some suggest tiles far from square (Juricevic & Kennedy, 2003, 2005). This is known as "distortion" (Kubovy, 1986). In contrast to the predictions of perspective, there may be constancy and distortion simultaneously in a perspective picture.

Figure 1.

Few theories reconcile constancy and distortion in one picture. To this end, consider an Angles and Ratios Together (ART) theory (Juricevic & Kennedy, 2003, 2005). Gibson (1979) argues perception is a function of the optic array. Likewise, the ART theory proposes that the perception is determined by a combination of "visual angle ratio" and "angle from normal." The first is the ratio of the visual angle of the depth of an object divided by the visual angle of the width of an object. The "angle from normal" is the angle between the line of sight joining the observer to the central vanishing point and the line of sight to the object. For convenience, the line of sight intersects the object on the base of the object where it is farthest laterally from the observer.

The ART theory postulates that the "visual angle ratio" and the "angle from normal" must fall within certain ranges for a tile to appear square. We found these ranges for square tiles (Juricevic & Kennedy, 2003). Here we test the generality of the ART theory with diamond-shaped tiles, i.e., square tiles at 45° to the picture plane (see Figure 2). Will the ART theory's ranges apply? Will both constancy and distortion be evident?

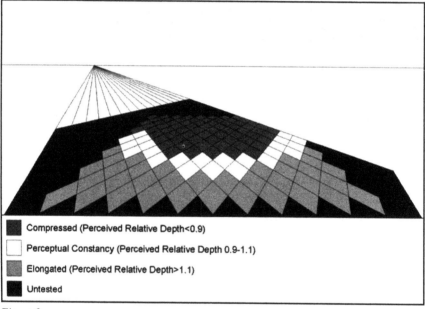

Figure 2.

Method

Subjects

Nine female third-year psychology students (*M* age = 21.7, *SD* = 1.2), all with normal or corrected-to-normal acuity and naïve to the study's purpose, participated.

Stimuli

The pictures were projected as panoramas onto a back-projection screen using an EPSON PowerLite 51c LCD projector (model: EMP-51). Each picture measured 0.64 m (high) x 1.28 m (wide), and subtended 79.3° x 121.3° of visual angle when viewed at a distance of 0.36 m.

The diamond-shaped tiles were in rows numbered from 1 (near and lowest on the screen) to 9 (far) (see Figure 2). The columns ran from 1 (center) to 7 (left).

The tiles were depicted in two-point perspective using 3 different vantage points with distances of 0.09, 0.36, and 0.63 m from the picture plane, all on the normal to the picture plane (an orthogonal from the central vanishing point on the horizon), and in front of the central column of tiles (column 1).

Tiles tested were located in the factorial combinations of rows 1, 3, 5, and 7, and columns 1, 2, 3, 4, 5, and 6. These tiles were indicated to the subjects by adding two lines to a given diamond, one line just below the diamond and oriented horizontally and the other an oblique just to the right, corresponding to the width and depth of the tiles. One tile was so highlighted per trial.

Procedure

Each subject, tested individually, judged the depth of an indicated tile relative to the width, with the width of every tile set at 100.

The subject viewed each picture monocularly, directly opposite the central vanishing point, 0.36 m from the picture plane. Subjects were free to turn their eyes and head. Once a subject made his or her judgment, the screen went black for 2 s. and the next picture was displayed.

Results

Dependent measure

The dependent measure was perceived relative depth, as ratios of depth to width. Tiles judged as being longer than their width have perceived relative depth ratios greater than 1, shorter than their width have ratios less than 1, and tiles judged perfectly square a ratio of 1.

Repeated Measures ANOVA

Three independent variables were tested: Vantage Point, Column, and Row in a 3 (Vantage Point) x 6 (Column) x 4 (Row) Repeated Measures ANOVA. In brief, both perceptual constancy and distortions were evident (see Figure 2). The ANOVA revealed a main effect of Vantage Point, $F(2,16) = 54.26$, $p < 0.001$. Perceived relative depth increased as the depicting-vantage-point distance increased.

The main effect of Column was significant, $F(5,40) = 30.20$, $p < 0.001$. Perceived relative depth increased from Column 1 (center) to Column 7 (left) (see Figure 2).

The main effect of Row was also significant, $F(3,24) = 46.62$, $p < 0.001$. Perceived relative depth increased from Row 1 (center) to Row 7 (left) (see Figure 2).

ART Theory Ranges

15 tiles were judged as square and 57 as either elongated or compressed. 14 of the 15 tiles (93%) judged as square in this study fell within the ART theory

ranges from Juricevic and Kennedy (2003). By contrast, only 15 of the 57 tiles (26%) that were elongated or compressed fell within the ART theory ranges.

Discussion

The ART theory applies well to diamond-shaped tiles. As evident from the main effects of column and row, perceptual constancy and distortions occurred in a given perspective picture. Interestingly, the overwhelming majority of the diamond-shaped tiles that were perceived as square (i.e., perceptual constancy) all fell within the ART theory ranges, devised originally for squares. Further, most of the tiles judged as either compressed or elongated fell outside of the ART theory ranges. The ART theory ranges, then, may be general across changes in the orientation of the objects being viewed. This offers a base for reconciling perceptual constancy and distortion in the same perspective picture with shapes at any orientation.

References

Gibson, J.J. (1979). *The ecological approach to visual perception.* Boston, MA: Houghton Mifflin.

Juricevic, I., & Kennedy, J. M. (2003, November). *Foreshortening and forelengthening: Underestimated much more than perspective predicts.* Poster presented at the annual meeting of the Psychonomic Society, Vancouver, British Columbia.

Juricevic, I., & Kennedy, J. M. (2005). Object constancy: Object orientation affects relative depth in perspective pictures? In H. Heft & K. L. Marsh (Eds.), *Studies in perception and action VIII: Thirteenth International Conference on Perception and Action* (pp. 249-253), Mahwah, NJ: Lawrence Erlbaum Associates, Inc.

Kubovy, M. (1986). *The psychology of perspective and renaissance art.* Cambridge, MA: Cambridge University Press.

Studies in Perception and Action VIII
H. Heft & K. L. Marsh (Eds.)
© 2005 Lawrence Erlbaum Associates, Inc.

Object Constancy: Object Orientation Affects Relative Depth in Perspective Pictures?

Igor Juricevic & John M. Kennedy

University of Toronto, Scarborough, Canada

Our experiment examined the perception of a perspective picture of square tiles turned 45°, producing diamonds. It is well known that the same shape can be perceived as a diamond or a square with a change in orientation. We offer a major challenge to theories of perceptual constancy by demonstrating a possible effect of orientation on perceived relative depth.

Figure 1, devised using linear perspective, shows square tiles oriented as diamonds on a ground plane. Tiles project many different shapes in the picture. If the shapes in some regions of the picture are seen as depicting square tiles turned 45° (producing diamonds), then "perceptual constancy" obtains. Strikingly, in some regions the shapes may be seen as tiles deviating from a square shape, revealing "distortion" (Kubovy, 1986). Alas for perspective geometry, which predicts uniform perception of the tiles in a given picture, there may be constancy and distortion simultaneously in the picture (Juricevic & Kennedy, 2005).

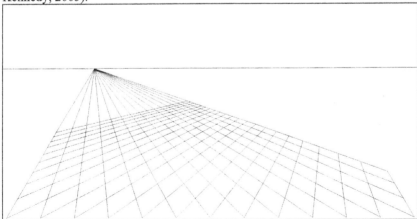

Figure 1.

Theories explaining perceptual constancy, regularly experienced by anyone looking at ordinary snapshot pictures, are widely celebrated. Gibson (1979) argued that "invariant" relations within optic arrays produced by a picture (or, more generally, by any scene) are information for spatial properties. That is, a certain size or shape produces a specific optic invariant for all observers in any direction in front of the picture despite projective transformations. Putative examples include: relative rate of change of density of the light from the ground texture specifies relative rate of change in distance (Gibson, 1979); the horizon-ratio relation indicates height relative to eye-height (Rogers, 1996; Sedgwick, 2001); and the cross-ratio, which is information for rigidity of a rotating object (Cutting, 1986).

The "Projective" approach of Niall and Macnamara, and such distinguished theorists as Helmholtz, Rock, and Ullman (Niall & Macnamara, 1990), hold that vision undertakes "inverse projection", determining the scene by inverting the projection. Projective theories predict that an observer positioned farther than the correct vantage point will perceive elongated tiles whereas from too close a vantage point they will perceive compressed tiles.

"Compromise" theories argue perception of a picture has two sources: first, inverse projection of depicted depths and, second, the flatness of the picture surface, which diminishes percepts (Sedgwick & Nicholls, 1993).

None of these theories predict that the perceived orientation of an object affects its perceived relative depth (i.e., the ratio of the perceived depth and width of the object). Perceived orientation cannot affect perspective projections, invariants, or surface flatness. But if orientation does affect perceived depth, then diamond-shaped tiles could result in two kinds of responses, because they can be perceived as diamonds or squares, the same form seen with two orientations.

Method

Subjects

Fourteen introductory psychology students (M age = 19.2, SD = 1.8, 7 female), all with normal or corrected-to-normal acuity and naïve to the study's purpose, participated.

Stimuli

The pictures were panoramas on a back-projection screen, via an EPSON PowerLite 51c LCD projector (model: EMP-51). Each picture measured 0.64 m (high) x 1.28 m (wide), and subtended 79.3° x 121.3° at a distance of 0.36 m.

The diamond-shaped tiles were in rows numbered from 1 (near and lowest on the screen) to 9 (far) (see Figure 1). The columns ran from 1 (center) to 7 (left).

The tiles were depicted in two-point perspective using 7 different vantage points with distances of 0.09, 0.18, 0.27, 0.36, 0.45, 0.54, and 0.63 m from the picture plane, all on the normal to the picture plane (an orthogonal from the central vanishing point on the horizon), and in front of the central column of tiles (column 1).

The tiles tested were located in the factorial combinations of rows 1, 3, 5, 7, and 9 and columns 1, 2, 3, 4, 5, 6, and 7. They were indicated to the subjects by adding the diagonal lines depicting the width and depth of the tiles. One tile was so highlighted per trial.

Procedure

Each subject, tested individually, judged the depth of an indicated tile relative to the width as a ratio of the diagonals. The width diagonal of every tile was set at 100.

The subject viewed each picture monocularly, directly opposite the central vanishing point, 0.36 m from the picture plane. Subjects were free to turn their eyes and head. Once the subject made a judgment, the screen went black for 2 s. and the next picture was displayed.

Results

Dependent measure

The dependent measure was perceived relative depth, as ratios of depth to width. Tiles judged as being longer than their width have perceived relative depth ratios greater than 1, shorter than their width have ratios less than 1, and tiles judged perfectly square, a ratio of 1.

Inter-Subject Correlations

A 3-means Cluster Analysis revealed two groups with high inter-subject correlations within the groups, and low inter-subject correlation between the groups. The third group contained only two subjects and did not correlate highly even within the group and was excluded from any further analysis. To test for differences between the two remaining groups, the between-subject variable "Group" was added to the analysis.

Repeated Measures ANOVA

Four independent variables were tested: Group, Vantage Point, Column, and Row in a 2 (Group) x 7 (Vantage Point) x 7 (Column) x 5 (Row) Repeated Measures ANOVA. In brief, the perceived relative depth patterns varied enormously between the two groups (see Figure 2). Specifically, all two-way interactions with Group reached significance: (1) Group x Vantage Point, $F(6,60) = 22.5, p < 0.001$, (2) Group x Column, $F(6,60) = 3.5, p = 0.005$, and (3) Group x Row, $F(4,40) = 4.1, p=0.007$.

Discussion

The two groups vary widely in their response patterns. What can be causing this split? We speculate that the cause is the perceived orientation of the diamond-shaped tiles. The major axis of any tile can be selected in two distinct ways: as one pointing towards the central vanishing point (diamond tile) or as one pointing towards the distance point of the picture to one side of the vanishing point (square tile). Consider the tile in Figure 1 located in the center column, row 2. If this tile is perceived as pointing towards the central vanishing point (diamond tile), the diagonals highlighting the depth and width of the tile

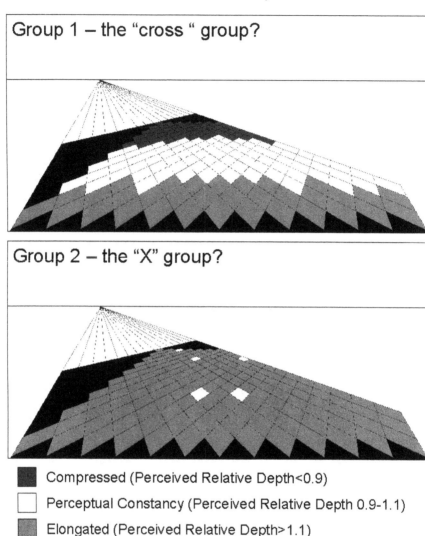

Group 1 – the "cross " group?

Group 2 – the "X" group?

■ Compressed (Perceived Relative Depth<0.9)

☐ Perceptual Constancy (Perceived Relative Depth 0.9-1.1)

■ Elongated (Perceived Relative Depth>1.1)

■ Untested

Figure 2.

can be thought of as forming a "cross" on the ground plane. If, on the other hand, the tile is perceived as pointing towards the distance point (square tile), they form an "X" on the ground plane. Phenomenologically, the ratios of the lines making up the "cross" and those making up the "X" appear to differ, even though they are the same lines! Group 1 may be the "cross" group (see Figure 2). This orientation effect is not predicted by projective, invariant, or compromise theories, and requires an additional factor to be added to theories of constancy.

References

Cutting, J.E. (1986). *Perception with an eye to motion.* Cambridge, MA: MIT Press.

Gibson, J.J. (1979). *The ecological approach to visual perception.* Boston, MA: Houghton Mifflin.

Juricevic, I., & Kennedy, J. M. (2005). Perspective picture perception: A test of the ART theory. In H. Heft & K. L. Marsh (Eds.), *Studies in perception and action VIII: Thirteenth International Conference on Perception and Action* (pp. 245-248), Mahwah, NJ: Lawrence Erlbaum Associates, Inc.

Kubovy, M. (1986). *The psychology of perspective and renaissance art.* Cambridge, MA: Cambridge University Press.

Niall, K.K., & Macnamara, J. (1990). Projective invariance and picture perception. *Perception, 19,* 637-660.

Rogers, S. (1996). The horizon-ratio relation as information for relative size in pictures. *Perception & Psychophysics, 58,* 142-152.

Sedgwick, H. A., & Nicholls, A. L. (1993). Cross talk between the picture surface and the pictured scene: Effects on perceived shape. *Perception, 22* (supplement), 109.

Sedgwick, H. A. (2001). Visual space perception. In E. B. Goldstein (Ed.) *Blackwell handbook of perception* (pp. 128-167). Oxford: Blackwell Publishers.

Pedagogy

Studies in Perception and Action VIII
H. Heft & K. L. Marsh (Eds.)
© *2005 Lawrence Erlbaum Associates, Inc.*

Using EPAID to Design Doctoral Minors

Judith Effken[1], Gerri Lamb[1], Marylyn McEwen[1], Joyce Verran[1], Deborah Vincent[1], & Michael Young[2]

[1]University of Arizona, Tucson, AZ, USA
[2]University of Connecticut, Storrs, CT, USA

J.J. Gibson and his followers developed a robust perceptual psychology that relies on the duality of perception and action. As goal-directed organisms, we perceive in order to act in ways that allow us to achieve our goals; and we act in order to improve our ability to perceive goal-relevant information. Eleanor Gibson and her colleagues demonstrated that perceptual learning is fundamentally the discrimination of finer and finer differences in available information (perception) and the execution of finer and finer-grained control (action). For that reason, perceptual learning is often cited as the basis for "situated cognition" or "situated action" approaches to learning. The Ecological Approach to Instructional Design (EPAID) applies fundamental principles of ecological psychology to instructional design (Effken & Kadar, 2001; Shaw Kadar, Sim, & Repperger, 1992; Young, 2003; Young, Barab, & Garrett, 2000). We are using EPAID to design four courses that vary a great deal in substance and style for our online Nursing PhD program.

In this presentation, we define the ecological psychology principles being used to design two of the courses then describe how we have applied and adapted those principles into instructional design strategies that immerse the online student in the rich context of a very complex healthcare environment and enable them to interact with that environment and each other to accomplish targeted learning outcomes.

Principles of EPAID

EPAID anchors learning in the complexity of real-life situations, which makes it both appealing and challenging for online doctoral education. EPAID is similar to other learning theories in assuming that learners are self directed by their personal goals and that learning improves with practice and feedback, but differs from other approaches because it holds that learning is the education of intention and attention:

- Educating *intention* requires helping students align their learning goals with those of the curriculum by first engaging students through authentic, contextually-rich situations presented through videos, stories of real-world problems, and associated social constructivist interactive online activities.

- Educating *attention* means helping students learn to detect aspects of their environments that have functional value by presenting exemplars through which they can "tune" their detection skills.

- Learning emerges from the interaction of learner and environment. Action (both physical and cognitive) is a necessary component of learning.

Applying EPAID

To date, we have used EPAID to develop three very different web-based nursing doctoral courses:

- Workforce and Healthcare Delivery Environments
- Border Health Issues and Policy
- Technology for Increasing Healthcare Capacity

We began the endeavor with a workshop in which Dr. Young oriented faculty to fundamental principles of ecological psychology and how they were operationalized in EPAID. As part of the workshop, Dr. Young presented concrete examples of using EPAID.

As a general design strategy, we are developing each course as a set of challenges, each of which builds on the previous. Challenges begin by immersing students in an authentic situation to which they will be asked to develop (usually as a dyad) a specific response. Initially, they are asked to respond individually to the situation, based on their own previous experience or knowledge. In this way we begin to engage the student's own effectivity structure with the affordances of the particular situation. Students share their initial responses in an online discussion forum. Additional information is provided, typically as a rich set of resources (readings, videotapes, poetry, music, interviews) that the dyads then explore and use as a basis for their group response to the challenge. Students post their responses and then interact by asking questions, making suggestions, or even challenging the responses of others. Students use that feedback to develop their final response, which is then posted and submitted to the instructor for grading.

The Workforce and Healthcare Delivery Environments course requires student immersion in both the science and the lived experience of workplace shortages and turbulent working conditions. Students are exposed to a broad range of current media and scientific literature on the context and content of workforce and working conditions issues to focus their attention and clarify goals for the course. The challenges for this course engage the students as research consultants for the chief nursing executive of a local hospital. Students see a video in which the nurse executive discusses the problems facing the hospital and her goals for addressing staffing shortages and improving quality of care. Working in dyads, students analyze current research and propose solutions to achieve the hospital's goals. The solutions require that students incorporate theories and methods from research, organizational theory, economics, and policy, as well as their knowledge of change management. The faculty role is to help students detect, from the rich environmental problem, the relevant information they will need to develop a scientifically sound and realistic solutions. Student assignments require that they prepare documentation that supports their recommendations for both academic and administrative audiences. Students and faculty critique recommendations and justification in both on-line and real-time discussions.

In the Border Health course, students are exposed to the unique challenges present in the U.S.-Mexico borderlands. Students are introduced to the cultural, historical, social, economical and political contexts of the U.S.-Mexico border through poetry, art, music, and interactive websites. The first challenge will provide an immersion into the rich border context through introspection, reflection, and critical analysis of the factors that contribute to the health of borderlanders. The second challenge is situated within the health care systems in the border region. Students will use the binational agenda, *Healthy Gente* 2010 to examine U.S.-Mexico collaborative efforts, both formal and informal, that impact selected Healthy Gente objectives. For example, if injury prevention was selected, students would explore binational efforts that address reducing vehicle mortality rates by 25% (U.S.) or 20% (Mexico). One example related to this particular objective would be the discovery of a collaborative partnership between Arizona border hospitals and *Hospital General* in Sonora, Mexico. The outcome of this binational effort was the development of a triage unit for trauma victims in Nogales, Sonora. The final challenge requires the learner to integrate knowledge from previous challenges with new knowledge required to produce culturally competent scholarship. The final challenge requires students to integrate concepts, research design and research methodologies into a binational proposal that will respond to one of the *Healthy Gente* 2010 objectives. Consistent with the principle of educating intention, at the end of each challenge students will have the opportunity to reflect on the meaning and potential application of new knowledge beyond the U.S.-Mexico border.

In the Technology course, the focus is on applying information technology to improve our ability to deliver health care to underserved areas. The exemplar used is Diabetes care at the U.S.-Mexico Border. Diabetes is rampant at the border and care is hampered by physical distance, disparities in healthcare access, economic and policy issues, to name a few. The course is structured as four challenges. The first challenge asks students to write an article for a local paper that characterizes problems associated with living with diabetes along the Mexican-American Border and our current capacity for delivering healthcare to this population. Resources for challenges are presented as infographics (Van der Lugt, 2004) in which each icon is a link to additional resources (Figure 1). The infographic allows students to explore the information in their own ways. In the second challenge, students are asked to propose criteria and use them to evaluate potential telehealth solutions. In the third challenge students prepare a presentation in which they critically analyze one of the conceptual frameworks or theories that have been used to support telehealth innovations. In the fourth challenge, students critique the research methods proposed for evaluating (or used to valuate) an existing telehealth intervention that is, or could be applied to the diabetic population. In the final challenge, students use information from the previous challenges to write their own supplementary grant to seek funding for a telehealth innovation that meets current research priorities and is a potential solution for a problem identified in Challenge 1. This is precisely the kind of

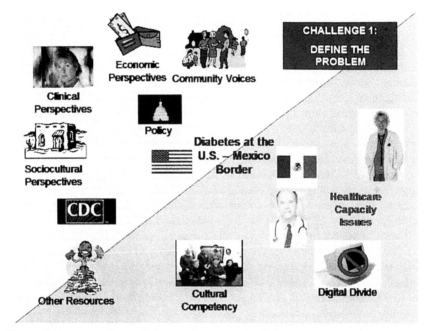

Figure 1. Prototype for an Infographic presenting links to resources for Challenge 1 in the Technology course.

activity that students will face as they build their own programs of research.

References

Effken, J. A., & Kadar, E. E. (2001). Learning as progressive biasing of a random walk process: Toward an ecological theory of exploratory learning. *Ecological Psychology, 13*, 1-30.

Shaw, R. E., Kadar, E., Sim, M., & Repperger, D. W. (1992). The intentional spring: A strategy for modeling systems that learn to perform intentional acts. *Human Movement Science, 7*, 155-200.

Van der Lugt, R. (2004). Visualizing information via infographics. Presented at the Cognitive Work Analysis Workshop, Seattle, WA.

Young, M. (2003). An ecological psychology of instructional design: Learning and thinking by perceiving-acting systems. In D.H. Jonassen (Ed.), *Handbook of research on educational communications and technology, 2nd ed.* (pp. 169-177). Mahwah, NJ: Erlbaum.

Young, M. F., Barab, S., & Garrett, S. (2000). Agent as detector: An ecological psychology perspective on learning by perceiving-acting systems. In D. H. Jonassen & S. M. Land (Eds.), *Theoretical foundations of learning environments* (pp. 147-172). Mahwah, NJ: Erlbaum.

Acknowledgements. This project is funded by a grant from the Health Resources and Services Association (HRSA 1 D09HP03116-01-00). We are deeply indebted to Rudy Valenzuela and Zu-Chun Lin who contributed to the development of the Border and Technology courses, respectively, as well as to the TRIAD technology team at the University of Arizona.

Author Index

Akita	87	Gray	129
Amazeen, E.	91	Grove	111
Amazeen, P.	191	Gunderson	181
Anderson	59	Hajnal	103, 136, 211
Aoyama	77	Harrison	103, 125, 136
Arzamarski	125, 214	Hayashi	45
Bahrick	37	Hirata	10
Baker	41	Hirose	199
Bardainne	207	Hong	203
Bardy	31, 169, 173, 177, 195, 221, 225	Hopkins	162
		Hove	115
Baron	54	Hyde	181
Batista	37	Isenhower	49, 54, 103, 136, 211
Biggs	111	Issartel	207
Bonnet	221	Ito, A.	77
Bootsma	225	Ito, K.	77, 87, 169
Bril	3, 10, 157	Jackson	241
Bruggeman	65	Juricevic	245, 249
Cadopi	207	Kadar	82
Carello	54, 91, 191	Kay	211
Castaneda	129	Kennedy	245, 249
Castellanos	37	Kim	169
Chan	95	Kinsella-Shaw	91, 103
Chin	59	Kirkwood	145
Cornus	7	Kojima	77
Cummins-Sebree	99	Komatsu	87
Davis	15	Lamb	257
Doi	69	Lopresti-Goodman	103
Dolgov	132	Mantel	173
Effken	257	Marin	207
Fajen	73	Mark	23
Faugloire	195	Marsh	49, 54
Fisher	82	Matsuishi	77
Flom	181	McBeath	132
Foucart	3, 10	McEwen	257
Fowler	41	Michaels	125, 136
Furuyama	45	Minarik	162
Fuwa	10	Mishima	45
Gaillot	207	Miyashita	77
Goasdoué	157	Moreno	214
Goodman	49	Morice	177
Gordon	181	Newell, K.	203

Newell, L. 37
Okamato 87
Olmstead 214
Ono 87
Oullier 225
Pagano 107
Pellecchia 191, 214
Pepping 19, 139
Ramenzoni 15, 229
Rasseneur 7
Rhodes 211
Richardson 41, 49, 54
Riley 15, 115, 229, 234
Robart 149, 153
Rosenblum 149, 153
Rupp 7
Sachtler 111
Saunders 234
Schmidt 49
Schmutz 181
Schwartz 59
Shockley 41, 99, 185
Shuman 37
Siegler 177
Smith 19, 139

Snyder 15
Sosnoff 203
Stasik 23
Stoffregen 31, 169, 173, 195, 221, 225
Streit 185
Students in Psychology 331.04 119
Sugar 132
Taylor 27
Tollner 99, 115
Turvey 191
Ueda 69
Vaillant-Molina 37
Valenti 59
Verran 257
Vincent 257
Virk 82
von Wiegand 111
Wagman 27, 119, 162
Walther 7
Warren 65
Williams 37
Yang 31
Young 257

Keyword Index

action   45
adolescents   59
affordances:
  ball-posting through holes   19
  for others   15
  hockey sticks   115
  interpersonal   54
  reaching   23
  step-acrossability   7
  step-reachability   15
  tools   3, 10, 99
  tripping avoidance   27
analysis:
  nonstationary signals   207
attention   129
attractors   177
auditory perception:
  length   145, 162
  shapes   149
  space   153
ball-catching   136
ball-posting through holes   19
baseball batting   129
braking   73
calibration   73
children   3
cognitive task:
  concurrent   214, 229, 234
conversational patterns   59
coordination: 31, 214, 234
  interpersonal   49
  rhythmic   191
coordination dynamics   211, 225
coupling strength   203
cross-wavelet transform   207
CyARM   87
development   3, 99, 181
disclosure reciprocity   59
dual task performance   214, 229, 234
dynamic touch   87, 91, 95, 103, 107, 115, 185
education   257
EPAID   257

event perception   132
exercise test, maximal   7
eye movements   221
face perception   37
force production   203
global array   173
global dynamics   203
haptic perception   95, 99, 191
haptic space   111
haptics   27, 103, 119, 185
heaviness perception   185
human-machine interface   87
inertia tensor   103, 107
infants   37, 181
instructional design   257
intention to sway   225
interception   132, 136
intermodal   173
intermodal patterns   177
interpersonal analysis   207
interpersonal coordination   45, 49, 59
  crossmodal   45
  speech   41
joint attention   87
language   41
length perception   145, 162
locomotion   65, 73
memory:
  dynamic events   181
microslips   199
motor control   203
multimodal   181
music   157
navigation   82
neuropathy   91, 191
non-rigid objects   69
non-stationary signals   207
obstacle avoidance   65
optical gain   185
orientation   245
perceived heaviness   103
perception:
  tactile space   111

perception-action	54, 129	robotics	82
peripheral neuropathy	91, 191	room perception	153
perspective	245, 249	self-disclosure	59
physiological factors	7	shape constancy	245, 249
picture perception	245, 249	smell	82
porpoises	77	speech	45
postural control	225	step-reachability	15
postural dynamics	41	synchrony	49
postural sway	225, 229	time-to-collision	69
posture:	195	time-to-contact	77
stabilization	221	tool use	3, 10, 99
primates	10	trajectories	177
reachability	15	velocity control	77
reaching	173	visually impaired	87
representation (cognitive)	69	walking speed shifts	211

www.ingramcontent.com/pod-product-compliance
Ingram Content Group UK Ltd.
Pitfield, Milton Keynes, MK11 3LW, UK
UKHW020433010325
455677UK00029B/1129

9 780415 652100